I0815619

Acclaim for

"This is a stunningly original book, rooted in a deep respect for Asian traditions, philosophies, and ingredients and at the same time genuinely progressive in its approach. Pamelia's extensive knowledge of cuisine has enabled her to contextualize her stories and vegetable-starring recipes in a way which demystifies and excites."
—Helen Goh, coauthor of *Ottolenghi Comfort*

"What an incredible book! If you're looking to move away from meat but aren't sure where to begin, look no further. These recipes are vibrant, beautiful, and full of love for the cultures that inspired them."
—Tim Anderson, chef and author of *JapanEasy* and *Hokkaido*

"Pamelia captures the heart and soul of vegetarian Asian cuisine. Diving into her book will leave you inspired to get into the kitchen."**—Dr. Sheil Shukla, author of James Beard Award–nominated *Plant-Based India***

"Pamelia has written a vibrant and scrumptious ode to the vegetables of Asia. Her cookbook both honors tradition and pushes the boundaries on what a plant-based feast can look like."
—Clarissa Wei, coauthor of *Made in Taiwan: Recipes and Stories from the Island Nation*

"*PlantAsia* provides an abundance of umami-rich, multidimensional vegetable-forward recipes. [Pamelia's] dishes and interviews with other cooks will inspire your next meal to be both deliberate and delicious."
—Abi Balingit, blogger at *The Dusky Kitchen* and James Beard Award–winning author of *Mayumu: Filipino American Desserts Remixed*

"*PlantAsia* could not be more timely. Chia and her more than two dozen expert contributors understand that plants are no less capable of supplying depth of flavor, texture, and interest than meats; they just need a little coaxing. This is a gorgeous and inspiring handbook."**—Andrew Janjigian, head baker at the IACP-nominated newsletter *Wordloaf* and author of the forthcoming book *Breaducation***

"*PlantAsia* provides a beautiful and practical cornucopia of diverse delights. It is an excellent guide for what you might wish to eat, and provides the means for understanding how technique can be used to produce complex, balanced deliciousness."**—Holly Davis, author of *Ferment: A Guide to the Ancient Art of Culturing Foods***

"If you equate Asian food with meat-centered dishes, avail yourself of this book! Meat has never been required, and this book proves that with each page."**—Abra Berens, chef and author of *Ruffage, Grist, and Pulp***

"This authoritative guide through Asian techniques and flavors will revolutionize your cooking. Brilliant, innovative, and incredibly inspiring!"**—Mandy Yin, author of *Sambal Shiok: The Malaysian Cookbook***

"I love everything about *PlantAsia*. I want to cook it all and will happily turn vegetarian for months to do so!"
—Karan Gokani, author of *Hoppers: The Cookbook*

"An absolute joy to read. Pamelia's gift for tasty prose and captivating visuals, along with a liberal seasoning of helpful cooking tips and Asian cultural anecdotes, make this a real gem of a cookbook."
—Loh Yi Jun, writer and founder of *Jun & Tonic*

"[*PlantAsia*] takes us on an exhilarating journey to Asian vegetable heaven. This cookbook is a must-have for vegetable lovers and Asian food lovers alike."**—Maureen Tan, culinary teacher and author of *Java***

RENGHAN REVEYA,
PAGE 115

PLANT ASIA

Asia's Vegetable Wisdom in Recipes, Stories, and Techniques

Pamelia Chia

NEW YORK

New York, NY 10010-4658
theexperimentpublishing.com

Library of Congress Cataloging-in-Publication Data available upon request

ISBN 979-8-89303-087-7
Ebook ISBN 979-8-89303-088-4

Cover and text design by Beth Bugler
Illustrations by Shreya Parasrampuria

Manufactured in Malaysia

First printing October 2025
10 9 8 7 6 5 4 3 2 1

The authorized representative in the EU for product safety
and compliance is Easy Access System Europe,
Mustamäe tee 50, 10621 Tallinn, Estonia | easproject.com | gpsr.requests@easproject.com.

PODI-RUBBED
ROASTED CAULIFLOWER, PAGE 233

Contents

Introduction

When I was growing up in Singapore, meat and seafood were on the table at every meal, sometimes in every dish. So integral are they to Singaporean food culture that even the most innocent-looking plate of greens would be laced with fermented shrimp paste (belacan) or dried shrimp. When I started cooking professionally, it was not uncommon for vegetarian guests to be met with sniggering from the kitchen. The sentiment was that these people were missing the point. How can food be delicious without the gratifying flavor of bones, meat, or seafood?

2019 was a profound year of change for me, as it marked a move to Australia. During this year, the country experienced bushfires of unprecedented intensity due to climate change. Elsewhere in the world, the Amazon rainforest was set ablaze to fulfill a rising global demand for meat.

I first became aware of the horrors and atrocities behind modern, industrialized animal agriculture when I read Eric Schlosser's *Fast Food Nation* and Jonathan Safran Foer's *Eating Animals* as a teenager. The scale of suffering—both animal and human—exposed in these books led me to abstain from fast food, seeing it as a direct enabler of factory farming. Still, I'd remained an obstinate lover of all things meat and couldn't stop myself from continuing to consume immoderate amounts of it daily. But, as I watched the news in 2019 and saw how many lives were impacted by the Australian bushfires, something inside me shifted. I knew that the world was facing an international crisis, and I could no longer deny the impact that my meat-heavy diet was having on the environment.

Changing the way that I ate seemed so simple and yet it wasn't. I had grown accustomed to relying on animal products as a crutch. Every time I wanted more flavor in a dish, I'd add dried shrimp, use some stock, or brown some meat. Without meat or seafood to inject umami into food, I was stumped.

I doubted that I could give up meat for a meal, let alone a day. I knew that if I were to make a lasting change to my diet, the vegetable dishes that I cooked had to offer the same satisfaction as their meat-based counterparts.

Ironically, it was my work as a professional cook in Melbourne, and subsequently in Daylesford (a town about ninety minutes' drive from the city), that opened my eyes to what Asia could offer with regard to vegetable cooking. With vegetarianism and veganism becoming part of mainstream culture, chefs there were constantly reaching for ingredients such as kombu, or employing Asian cooking techniques, to make their vegetables sing.

A popular item at one restaurant I worked at, Carlton Wine Room, was deep-fried cauliflower on soy and sesame cream, drizzled with chili oil, then topped with puffed wild rice and crispy chickpeas. It was punchy, full of texture, and reminiscent of flavors I knew and loved—and it just so happened to be vegan. A light bulb flicked on in my mind.

Looking to Asia

Vegetarianism and veganism are commonly thought of as fads from the West, even though many Asians have been eating this way for centuries. In many Asian food cultures, plants traditionally provided the primary source of nutrition. Meat was an expensive luxury, so it was reserved as the centerpiece for celebratory meals or used sparingly in daily dishes.

In regions such as Taiwan and India, vegetarianism is a way of life. Tempeh and young jackfruit are deeply embedded in Indonesian food culture, but are only just seeing a rise in popularity in the West with the growing plant-based movement. It is clear that there is a deep well of knowledge in Asia on vegetable preparations that yield flavorful, satisfying results.

Using This Book

This book will open your eyes to textures, flavors, and techniques from Asia and jumpstart your discovery of just how dynamic and delicious plants can be. I believe that this is something relevant to everyone, regardless of your diet or stance on eating meat.

If you're an omnivore, think of the dishes in *PlantAsia* as exciting accompaniments to the meat in your meal. If you're apprehensive about forgoing meat and seafood

entirely, you can cook these recipes with a little addition of animal protein, gradually omitting it over time. Good news if you're vegan or vegetarian—you will find plenty of inspiration within these pages.

A Few Notes About the Recipes in This Book

- An instant-read thermometer is handy to have on hand, particularly for the recipes in this book that require deep-frying. If you don't have one, you can gauge if the oil is hot enough by dipping a wooden chopstick into the heated oil. When it is sufficiently heated, bubbles will stream readily from the chopstick.
- A rice cooker makes cooking rice a breeze, as there is no need to watch the pot and no risk of scorching. If you do not own one, select a pot just big enough to allow the rinsed and drained rice to come up to a height of at least 2 inches (5 cm). Add the other ingredients and set the pot over high heat, stirring occasionally to prevent the rice from sticking to the bottom. When the liquid comes to a simmer, cover and cook over low heat for 15 to 20 minutes, or until the rice is tender and all of the liquid has been absorbed.
- The size of skillets used is 10 inches (25 cm) in diameter, unless otherwise specified.
- A powerful blender is an essential piece of equipment in my kitchen. What I use and recommend is an Indian grinder, also known as a wet grinder. Typically fashioned out of stainless steel, it combines the function of a spice grinder and a blender, and thus is great for grinding whole spices into powder and pulverizing fibrous aromatics with little to no water. Indian grinders also happen to be very cost-effective compared to fancy blenders. The brand that I use is Preethi.
- All recipes were tested using full-fat dairy.
- Salt used is table salt, unless otherwise specified.
- Sugar used is caster or superfine sugar, unless otherwise specified, as this type of sugar dissolves and incorporates easily—especially important when making dipping sauces and desserts. Granulated sugar can be substituted if you can't find superfine sugar, but be aware that it won't dissolve as easily.
- Eggs used weigh 2 ounces (55 g) each, and are at room temperature.
- Oil refers to neutral cooking oil such as peanut oil, canola oil, grapeseed oil, or vegetable oil, unless otherwise specified.
- All aromatics and vegetables except eggplant are peeled before use, unless otherwise specified. When shallots are called for, I am referring to purple-skinned Asian shallots.
- While the quantities of ingredients are expressed in multiple ways in this book, I highly recommend using metric measurements for best results. This is especially crucial when attempting any recipe involving batter or dough.
- The quality of the coconut cream and milk you use can make or break your dish. I recommend using fresh products if you can source them. Otherwise, Asian brands are generally very good. I like using Kara cartoned coconut cream and Ayam canned coconut milk and cream.
- Always opt for fresh soy milk over cartoned—you will find this in the refrigerated aisles of Asian grocers.
- Recipes in this book were tested with Lee Kum Kee soy sauce, unless otherwise specified. I do not recommend Kikkoman for them, as it has a milder and sweeter profile whereas Chinese soy sauces like Lee Kum Kee pack a saltier, more umami punch.
- The produce is the star of these dishes, so it is worth sourcing the best.

Learning about Asia's diverse food cultures and cuisines has immensely improved my own relationship with vegetables. I am not a full-time vegetarian, but there are many days when there is not a shred of meat or seafood on the table, and I scarcely notice. I hope the recipes and stories in this book can do the same for you.

CHICKPEA TOFU SALAD, PAGE 29

The Flavor Compass

Compared to meat, a vegetable or plant-based product like tofu often lacks the inherent savory qualities that are so abundant in animal flesh. Meat is also a rich source of reducing sugars (simple sugars like glucose and fructose that can react with other molecules) and amino acids that, when heated, react to provide even more complexity in flavor.

If handled correctly, meat is also more texturally compelling. Barbecued pork with its tender meat, wobbly fat, and crunchy charred bits is far more enticing than braised cabbage or raw carrots that have a singular texture.

In short, you can sear a simply seasoned piece of meat in a pan and have an amazing eating experience, but vegetables often need more help. I developed my own compass for cooking vegetables well—**Flavor**, **Accent**, **Process,** and **Texture**. Additional flavor-packed ingredients lend their own deliciousness to vegetables. An aromatic accent brings a new dimension—brightness, freshness, sensuality—to a dish. The right cooking process further amplifies flavors. And finally, a contrasting texture makes the vegetable exciting to eat; like the crispy skin on a piece of fish.

Flavor, **Accent**, **Process,** and **Texture** manifest in various forms throughout Asia. Indian cooks pack flavor into their vegetables through the deft use of spices; Japanese cooks sprinkle shichimi togarashi (七味唐辛子) as a finishing accent. Korean cooks enhance the savory attributes of vegetables through fermentation. Burmese cooks deep-fry lentils, onion, and garlic to add crunch. The formula below is one that I use, and one that can be applied to all vegetable cooking, even beyond the recipes in this book.

1. Add a flavor-packed ingredient.

Spices / Dairy and eggs / Alliums / Umami-rich plants and their derivatives / Preserved and fermented products

2. Add an aromatic accent.

Herbs / Fragrant spices / Flowers and essences / Citrus

3. Boost the flavor through a preparation or cooking process.

Aging / Browning / Blooming / Charring

4. Add a contrasting texture.

Juicy / Silky / Creamy / Chewy / Crunchy

Flavor

Good cooking begins with a well-stocked kitchen. Peek into any Asian pantry and you will see jars, bottles, or packets of powerhouse ingredients that lend a ton of flavor to food.

1. Spices

Spices are parts of plants that are rich in flavor compounds; these phytochemicals originally evolved in plants as a form of defense against herbivores and pathogens. Whether used whole or ground, spices can impart a massive amount of flavor to dishes in an instant. The world of spices is vast and you could fill all your cupboards with them, but the ones that I reach for the most often are cumin, cinnamon, mustard seeds, coriander, red chiles, and turmeric. Apart from individual spices, I also use blends such as garam masala and five spice powder for their ability to give dishes a harmonious, distinctive character with a single sprinkle.

2. Dairy and Eggs

Dairy products—such as butter, cheese, yogurt—and eggs, are rich in umami. I am partial to using ghee in my cooking. It is made by allowing the milk solids in butter to caramelize, producing a wonderful nutty aroma. Unlike brown butter, the milk solids are removed from the fat, allowing ghee to have a high smoke-point and be used in all applications, including deep-frying. Another noteworthy ingredient in this category is salted egg yolks. When duck eggs are brined, salt penetrates the eggshell, causing the yolk to solidify and develop a deep, savory flavor reminiscent of Parmesan.

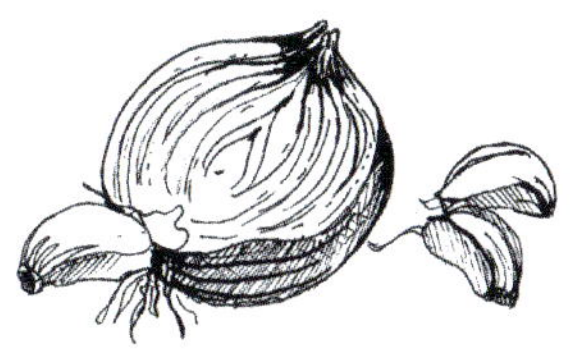

3. Alliums

There is something truly delicious about alliums, a botanical genus that includes garlic, onion, chives, green onions, and shallots. Alliums contain pungent sulfur-rich compounds that can be transformed through cooking. While they have a sharp bite when eaten raw, they turn mellow and sweet when cooked gently. Deep-fry or char them, and their natural sugars caramelize and the flavors become remarkably complex.

4. Umami-rich plants and their derivatives

It is a misconception that umami can be found only in meat, seafood, or animal products. Tomatoes, seaweed, and mushrooms are rich sources of glutamic and aspartic acids—compounds that stimulate our umami taste receptors. When these plants are dehydrated or concentrated, the amount of umami compounds per unit increases. This is why ingredients such as ketchup, nori, kombu, and dried shiitake mushrooms are all powerhouse ingredients in a plant-based kitchen.

5. Preserved and fermented products

Anything preserved or fermented guarantees flavor. In Asia, these ingredients are ubiquitous. When it comes to seasoning a dish, there are products such as soy sauce, gochujang, miso, and fermented tofu (fǔ rǔ/腐乳) that can be easily dissolved or mixed into broths, stews, and dressings. Preserved vegetables such as preserved radish (cài fǔ/菜脯), fermented black beans (dòu chǐ/豆豉) and preserved mustard stem (zhà cài/榨菜) can be added to stir-fries for an instant flavor boost. Aged ingredients, like nattō and tempeh, can be stars on their own. Properly made tempeh tastes so good that it can be enjoyed simply fried with salt.

Accent

Aromatic ingredients create layers of flavor, add interest, and lend the dish a distinctive regional taste. Just as the smell of yuzu is evocative of Japan, a whiff of pandan transports one to Southeast Asia.

1. Herbs

Herbs are used in abundance in many parts of Asia. There are three broad categories. First, you have delicate herbs like cilantro, shiso, or mint, which are heat-sensitive and best reserved for scattering toward the end of cooking or as a garnish. Others, such as curry leaves and green onions, are hardier and can be used at the start of cooking to build a foundation of flavor. Finally, there are those that release their flavors as a dish cooks, whether they are used as a herb or an edible wrapper; these include pandan leaves, banana leaves, lotus leaves, and betel leaves.

2. Fragrant spices

Some spices can act as a way to add a final, fragrant flourish to a dish. Of these, perhaps the most economical and accessible are sesame seeds, which take hardly any time to be toasted and sprinkled over the dish. When I prefer the flavor of sesame to be more assertive, I use toasted sesame oil. Similarly, perilla oil (deulgireum/들기름) finds a place in my kitchen cupboard. Another spice of note is Sichuan peppercorns, which carry aromatic floral and citrus notes and impart an irresistible numbing quality to food. Many Asian grocers also carry Sichuan peppercorn oil.

3. Flowers and essences

An oft-overlooked category of ingredients are flowers and essences, which sit at the intersection of perfumery and cookery. The ones that you will encounter in this book include dried rose petals and rosewater—popular in Indian cooking—which add intrigue and sensuality to dishes.

4. Citrus

Citrus is a valued ingredient in my kitchen for its ability to add brightness to dishes. There is lemon and lime, but I also love yuzu and calamansi. While it might seem that one citrus can be used interchangeably with another, each has its own distinctive perfume. Apart from using the fresh juice, another way to add an aromatic accent is with the zest. One of my favorite finishing touches for dishes is Japanese seven-spice seasoning (shichimi togarashi/七味唐辛子), a highly aromatic mixture that contains dried orange peel in addition to sesame seeds, nori, and dried red chiles.

Process

While preparation processes and cooking techniques can serve practical functions such as promoting the digestion of food and absorption of nutrients, they also allow for depth of flavor through the harnessing of heat and smoke or the passage of time.

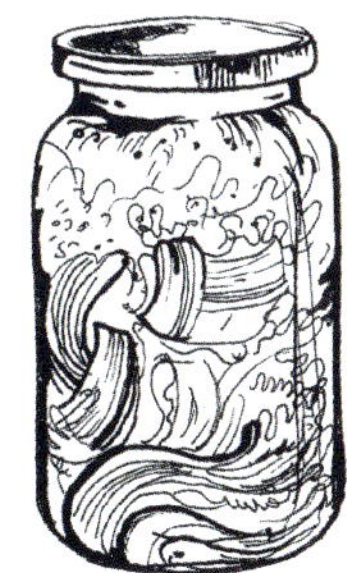

1. Aging

The act of preserving food is a common tradition in many parts of the world, as it was used to prolong the shelf lives of perishable foods before the advent of refrigeration. Preserving plays a less important role today than it did in the past, but it has regained popularity for its ability to coax flavors out of ingredients. During fermentation, microorganisms metabolize food, breaking down proteins into smaller, flavorful, and more easily digestible molecules that contribute to the savoriness of fermented products. In the making of kimchi and other vegetable ferments, this process results in a complex blend of sour, sweet, and savory flavors.

2. Browning

When food browns, it is usually the result of caramelization and/or the Maillard reaction. Both describe a cascade of chemical reactions happening at high temperatures that trigger the formation of hundreds of flavor compounds. As the saying goes, "more color, more flavor." The cooking techniques that promote browning in foods include toasting, searing, deep-frying, and roasting.

3. Blooming

Blooming is the act of releasing the fragrance of an ingredient with hot oil, without necessarily browning it. In Indian cuisine, spices are added to hot fat in a process known as tempering, causing their aroma to evolve, becoming intense and toasted. The spices and fat are then used to start or finish a dish. Similarly, in Chinese cuisine, the technique of drizzling oil over aromatics is an easy way to amplify flavors without the risk of burning delicate seasonings such as Koran chili flakes and garlic.

4. Charring

Humans began cooking over open fire, and the smoky scent of charred food remains a profound stimulus. The bitter notes of charred food heighten the perception of its natural sweetness. Vegetables can be charred within their coverings, like eggplant in its skin. In certain parts of Asia, coconut flesh is traditionally charred either in grated form or in chunks roasted over burning coconut husks. This process gives the finished dish an overall smokiness and nutty sweetness.

Texture

A dish may taste delicious, but it is bound to get boring if there is only one texture. Contrast is the antithesis of monotony. Having a range of different textures in a dish keeps things interesting and enhances our enjoyment.

1. Juicy

Juiciness, or freshness, is a quality I gravitate toward, particularly in warm-weather dishes. Vegetables like tomatoes, lettuce, and cucumber are great for adding a burst of freshness, and are best enjoyed raw or pickled. Juicy fruits such as grapefruit, pomegranate, and pomelo are also great additions to savory dishes.

2. Silky

When I think of silky textures, my mind goes to tofu, especially silken, medium-firm, and egg tofu, the latter of which is made from a combination of egg and soymilk. Other than soybean-based tofu, there are tofus made from lentils and other legumes. Chickpea tofu, for instance, is unique to Burma and can be enjoyed hot as a porridge or cooled and set, where it takes on a slippery-smooth, almost melt-in-your-mouth consistency.

3. Creamy

A creamy mouthfeel provides a sense of richness and fattiness. Part of the reason why we crave meat is because of its inherent fat content; fat is energy-dense and we are evolutionarily wired to desire it. Fat is something many vegetables lack, but we can prepare them in tandem with fatty ingredients such as avocado, coconut milk, mayonnaise, and dairy. Products like peanut butter, tahini, and sesame paste are also great options. An underrated ingredient in this category is fermented tofu (fǔ rǔ/腐乳), a jarred condiment that comes in white or red varieties and is spreadable like soft cheese. When dissolved, fermented tofu has the ability to enrich and add body to broths, stews, and braises.

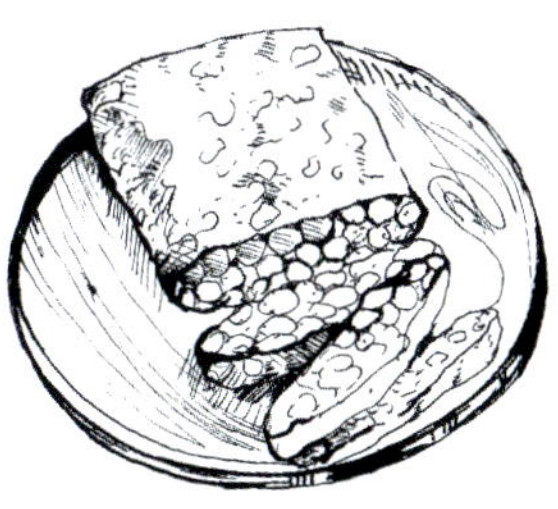

4. Chewy

This is a texture not to be overlooked, especially when we consider that a big part of the pleasure we derive from meat is its chew. For this reason, firm tofu—the chewiest of all tofu—is often described as a meat substitute. Other ingredients in this category include tempeh, seitan, dried tofu sticks (fǔ zhú/腐竹), and noodles. In some Asian food cultures, we also talk about Q, a coveted texture that describes something that goes beyond chewy to the extent of being springy or bouncy. This can be obtained from ingredients such as Korean rice cakes (tteokbokki/떡볶이), sago, or sweet potato noodles.

5. Crunchy

Everyone knows the pleasure derived from crunchy foods: just think of potato chips. Anything deep-fried can add crunch to a meal. I tend to reach for crispy fried shallots or sev (सेव), thin deep-fried chickpea noodles from India. Nuts are also a great addition to a dish; my favorites are peanuts and cashews fried in ghee. In Indonesia, kerupuk (Indonesian deep-fried crackers) are essential components of dishes such as gado gado, a vegetable salad with peanut sauce. Raw vegetables, such as cucumber and celery, are fantastic at providing juiciness and crunch in the same bite.

Expanding Your Asian Pantry

Cooking stand-out vegetable dishes begins with building your pantry. When doing so, consider whether an ingredient fulfills at least one component of the Flavor Compass (pages 5–13). A certain ingredient could be inherently rich in flavor (F), add an extra layer of aroma (A), gain depth of flavor through a processing method (P), offer a unique texture (T), or bring a combination of these qualities. Here are some of the ingredients I rely on—and how they map onto the Flavor Compass.

 = FLAVOR  = ACCENT  = PROCESS  = TEXTURE

Asafoetida (hing/हींग) is a spice extracted from ferula, a variety of giant fennel. It resembles a yellowish white powder and has an oniony and garlicky aroma. Asafoetida is typically used in Indian vegetarian dishes that lack alliums. It is usually fried in oil at the start of a recipe to release its fragrance (see Chayote Paruppu Poriyal on page 69). It is available in small containers with slide-to-open caps at Indian grocers. In the absence of asafoetida, assuming that you consume alliums, add a little chopped garlic and shallot to your recipe. Read more about asafoetida on page 66. (F)

Chili crisp and chili oil are blends of crispy bits of chile, onion, and garlic stored in fragrant oil, delivering as much crunch as savory heat. It is made by patiently frying thinly sliced or minced aromatics and toasting spices and dried chiles in oil. This technique browns and crisps the solids while also helping the oil absorb their flavors, turning red and aromatic. While it originated as a Sichuanese condiment, it is a versatile pantry staple that can be a key component in salad dressings (see Celery and Black Fungus Salad on page 63), incorporated into stews, or drizzled over dishes as a finishing touch (see Chayote and Glass Noodle Dumplings on page 73). Given its recent explosion in popularity in the West, there are many brands of jarred chili crisp to choose from. One of the most popular brands both in and out of China is Lǎo Gān Mā (老干妈), which is available at Chinese grocers. I typically reach for the variant labeled "peanuts in chili oil," which promises mellow heat, abundant crunch, and lots of umami. On days where I'm craving something mind-bendingly numbing, I reach for a chili crisp with Sichuan peppercorns. The main thing is to go with a variety that you enjoy. (F) (P) (T)

CHILI CRISP AND CHILI OIL

Chinkiang black vinegar is an essential seasoning in Chinese cooking. It is made by fermenting glutinous rice over a long period of time to produce a dark, complex vinegar with a rich, malty flavor and a hint of sweetness. It can be used in dressings (see Watercress Noodles with Split Pea Fritters on page 79) or to season sauces and stir-fries (see Tempeh Chili Pan Mee with Thai Basil on page 23). It is available at any Chinese grocer, but balsamic vinegar can be used as a substitute. (F) (T)

Coconut cream is the fat-rich layer that floats to the top of coconut milk when it is left to stand. It is creamy, white, and thick like heavy cream, and possesses a slightly sweet and rich flavor. Coconut cream can be used in both sweet (see Ginataang Bilo-Bilo on page 273) and savory dishes (see Sambal Goreng on page 211) to add a rich creaminess. It is usually added as a final step, and is rarely allowed to come to a full boil to prevent it from splitting. Coconut cream is available in cans or cartons at Southeast Asian or Indian grocers. My favorite brands are Kara or Ayam. Because different brands of coconut milk vary widely in terms of dilution, you may want to try substituting coconut cream and some water for coconut milk. A good rule of thumb is to substitute 3 parts coconut cream to 2 parts water for the same weight of thick coconut milk. If you can't find coconut cream in stores, you can leave coconut milk to stand and skim off the fatty layer on top. Do not confuse coconut cream with creamed coconut, which is made by grinding the dehydrated flesh of mature coconuts into a solid paste and sold as a hard block or in jars. (T)

Crispy gram flour noodles (sev/सेव) are a popular Indian snack food made by forming thin noodles out of chickpea flour and spices, and deep-frying them to achieve a crispy texture. Sev has a nutty, savory flavor that can range from mild to spicy. It is sprinkled over

CURRY LEAVES

dishes, typically snacks known as chaat, to add a light crunch (see Spinach Leaf Chaat on page 171). Sev can be found at Indian grocers, where it is sold in plastic bags or containers. In place of sev, you can deep-fry dried rice vermicelli until crispy to mimic the crunchy texture. P T

Curry leaves, the small green leaves of the curry tree, have a citrusy, peppery flavor. They are never eaten raw and have to be bloomed in oil to release their fragrance; this step can be performed at the start of the recipe as a foundation for flavor (see Polos Ambula on page 103), or as a final flourish (see Butternut Squash Kootu with Spiced Chickpeas on page 99). Pull the leaves off the stem before adding them to hot oil, then stand back as they can splutter quite aggressively. It takes only seconds for curry leaves to turn from attractively glassy and fragrant to burnt and bitter, so be vigilant when blooming them. You will find curry leaves, fresh or frozen, at Southeast Asian or Indian grocers. Because their fragrance is so unique, there is no good substitute. A

Dark palm sugar is a rich, complex sweetener that has a strong caramelized and smoky flavor. Almost every Southeast Asian country has a palm sugar–making history that predates the European introduction of cane sugar to the region. The sap of palm trees is collected, then boiled in cauldrons for hours to concentrate and caramelize the sugars. Poured into molds and allowed to cool, the molten lava sets into solid pucks. As there is a whole gamut of palm tree varieties, each type of palm sugar has its own host of notes that go beyond sweetness. Some palm sugar varieties include kithul, gula melaka, and gula jawa. This sugar works well in both sweet and savory dishes (see Garden Greens Sambol on page 49). You will find dark palm sugar sold in block or granulated form at Southeast Asian grocers. Each palm sugar block weighs 1.75 ounces (50 g); you can shave what you need off the block with a knife. Do not mistake it for the blond pucks of palm sugar from Thailand; you want it to be as dark as chocolate. In a pinch, you can substitute granulated coconut sugar. F P

Dried black fungus, also known as dried wood ear mushroom or dried cloud ear mushroom, is an ear-shaped mushroom that is valued primarily for its unique texture rather than its relatively bland flavor. The slippery yet delicately crunchy texture of dried black fungus is appreciated in salads (see Celery and Black Fungus Salad on page 63), braises (see Buddha's Delight on page 105), and dumpling fillings (see Vegetable Rolls, Two Ways on page 187). Before use, soak the pieces in room-temperature water for 30 minutes before draining. Once soaked, they require only a quick blanch, stir-fry, or simmer to cook through. Dried black fungus is available at Southeast Asian or Chinese supermarkets, either whole or thinly sliced. For the recipes in this book, any whole dried black fungus can be used, but I prefer those that resemble the shape and size of black kittens' ears. T

Dried glass noodles are an ingredient embraced by multiple Asian food cultures, including Chinese, Filipino, Thai, and Vietnamese. Made from starch, they are sold in small bundles of white, wiry strands. Their biggest benefit is how quickly they cook—about a minute or so—taking on a slippery, slightly chewy texture and a neutral taste that easily absorbs seasonings. They can be stir-fried (see Stir-Fried Glass

DRIED BLACK FUNGUS

Noodles with Cilantro and White Pepper on page 133), slipped into simmering stews (see Buddha's Delight on page 105), or snipped into small pieces and used as a filling ingredient in dumplings (see Chayote and Glass Noodle Dumplings on page 73). Sold in plastic packaging, you will find them at Chinese or Southeast Asian grocers, where they may be sold as cellophane noodles or bean thread noodles. T

Dried shiitake mushrooms are made by drying fresh shiitake mushrooms. The drying process triggers enzymes within the mushrooms to produce guanylic acid, an umami compound that becomes even more potent when the mushrooms are used in tandem with other umami sources, such as kombu. To prepare the mushrooms, soak them in boiling water until they have softened, about 30 minutes, before use. The tough stems should be snipped off with scissors and discarded (or turned into a meat substitute; read more about this on page 52). The caps can be sliced and fried to build a flavor foundation (see Stir-Fried Glass Noodles with Cilantro and White Pepper on page 133), steeped whole to make dashi (see Whole Tomato Rice on page 77), or braised in large chunks so that their meaty texture can be appreciated (see Buddha's Delight on page 105). The soaking liquid is akin to instant mushroom stock and can be used in dishes in place of water. Dried shiitake mushrooms are available at Southeast Asian, Chinese, Japanese, or Korean grocers, where they come in a range of sizes. The ones that I love are known as huā gū/花菇 ("flower mushroom"), and are instantly recognizable by the large fissures on their caps. These mushrooms have a juicy and uniquely al dente texture when cooked, akin to abalone. For the recipes in this book, use medium whole dried shiitake mushrooms that are roughly 1½ inches (4 cm) in diameter. F P T

FERMENTED BLACK BEANS

Dried tofu sticks (fǔ zhú/腐竹), also known as yuba, are fresh tofu skins that have been bunched up on poles and allowed to dry until they are creamy yellow, stiff, and brittle. These sticks are long; before use, soak or steam the tofu sticks before snipping them into neat lengths. Alternatively, snap them into pieces with your hands. Their fragrance can be heightened by shallow- or deep-frying them in oil (see Charred Brussels Sprouts with Grapefruit and Yuba on page 193). Dried tofu sticks are sold in sealed clear packages at Southeast Asian or Chinese grocers. T

Fermented black beans (dòu chǐ/豆豉), used frequently in Chinese cooking, are black soybeans that have been preserved in salt. They look like dull-black, soft, shriveled pellets, often with tiny salt crystals on them, and have a pungent and salty flavor. To use them, first rinse them to remove excess salt, then chop them. Fermented black beans are great as an addition to stir-fries or as a base for sauces and stews (see Egg Tofu with Mapo Mushroom Sauce on page 93). Sold in plastic bags, you will find them at Chinese grocers. In lieu of fermented black beans, you can use jarred black bean sauce. Read more about them in Cathy Erway's interview on page 134. F P

Fermented broad bean paste (dòu bàn jiàng/豆瓣酱), sometimes also known as fermented chili bean sauce, is a thick, chunky paste made by fermenting broad beans with chiles, soybeans, salt, and flour. Being deeply umami and complex, this paste is typically fried in oil to release its aromatic flavors and used as a base for many Sichuan dishes (see Egg Tofu with Mapo Mushroom Sauce on page 93). You will find it jarred or in plastic containers at Chinese grocers. In the absence of fermented broad bean paste, you can use another type of fermented bean paste, such as soybean sauce, miso, or doenjang, in tandem with some chili crisp to compensate for their lack of heat. F P

Five-spice powder is a mixture of ground spices used extensively in Chinese cooking. Despite the name, some blends contain more than five spices. My favorite blend comes from Pok Oy Thong in Penang and contains cinnamon, aniseed, star anise, lime peel, cloves, coriander seeds, nutmeg, rice, and pepper. Five-spice powder is wonderful when dusted over deep-fried food (see Typhoon Shelter Mushrooms on page 185) or used

GALANGAL

as a seasoning in tandem with soy sauce and toasted sesame oil (see Vegetable Rolls, Two Ways on page 187). You will find it in small glass jars or plastic containers at Chinese and Southeast Asian grocers. F A

Fried shallots, an essential garnish in many Asian cuisines, are made by frying thinly sliced shallots in a generous amount of oil. This ingredient can be used to top anything from salads (see Kohlrabi and Carrot Salad on page 35) to snacks (see Quail Egg Bhejo with Palapa on page 145), to steamed rice rolls (see Mushroom Rice Rolls with Bean Sprout Salad on page 83). Fried shallots can be found at any Chinese or Southeast Asian grocer. Indian grocers also sell a variant—fried red onions—known as birista.

Homemade fried shallots are laborious but not difficult to make, and the reward is that you additionally get a jar of richly flavored shallot oil. Heat 2½ cups (600 ml) neutral oil in a large saucepan or wok to 400°F (200°C). Thinly slice 1 pound (450 g) shallots into rings using a mandoline and add them to the oil. Cook on medium heat, stirring occasionally, for about 3 minutes, or until the shallot rings are translucent, tender, and slightly shrunken. Continue frying over low heat, stirring frequently, until the shallot rings begin to turn a light golden brown, about 15 minutes. Turn off the heat and leave the shallots to fry in the residual heat until they turn the color of hash browns. Line a baking sheet with paper towel. Pass the contents of the pan through a fine-mesh strainer set over a bowl, then spread the fried shallots out in an even layer on the prepared baking sheet to drain. Cool the shallot oil and fried shallots completely before jarring separately. This makes about 2 ⅓ cups (140 g) fried shallots that will keep for 2 weeks at room temperature. F P T

Galangal is a pink-tinged rhizome that resembles ginger in appearance and has a citrusy, piney flavor. Cut into thick coins, galangal can be infused into curries, stir-fries, or braises (see Sambal Goreng on page 211). It can also be ground into a paste with other aromatic ingredients and used as the foundational flavor of a dish; the tough skin should be removed with a knife before grinding. Galangal is available fresh or frozen at Southeast Asian grocers. A

Garam masala is a complex mixture of ground spices—typically cumin, coriander, cardamom, cloves, cinnamon, nutmeg, and black pepper—used to add depth and warmth in Indian cuisine. A multipurpose spice blend, it is suitable for anything from raita (see Smoky Eggplant Raita with Focaccia on page 217) to brines and marinades (see Podi-Rubbed Roasted Cauliflower on page 233). You will find it sold in plastic bags at Indian grocers. F

Garlic chives, also known as Chinese chives, is an herb with garlicky flavor and delicate crispness. It resembles tall straight grass in appearance. The bottom inch of the stalks tends to be fibrous and should be trimmed off and discarded. The best way to celebrate the texture of this unique vegetable is to enjoy it simply stir-fried (see Tteokbokki with Soybean Sprouts and Garlic Chives on page 131). A few brisk tosses in a pan to wilt the chives is sufficient. Garlic chives are usually sold in fresh bundles at Southeast Asian or Chinese grocers. If unavailable, regular chives, or the green sections of green onions cut lengthwise into long thin strips, make good substitutes. F T

GARLIC CHIVES

GHEE

Ghee is a fat used extensively in South Asian cooking, traditionally made with cultured butter that is obtained from the churning of yogurt; the fermentation is what sets the flavor of ghee apart. In the making of ghee, butter is heated until its milk solids caramelize, producing a rich and nutty flavor. Strained, the resulting fat has such transparency and glow that the word "elixir" often springs to mind. The benefit of using ghee is that you get the flavor of brown butter without any risk of it burning, since the milk solids have been removed. Use it in the same way you use oil—to bloom spices (see Spanakopita with Spiced Ghee and Fried Onions on page 241) or for frying (see Egg Bhurji with Peas on page 155), for example. Ghee is available at health food stores or Indian grocers, though it is often more economical to make at home.

To make ¾ cup (180 ml) of ghee, add 1 cup (225 g) unsalted, preferably cultured, butter to a saucepan and set it on low heat. Without stirring, allow the butter to melt and come to a gentle simmer. As foam forms on the top, stir the surface gently to encourage the milk solids to sink to the bottom. When the butter smells nutty and the milk solids are a rich golden brown, pass the contents of the saucepan through a fine-mesh strainer lined with cheesecloth set over a bowl. The milk solids are delicious and can be enjoyed over yogurt or a chopped banana. Cool the ghee completely before jarring. It will keep for up to 2 weeks in the refrigerator. F P

Ginger flower, also known as torch ginger, is the pale pink bud of the ginger plant that is sometimes sold on a thick green stalk. Only the bud, which has a citrusy flavor, is used in the Singaporean kitchen; the stem is discarded. The entire bud can be halved and added to stews to infuse. Otherwise, the petals can be pulled off the bud, sliced or chopped finely, and enjoyed raw or lightly scalded in oil (see Tempeh Satay with Sambal Matah on page 215). This ingredient is available at Southeast Asian grocers, where it is sold, frozen, as closed buds. A

Grated coconut is the raspy, finely grated flesh of mature coconut. Being fresh-tasting and subtly sweet, it is wonderful in both desserts and savory dishes (see Beet Curry with Coconut Sambol on page 97). It can also be toasted to enhance its nutty aroma (see Urab Kacang on page 199). In Asia, dedicated cooks purchase this ingredient from market vendors who employ an electric grater and grate coconuts to order. There are two varieties that one can request at the market: grated coconut that is white as snow, or grated coconut that is speckled with bits of brown. For the recipes in this book, choose the former, which is also available fresh or frozen at Southeast Asian or Indian grocers; thaw frozen coconut in the refrigerator before use. The latter, being more oil-rich, is better for extracting coconut milk. Do note that grated coconut is not the same as desiccated coconut, sweetened shredded coconut. Grated coconut should resemble finely grated shavings rather than long thin shreds. T

Japanese salted plums (umeboshi/梅干し) are unripe ume—a variety of Japanese plum similar to apricots—that are pickled in salt and dried in the sun. These can be light brown or red if red shiso leaves have been added for color and flavor. Remarkably sour and salty, salted plums can be added as an appetizing topping for porridge or noodle soups; mash the umeboshi to disperse its flavor. Otherwise, they can be chopped or combined with rice (see Umeboshi Onigiri

JAPANESE SALTED PLUMS

KOMBU

with Marinated Yolk and Shiso on page 209). Japanese salted plums are typically sold whole in small plastic packets or as a jarred paste (labeled "umeboshi paste") at Japanese grocers, and should not be confused with dried salted plums that are sold as snacks. Chinese salted plums make a fine substitute; these tend to be larger and are jarred in brine. F P

Japanese seven-spice seasoning (shichimi togarashi/七味唐辛子) is a nutty, citrusy blend that typically consists of ground red chiles, sansho pepper, sesame seeds, seaweed, ginger, and orange peel. Its fragrance is very delicate, so it is typically used as a finishing sprinkle (see Butternut Squash Dengaku on page 251). This seasoning can be found at Japanese grocers, where it is sold in small glass jars. A

Kecap manis is a sweet and thick soy sauce that originates in Java, Indonesia. It is made by fermenting soybeans and combining them with palm sugar, producing a condiment that is deeply sweet, savory, umami, and thick as honey. Kecap manis works terrifically in dishes as a key seasoning to provide nuanced sweetness (see Hot Butter Mushrooms on page 161), as the core component of a dip (see Fried Tempeh with Sambal Kicap on page 183), and as a glaze for grilled foods (see Tempeh Satay with Sambal Matah on page 215). You can find kecap manis at Southeast Asia grocers. I typically reach for the ABC brand, which is labeled as sweet soy sauce. F P

Kombu is a type of edible kelp that is typically sold dried as thick, dark green sheets. The drying process breaks down its proteins into free glutamate, the primary umami compound, which forms a white powdery coating on the kelp. Thus, for maximum flavor, avoid rinsing the kombu before use. Kombu is a cornerstone ingredient in Japanese cuisine, where it is used to make dashi, the umami-rich soup stock that forms the base of many Japanese dishes. To release its flavor, kombu can be steeped in water overnight (see Whole Tomato Rice on page 77) or simmered in water. Because kombu can impart bitter flavors if it is boiled, it is good practice to remove it from the pot before the liquid reaches a boil. You can find kombu sold in plastic packets or as bottled kombu dashi (sometimes also labeled kombu stock extract) at Japanese grocers. F P

Korean fermented plum syrup (maesil-cheong/매실청) is made by packing green plums in sugar and leaving them to ferment for months, resulting in a sweet syrup. Slightly tangy and fruity, this sweetener truly shines in simple preparations with few ingredients (see Soba Salad with Tahini Dressing on page 51). It is sold in glass jars or plastic squeeze bottles at Korean supermarkets. A combination of brown rice syrup and mashed Japanese salted plum or plum sauce (I'm partial to Lee Kum Kee) can work as a substitute. Otherwise, you can approximate Korean fermented plum syrup by roughly chopping some plums and mixing them with an equal weight of sugar in a glass jar. Leave the jar at room temperature for 2 to 3 weeks, or until the fruit releases liquid and the sugar is completely dissolved. Stir the mixture every few days to help dissolve the sugar completely. Pass the syrup through a fine-mesh strainer set over a large bowl; discard the solids or have them with yogurt. The syrup will keep in the refrigerator for up to a year. F P

KOREAN FERMENTED PLUM SYRUP

MAKRUT LIME LEAVES

Korean chili paste (gochujang/고추장) is one of the mother condiments in Korean cuisine. The savory, sweet, and spicy paste is made by fermenting a mixture of Korean chili flakes, fermented soybeans, glutinous rice, and salt in earthenware pots for months. This ingredient is incredibly versatile and can be used in dipping sauces (see Mini Kimbap with Ssamjang Mayonnaise on page 41), stews, or glazes (see Fried Cauliflower with Gochujang Glaze on page 179). You can find gochujang sold in plastic containers on the shelves of Korean grocers. F P

Korean soybean paste (doenjang/된장) is another foundational condiment in Korean cuisine. To make doenjang, soybeans are boiled and mashed into a paste. This paste is then molded into firm brown bricks, hung to air-cure, and left to ferment in salted water. While doenjang has the same paste-like consistency as miso, it is more intensely earthy and funky. It is wonderful as a backdrop flavor in stews and dipping sauces (see Mini Kimbap with Ssamjang Mayonnaise on page 41). You can find doenjang sold in plastic containers at Korean grocers. If unavailable, you can substitute miso in a pinch. F P

Lemongrass is a sturdy grass with a citrusy, citronella-like flavor. It can be ground and cooked gently with other aromatics in a spice paste (see Steamed Okra with Sambal and Red Onion on page 71), minced and fried at the start of a recipe (see Lemongrass Tofu with Chiles on page 167), or thinly sliced and enjoyed raw or lightly scalded (see Tempeh Satay with Sambal Matah on page 215). The flavor of lemongrass is concentrated in the bottom half of the stalk, which is the only part typically used in applications involving grinding or thinly slicing. Fresh lemongrass is available at Southeast Asian grocers, and the stalks can also be found frozen. I don't recommend chopped or pureed lemongrass as the flavor diminishes once the lemongrass is cut. A

Makrut lime leaves, the dark green leaves of the makrut lime tree, carry an intense citronella-like aroma. When torn to release their fragrance, they can be steeped in stir-fries, braises, or curries (see Gaeng Tay Po on page 229). Alternatively, they can be enjoyed raw or lightly scalded (see Cauliflower Laab on page 117); because lime leaves are very tough, they have to be finely sliced before they can be used as a garnish. To do this, stack the leaves, fold them in half along their inner rib, then slice them crosswise, as thinly as you can. You will find lime leaves, fresh or frozen, at Southeast Asian grocers. A

Miso is a fermented soybean paste that is foundational to Japanese cuisine. Known for its umami flavor, miso comes in various types, ranging from light and sweet to dark and intensely savory. These include white miso (shiro miso), which is light in color and mildly sweet, and red miso (aka miso), which is darker and more robustly umami. Miso is incredibly versatile; it can be dissolved into soups or turned into a glaze (see Butternut Squash Dengaku on page 251), for example. A blend of red and white miso (awase miso) is a great all-purpose option that is ideal for the recipes in this book; it is available at Japanese grocers in plastic tubs or packets. Otherwise, any miso that you have on hand will work. Read more about miso on page 86. F P

LEMONGRASS

PRESERVED RADISH

Nori is paper-like, dried red algae. The drying concentrates its umami flavor, while the gentle heat generates roasted, nutty notes. These are widely used in Japanese and Korean cuisines and appreciated for their umami flavor and crispy texture. Nori is most commonly sold in sheets. A sheet is approximately 8 by 8½ inches (20 by 22 cm), making it suitable for rolls such as sushi and kimbap (see Mini Kimbap with Ssamjang Mayonnaise on page 41). Nori sheets can be shredded into nori strips and used for garnish (see Charred Brussels Sprouts with Grapefruit and Yuba on page 193). Both forms can be bought from Japanese and Korean grocers. The standard-size sheets are typically sold in plastic packages with a desiccant to prevent moisture absorption. Nori strips are often sold in plastic bags, but can also be made from store-bought seaweed sheets by snipping with scissors.

Pandan leaves are the long and blade-shaped leaves of the pandan shrub. Their unique fragrance that sits between jasmine rice, vanilla, and matcha lends them to both sweet and savory dishes. As these leaves are too tough and fibrous to eat directly, cooks drop them into pots to infuse (see Gaeng Tay Po on page 229), or juice them to obtain pandan extract (see Pandan Nián Gāo on page 265), where their bitter, matcha-like quality comes to the fore. Knotting pandan will keep the leaves from being an impediment to stirring. Knotting also partially crushes the leaves to help release their fragrance. To knot pandan, gather the leaves into a bunch, all oriented the same way, and loop the bunch around itself into a knot. Repeat the knotting once more so that you get a tidy bundle of pandan. You will find pandan leaves, fresh or frozen, at Southeast Asian grocers. While commonly used, store-bought pandan extracts and essences are not ideal as they turn desserts a garish neon green and lack the nuance of fresh pandan. Fig leaves are a good substitute for pandan leaves, as both pair well with coconut and are versatile enough to straddle sweet and savory applications.

Perilla oil (deulgireum/들기름) is oil extracted from the seeds of the perilla plant, commonly used in Korean cuisine. Perilla leaves, also known as shiso leaves, are also used in cooking, particularly in Korean, Japanese, and Vietnamese cuisines. Even though it is sometimes compared to sesame oil, perilla oil has a distinct grassy flavor and greenish-yellow hue that reminds me of extra virgin olive oil. Due to its low smoke point, perilla oil is typically used in moist-heat cooking methods (see Whole Tomato Rice on page 77) or as a finishing oil (see Naengmyeon with Watermelon Dongchimi on page 59). You will find this ingredient sold in glass jars at Korean supermarkets. In place of perilla oil, rather than using sesame oil, try high-quality extra virgin oil.

Preserved mustard stem (zhà cài/榨菜) is the swollen stem of the mustard plant that has been salted, dried, and fermented with chili paste. This Chinese ingredient is valued for its crunch as much as its salty, tangy, slightly spicy, and umami flavor profile. This is why I love pairing it with softer, custardy textures (see Steamed Eggplant with Preserved Mustard Stem, Garlic, and Soy on page 65). Preserved mustard stem is typically sold in strip form in vacuum-sealed pouches at Chinese and Southeast Asian grocers. Pickled mustard greens, stored in brine, are a passable substitute though these are significantly tangier.

Preserved radish (cài fǔ/菜脯) is fresh daikon radish cured in salt and dried in the sun until it turns brown and leathery. Rinse or soak the pieces in water to get rid of excess salt before draining and using. Because it brims with umami flavor, preserved radish is often fried in oil like an aromatic such as garlic or onion, though it has more of a pleasantly chewy, nubbly texture (see Chayote and Glass Noodle Dumplings on page 73). You will find preserved radish sold in small plastic packets at Southeast Asian or Chinese grocers. They are sold whole, in strips, or finely chopped; for the recipes in this book, use finely chopped preserved radish.

Red fermented tofu (hóng fǔ rǔ/红腐乳) is a Chinese ingredient made by fermenting tofu cubes in a brine of rice wine, salt, spices, and red yeast rice, which gives it its distinctive red color. Whereas red fermented tofu is robust and suited for enriching thick soups, stews, and braises, there is also a white variant made without red yeast rice (bái fǔ rǔ/白腐乳) that is milder and more suitable for vegetable stir-fries. Mashed with a fork, it has the creamy, spreadable consistency of soft cheese and can be used to make creamy dressings without dairy or dissolved in water for a rich, almost-instant broth (see Mushroom Ramen with Fermented Tofu Broth on page 125). It is available jarred or in plastic containers at Chinese and Southeast Asian grocers. White fermented tofu can be used if red fermented tofu is unavailable. Read more about fermented tofu on page 134. F P T

RED FERMENTED TOFU

Shiso leaves, also known as perilla leaves, are a heart-shaped aromatic herb with jagged edges, and can be found in two colors: green and purple (or red to some). Typically used in Vietnamese, Japanese, and Korean cuisines, the leaves have a unique fragrance that is simultaneously minty, herbal, and citrusy. To use them, pick them off their tough stems before chopping and incorporating into rice for a burst of flavor (see Umeboshi Onigiri with Marinated Yolk and Shiso on page 209), thinly sliced and used as garnish, or infused into beverages and desserts. You will find the fresh leaves at Vietnamese, Japanese, and Korean grocers. Instead of shiso, you can use basil or mint leaves, though their flavor profiles are different. A

SHISO LEAVES

Sichuan pepper (crushed or ground) is made from the dried berries of the prickly ash tree, and is the key ingredient in Sichuan cuisine, known for its citrusy aroma and numbing sensation. To release its flavor, scald it with oil (see Sizzling Cucumber Salad with Silken Tofu on page 31). Sichuan pepper powder is sold in small glass jars at Chinese grocers. Alternatively, you can grind your own powder from Sichuan peppercorns. A

Tamarind concentrate is a watery liquid made by dissolving the dark brown pulp derived from the tamarind fruit in water. It is used as a souring agent, offering a date-like sweetness and rounded tang to dishes (see Polos Ambula on page 103). Store-bought concentrate can be purchased from Southeast Asian and Indian grocers, but you can make your own with tamarind paste, which has the firm yet pliable texture of nougat and is studded with seeds.

To do this, place the tamarind paste in a bowl and cover with double its weight of boiling water. Set aside until it is cool enough to handle, then knead it by hand to loosen the seeds. Pour this through a fine-mesh strainer, discarding any debris, and store it in an airtight container in the refrigerator for up to 3 weeks.

In place of store-bought or homemade tamarind concentrate, you can use jarred seedless tamarind pulp. A

Tempeh is a traditional Indonesian food item made by fermenting cooked soybeans, resulting in a firm, cake-like block that is valued for its high protein content. The best way to cook tempeh, in my opinion, is to fry it; it crisps and browns spectacularly and its nuttiness is enhanced (see Fried Tempeh with Sambal Kicap on page 183). There is much poorly made tempeh on

the market. In good tempeh, the individual soybeans should be visible in the block and encased in pure white, rather than off-white, mycelium. The block should be dry—almost slightly furry—to the touch and should smell subtly yeasty, like a loaf of bread. Stay away from tempeh that smells musty or has been pre-marinated with seasonings such as soy sauce. High-quality tempeh can be bought from Southeast Asian grocers. Read more about tempeh on page 180.

Thai basil is a fragrant herb that is used in Thai, Vietnamese, and Taiwanese cuisines. Unlike sweet basil, it has pointed green leaves tinged with purple, and has prominent anise and licorice undertones. Stripped from the tough stems, the leaves can be enjoyed raw in salads (see Kohlrabi and Carrot Salad on page 35) or wilted into stir-fries and sauces (see Tempeh Chili Pan Mee with Thai Basil on page 119). You will be able to find fresh Thai basil at Southeast Asian grocers. Otherwise you can substitute sweet basil, though the flavor profile will be slightly different. A

Tofu is a versatile and nutritious soybean product that is widely enjoyed in Asian cuisines. Tofu is made by soaking and grinding soybeans to form soymilk, before adding a coagulant to curdle it. The curds are transferred into molds lined with cloth and pressed to remove excess whey. The amount of pressure determines the tofu's firmness. Silken tofu has a soft texture that allows it to be scooped out of its packaging with a spoon. It is typically served cold or at room temperature, with a punchy dressing (see Sizzling Cucumber Salad with Silken Tofu on page 31). Firm tofu, on the other hand, holds its shape

TAMARIND CONCENTRATE

THAI BASIL

well and is versatile for cooking (see Tofu Kimchi on page 123). Extra-firm tofu is dense and chewy, and is best for deep-frying (see Sambal Goreng on page 211). You will find all three varieties at most Asian grocers. Read more about tofu on page 164. T

Yellow bean paste (tau cheo/豆酱) is a dark brown condiment made by salting and fermenting soybeans before coarsely mashing them into a paste. It is incredibly salty and umami, and has a looser, less paste-like consistency compared to miso. It is perfect as a condiment, in stir-fries (see Eggplant Croquettes with Cilantro Mayonnaise on page 169), braises, or gravies. You'll find jars of yellow bean paste at Southeast Asian or Chinese grocers—I use Lee Kum Kee's "soybean sauce." Fermented soybeans are sometimes also sold as whole pellets rather than in paste form; these can be coarsely crushed with a mortar and pestle and used just like fermented soybean paste. F P

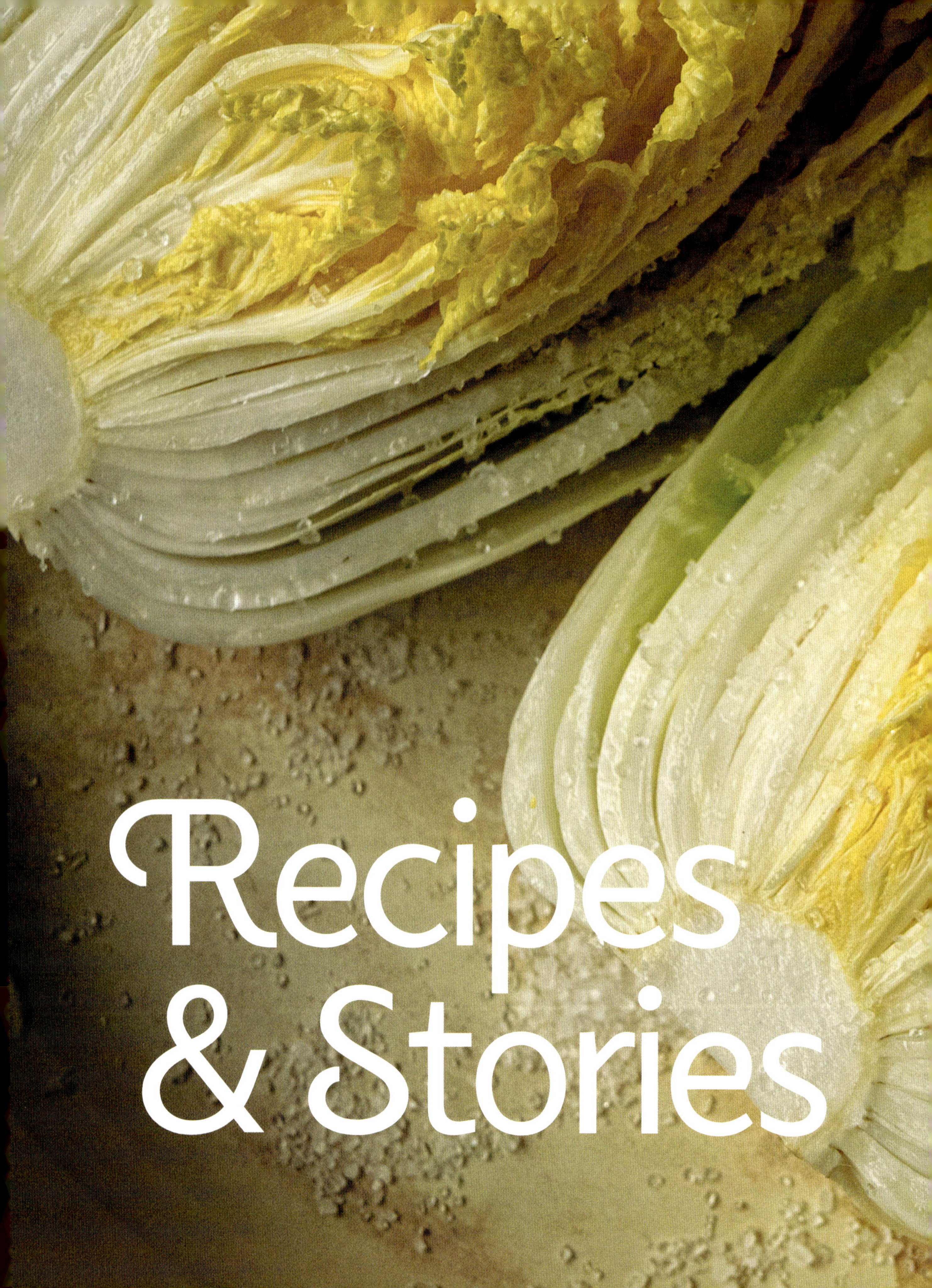
Recipes
& Stories

NAENGMYEON WITH
WATERMELON DONGCHIMI, PAGE 59

Raw

Chickpea Tofu Salad

SERVES 2

TOFU

Oil, for greasing

1 cup (140 g) chickpea flour

½ teaspoon ground turmeric

½ teaspoon salt

SALAD

6 garlic cloves, thinly sliced

¼ cup plus 3 tablespoons (100 ml) oil

3 ounces (85 g) purple or green cabbage, finely shredded

4 makrut lime leaves (see page 20), thinly sliced

2 green onions, thinly sliced

1 green chile, minced

¼ small red onion, thinly sliced

2 tablespoons lime juice

2 tablespoons soy sauce

1 tablespoon chili crisp (see page 14), optional

1 tablespoon sesame seeds, toasted

1½ teaspoons sugar

My gripe with leafy salads is that they demand to be dressed à la minute, since dressings pull moisture out of the greens once tossed and turn them limp. Not so with tohu thoke (တိုဟူးသုပ်). The star of this Burmese salad is chickpea tofu, also known as Burmese tofu or Shan tofu. It is made by simmering chickpea flour in water, similar to making polenta, except that this mixture thickens in a fraction of the time. Soft and porridge-like, it can be enjoyed with an assortment of toppings, or poured into a mold to set before slicing and adding to salads. Any leftovers can be deep-fried into fritters with crispy exteriors and custardy interiors. Its versatility is truly astounding and its neutrality allows it to function as a canvas for flavor. This salad with its slippery, cooling strips of tofu is one of my favorites for summer, and what truly makes it special are the makrut lime leaves, which provide a haunting fragrance.

1. **For the tofu,** the night before you plan to serve, oil a rectangular plastic container or loaf pan. Pour 1¼ cups (300 ml) water into a saucepan and set it on high heat. In the meantime, whisk together the chickpea flour, turmeric, salt, and 1¼ cups (300 ml) water in a medium bowl.
2. When the water in the saucepan boils, turn the heat to low. Pour in the chickpea mixture, scraping the bowl with a spatula to get it all out. Bring the mixture to a simmer while stirring frequently with a spatula. As the mixture thickens, diligently scrape the bottom and sides of the saucepan to ensure even cooking. It is ready when it resembles a thick custard and clings to the spatula, holding its shape when lifted.
3. Scrape the mixture into your prepared container or pan and spread it out evenly with a spatula. Allow to cool completely, then cover and refrigerate overnight. The tofu can be made up to four days in advance and kept refrigerated in an airtight container.
4. **For the salad,** combine the garlic and oil in a saucepan and set it on medium heat. When the garlic turns a light golden color, 2 to 3 minutes, pour the contents of the pan through a fine-mesh strainer set over a bowl. With a slotted spoon, transfer the crispy garlic to a wide bowl, along with ¼ cup (60 ml) of the fragrant oil.
5. Add the cabbage, lime leaves, green onions, green chile, red onion, lime juice, soy sauce, chili crisp (if using), sesame seeds, and sugar. Toss well.
6. Retrieve the tofu from the refrigerator and turn the container or pan upside down onto a cutting board. Tap its base firmly to unmold the tofu. Slice the tofu in half lengthwise, then slice crosswise into thin strips. Add the tofu to the bowl and toss gently. Serve.

Sizzling Cucumber Salad with Silken Tofu

SERVES 3 TO 4

- 1 large cucumber, halved lengthwise
- 1 teaspoon salt
- ¼ cup plus 1 tablespoon (75 ml) oil
- ⅓ cup (40 g) raw peanuts, with or without skin
- 3 tablespoons Chinkiang black vinegar (see page 14)
- 3 tablespoons soy sauce
- 3 teaspoons toasted sesame oil
- 3 garlic cloves, finely grated
- 2 teaspoons sugar
- 1 tablespoon plus 1½ teaspoons Korean chili flakes (gochugaru/고춧가루)
- ½ teaspoon ground Sichuan pepper (see page 22)
- 14 ounces (400 g) silken tofu (see page 23)
- 1 tablespoon sesame seeds, toasted

In Chinese food culture, there are dishes to "open your stomach" (kāi wèi cài/开胃菜). These are usually an assortment of little dishes eaten at the start of the meal, and this cucumber salad recipe is one of my favorites because it is so refreshing. The key to this dish is to smack the cucumber with the back of a cleaver (or another heavy object) until it splits open. This encourages it to imbibe any dressing of your choice, which, in this case, is made by scalding aromatics with hot oil to enhance their flavor and color. If you're after a richer, more luxurious alternative to silken tofu, stracciatella is an unconventional but great option.

1. Place the cucumber halves cut side down on a cutting board. Smack firmly along the entire length of the cucumber halves with the side of a large knife, preferably a heavy cleaver, until they split.
2. Slice the cucumber thickly, on a diagonal, and transfer to a mixing bowl. Toss with the salt.
3. Set a saucepan on high heat. Line a dish with paper towel. Add the oil and peanuts and toast until the skins begin to peel or the skinless peanuts turn golden, about 3 minutes. Using a slotted spoon, transfer them to the prepared dish. Set the pan with the oil aside for later use.
4. Drain the released water from the salted cucumber and toss the cucumber slices with the black vinegar, soy sauce, and sesame oil. Top with the garlic, sugar, chili flakes, and Sichuan pepper.
5. Set the pan with the reserved oil on high heat until the oil just begins to smoke. Pour it over the aromatics—they should sizzle upon contact. Toss the cucumber salad briskly. Add more soy sauce, black vinegar, or sugar to taste.
6. Scoop large chunks of the silken tofu onto a serving platter, then spoon the cucumber and dressing over the tofu. Scatter the sesame seeds and fried peanuts over and serve immediately.

Cameron Stauch

When I embarked on writing *PlantAsia*, one of the first cookbooks that I consulted was Cameron Stauch's *Vegetarian Việt Nam*, a 2019 James Beard Foundation Book Award Finalist. The recipes did not compromise on what I considered "real food," and the book showed depth of research and insight into Vietnamese food culture. Stauch's interest in vegetarian cuisine came from working as part of the kitchen team that cooked for Canada's Governor General, and having to prepare meals for guests with dietary restrictions. Fueled by a desire to refine his skills, Stauch explores and documents the ingredients and techniques that Vietnamese cooks use to prepare vegetarian standouts.

Why did you write *Vegetarian Việt Nam*?

Because of my wife's job as a Canadian diplomat, I was fortunate to have lived in Hanoi. I felt that the best way for me to learn about the language, culture, and people of my new home was to engage with them through food. So, early on in Hanoi, I made it a daily habit to visit a market each day to learn more about Vietnamese ingredients and dishes via the food stalls around the markets.

During our first year in Hanoi, my three-and-a-half-year-old son announced at dinner that he was a vegetarian and would no longer eat meat or fish. So, for him to sample dishes from a cuisine that appeared to contain many meat and seafood elements, I needed to search out what options there were for him and for the rest of the family by extension.

What did you glean from your time in Vietnam through writing the book?

I was lucky to cook with Nguyen Dzoan Cam Van, perhaps Vietnam's most well-known chef. She's extremely well-versed in the different regional cuisines and has authored over forty cookbooks. I also had memorable meals at monasteries and nunneries, where there were prayers before each meal. These were always a good signal to slow down, pause, and think about offering thanks for the ingredients, the people who grew them, and the purpose of the meal. Eating in silence was another way to reflect on the bounty before you.

While researching the book and learning from the many cooks throughout Vietnam, it became apparent to me that the cooks who ate and cooked the meat and seafood versions of dishes—including vegetarian cooks who had not always been vegetarians—could often make better-tasting vegetarian versions as opposed to lifelong vegetarian cooks, since they had the taste memory to figure out how to make the meatless version taste like the original.

What are some techniques that you've picked up?

Freezing and thawing tofu changes its texture and allows marinades to penetrate easily. When the same tofu is molded and wrapped in nori, it mimics the texture and taste of fish.

I also became a huge fan of using fresh tofu skin. Its texture and flavor are wonderful in vegetarian sausages. In soup, shallow-frying smaller pieces of tofu skin before adding it to the broth not only helps to retain the integrity of its texture, but the thin layer of fat from the shallow-frying also adds flavor to the soup. It's important to make sure there is some fat in the dish, especially if it's a soup, stew, or simmered dish. Fat is flavor. I think too many vegetarian and vegan cooks leave this element out and this makes the dish taste a little one-dimensional.

What are your favorite ways to add flavor?

I was amazed to see how Vietnamese cooks used dried mushroom powder or ground seaweed near the end of cooking to boost the umami of a dish. Freshly ground black pepper adjusts the flavors and adds a nice citrusy zing right before serving. Fermented tofu, or chao in Vietnamese, is another umami-enhancing ingredient—you can stir a little into a soup like bún bò huế chay, or add it to stir-fried morning glory (water spinach).

Kohlrabi and Carrot Salad

SERVES 4

*BY CAMERON STAUCH**

1 large kohlrabi or 1½ chayote, cut into thin matchsticks

1 carrot, cut into thin matchsticks

¼ cup plus 2 tablespoons (90 ml) Japanese rice vinegar

3 tablespoons sugar

1 tablespoon soy sauce

1 teaspoon salt

3 garlic cloves, finely chopped

1 bird's-eye chile, finely chopped

A small handful of Vietnamese balm, mint, or Thai basil leaves (see page 23), roughly chopped

A small handful of cilantro leaves, roughly chopped

3 tablespoons roasted peanuts, roughly chopped

3 tablespoons fried shallots (see page 17)

"I really enjoy Vietnamese salads. Green papaya salad in Vietnam features thin strips of crisp green papaya marinated in a sweet and sour dressing, topped with lemony herbs and crushed peanuts. You can also make it with kohlrabi or chayote."—*Cameron Stauch*

1. Mix the vegetables together in a medium bowl. Set aside.
2. In a small bowl, make the dressing by combining the rice vinegar, sugar, soy sauce, salt, garlic, and bird's-eye chile.
3. Pour the dressing over the vegetables and add the Vietnamese balm and cilantro leaves. Mix everything together, then transfer to a serving bowl.
4. Sprinkle with the peanuts and fried shallots, and serve.

* Adapted from *Vegetarian Viêt Nam* by Cameron Stauch, copyright © 2018. Published by W. W. Norton & Company.

Baechu Kimchi

MAKES APPROXIMATELY 4 POUNDS (1.8 KG) KIMCHI

SALTED CABBAGE

1 large whole Napa cabbage (about 2 pounds/900 g)

½ cup (140 g) fine sea salt

½ cup (125 g) coarse sea salt

SEASONING PASTE

5 dried shiitake mushrooms (see page 16)

1¼ cups (300 ml) boiling water

1 tablespoon plus 1½ teaspoons cornstarch

¾ cup (75 g) Korean chili flakes (gochugaru/고춧가루)

⅓ cup (80 g) unsweetened applesauce

¼ cup (60 ml) soy sauce

5 garlic cloves, finely grated

1 teaspoon finely grated ginger

1 large daikon radish (about 1 pound/450 g), cut into thin matchsticks

3.5 ounces (100 g) chives, cut into 1½-inch (4 cm) lengths

In the traditional practice known as gimjang (김장), families and neighbors gather to prepare Napa cabbage (baechu kimchi/배추김치) for the winter months ahead. Heads of Napa cabbage are salted, massaged with a thick seasoning paste, and stored in large jars. While many ferments from other parts of the world are enjoyed only after a period of aging, Koreans embrace kimchi as a living, ever-evolving food. When baechu kimchi is freshly made, the seasoning has yet to fully penetrate the cabbage leaves, acting more like a salad dressing. As the kimchi ages, it progressively sours and develops an assertively funky flavor, making it ideal for cooking in dishes like kimchi pancakes or stews. While chopped cabbage offers convenience, making whole-cabbage kimchi is a time-honored practice for good reason—the larger pieces allow fermentation to occur at a more gradual pace, so the kimchi can be stored longer without becoming overly sour.

1. **For the salted cabbage,** make a deep cut in the root end of the cabbage and then pull the two halves apart from the incision. ① This gives the leaves a beautiful naturally ruffled appearance.
2. In a large bowl, dissolve the fine sea salt in 3 quarts (3 L) water to make a brine. Dip the cabbage halves into the brine and place them in a large tray or wide bowl; moistening the cabbage will help the coarse salt adhere. Pulling back one leaf at a time, sprinkle the cabbage all over with coarse sea salt, focusing on the thick stems. ②
3. Place the salted cabbage in a snug pot and pour over the brine; the cabbage should be submerged. Weigh it down with a heavy plate and leave to soak overnight in the refrigerator.
4. The next day, the cabbage should be limp and soft enough to fold in half without breaking. Drain and rinse it in several changes of water, folding back the leaves as needed to flush out any trapped salt. Taste a sliver of cabbage. It should taste salty, but you should still be able to taste the natural sweetness of the cabbage. If the cabbage tastes like you just ate a mouthful of salt, continue rinsing with more changes of water.
5. When you are happy with the saltiness of the cabbage, squeeze the halves over a sink with your hands to expel excess liquid, then place them with their cores facing up in a colander to drain for 30 minutes.
6. **For the seasoning paste,** add the shiitake mushrooms and boiling water to a saucepan. Let cool completely, then squeeze the mushrooms to expel all of the excess liquid. Only the liquid will be used in this recipe; the mushrooms can be saved for other dishes.
7. Whisk the cornstarch into the mushroom liquid and bring to a boil on low heat, stirring constantly. The mixture should thicken to a slurry.

8. Stir in the chili flakes, applesauce, soy sauce, garlic, and ginger. Scrape this into a large tray or wide bowl and mix in the daikon and chives. Add more soy sauce or applesauce to taste.

9. Working one layer of cabbage leaves at a time, pull back the leaves and smear them with the seasoning paste by hand. If you prefer, you can wear gloves to prevent lingering odors and potential irritation from the chiles. ③

10. Pack the cabbage into snug jar(s) or container(s), along with any excess daikon mixture. I like to store each cabbage half in a 1.3-quart (approximately 1.2 L) glass container because this allows me to keep one in the refrigerator and one on my counter (see the next step). ④ The kimchi will produce carbon dioxide as it ferments, so make sure that the container(s) or jar(s) are not packed to the brim. The kimchi will not be submerged in sauce.

11. You can eat the kimchi right away, age it in the refrigerator, or leave it on your kitchen counter for one to two days for a riper flavor. It will keep for weeks and will continue developing in flavor and acidity. Cut it into bite-size pieces with a knife or scissors before serving.

3

4

Mini Kimbap with Ssamjang Mayonnaise

MAKES 20 MINI KIMBAP

Many meals in my house revolve around a pot of freshly steamed rice. And when it's time to pack a lunch box, I am just as likely to pack something like kimbap (김밥) as I am to pack a sandwich. These mini kimbap are bite-size versions of the traditional Korean seaweed rolls. Their size means that they are less fussy to assemble and wrap, and far easier to eat on the go. I serve mine with ssamjang mayonnaise on the side for dipping. Ssamjang (쌈장) is a traditional condiment made with gochujang and doenjang—two mother condiments in Korean cooking made from fermented soybeans. In this dip, the bold flavors are complemented by the mayonnaise, which lends fattiness and richness to what is otherwise a rather lean dish. Like all great lunchbox additions, these kimbap can be made in advance and stored in the refrigerator. Just make sure that they are stored in a snug airtight container, or the rice might dry out and lose its comforting stickiness.

RICE

1½ cups (300 g) Japanese or Korean short-grain rice, rinsed thoroughly and drained

1 teaspoon salt

1 teaspoon toasted sesame oil

CARROTS

1½ teaspoons oil

1 garlic clove, minced

2 carrots, cut into thin matchsticks

1 teaspoon soy sauce

1 teaspoon toasted sesame oil

BABY SPINACH

1½ teaspoons oil

9 ounces (250 g) baby spinach

1 teaspoon soy sauce

1 teaspoon toasted sesame oil

SSAMJANG MAYONNAISE

¼ cup (60 ml) mayonnaise

2 tablespoons Korean chili paste (gochujang/고추장; see page 20)

1 tablespoon Korean soybean paste (doenjang/된장; see page 20)

1 tablespoon honey

3 garlic cloves, chopped

2 teaspoons toasted sesame oil

ASSEMBLY

½ Japanese cucumber, about 8 inches (20 cm) in length

5 nori sheets (see page 21), cut into quarters

Toasted sesame oil, for brushing

1½ teaspoons sesame seeds, toasted

1. **For the rice,** combine the rice with 2 cups (480 ml) water in a rice cooker and allow to cook. (See page 3 for instructions on cooking rice without a rice cooker.) Once the water has been fully absorbed and the rice is tender, mix in the salt and sesame oil and set aside to cool while you prepare the other components.
2. **For the carrots,** set a skillet on high heat and add the oil and garlic. Stir-fry to release the fragrance, about 10 seconds, then add the carrot. Fry for 1 minute, or until the carrots slightly soften, then stir in the soy sauce and sesame oil. Tip the carrots out onto a plate to cool.
3. **For the baby spinach,** return the skillet to the stove and add the oil, baby spinach, and a splash of water. Fry for 3 minutes, or until the spinach wilts and the moisture in the pan dries up. Stir in the soy sauce and sesame oil before tipping the spinach out onto a separate plate to cool.
4. **For the ssamjang mayonnaise,** stir together the mayonnaise, chili paste, soybean paste, honey, garlic, and sesame oil in a small bowl.

RECIPE CONTINUED →

1

5. **For assembly,** cut the cucumber half lengthwise into quarters, then remove the seeds with your knife or by scraping them off with a teaspoon. Cut each quarter in half crosswise so that each piece of cucumber is roughly 3¼ inches (8.25 cm) in length, about as long as a nori quarter. Slice the cucumber lengthwise to produce ⅓-inch-thick (8 mm) batons. You will need 20 cucumber batons for this recipe.
6. Place one nori quarter on your work surface and top it with a heaping tablespoon of rice. Dip your fingers into a bowl of water to moisten them, then gently press the rice onto the seaweed to form a thin and compact layer, leaving a ½-inch (1.25 cm) border at the edge farthest from you. ① Dampen this border with a moistened finger, then top the rice with a cucumber baton, a generous pinch of carrot, and a generous pinch of spinach. ② Roll the kimbap up away from you like a cigar to enclose the filling. ③ Repeat until all of the vegetables are used up.
7. Lightly brush the kimbap all over with sesame oil and sprinkle with the toasted sesame seeds. Serve with the ssamjang mayonnaise on the side. ④

Sunny Lee

When I spoke with Korean chef and Brooklyn resident Sunny Lee, she had just completed her residency *Banchan by Sunny*, with dreams of converting it into a brick-and-mortar restaurant. Despite having a "very American childhood," she found a passion for Korean food after a decade of working in some of New York City's finest dining institutions such as Blue Hill at Stone Barns, Eleven Madison Park, Battersby, Estela, and Insa. When asked about her focus on the small side dishes in a Korean meal (banchan/반찬), she recalls post-shift Korean barbecues with colleagues: "You go to dinner and someone puts ten little plates of food in front of you; there is no stronger way to say, 'I love you' than that."

How does the approach to plant-based dining in the United States compare to Korea's?

The vegan cuisine that is trendy in Los Angeles specifically focuses on meat substitutes, cold bowls of lettuce, and raw fruits. My opinion is that this is not very healthy, as it focuses more on what shouldn't be on the plate, as opposed to creating a balanced meal.

When you go to a place that has a strong vegetarian food culture such as Japan, India, or Korea, you realize that they have built the entire cuisine around health and wellness—it is not a trend. The more I learn about Korean cuisine, the more I realize that it emphasizes the role of food as medicine. There's a reason why Korean food features ingredients like ginger, jujube, ginseng, or mountain vegetables—plants that are extremely beneficial to health—and has fermentation at its heart.

What percentage of your menu is vegan?

It is important to me that more than half of the banchan on my menu is vegan. An example is the stir-fried dish (bokkeum/볶음) of tubers—burdock, lotus root, kohlrabi—glazed in a soy-sauce caramel.

I used to work in kitchens where we would roll our eyes at vegan guests and they would get served things like shaved radishes on a plate. Who wants to eat that for dinner? What I would like in my restaurant is for a vegan to sit next to an omnivore and for both of them to have equally satisfying dining experiences.

What are some of your favorite techniques and ingredients to enhance vegetables?

I use a lot of miso and Korean fermented bean paste (doenjang/된장) as an umami-enhancer. Homemade soybean powder (konggaru/콩가루), made by deeply roasting soybeans for an hour and crushing them, also features prominently in my cooking. There is a banchan that I make where I coat chunks of squash with doenjang, sugar, and a little oil, and roast them until they are deeply caramelized. Out of the oven, they are tossed with Israeli date syrup (silan/סילאן), soybean powder, and sesame oil for a sweet, savory, and nutty flavor profile with just a bit of crunch.

The act of fermentation also lends vegetables lots of flavor—they take on a deep savoriness and you forget that you are not eating meat. When I make sauerkraut, I use the liquid to season my salads for extra flavor.

How does texture factor into your dishes?

The Sichuan dish called "husband and wife lung pieces" (fū qī fèi piàn/夫妻肺片), where you have different textures of meat and offal on the plate, is a perfect study on texture. I have played around with veganizing it by using mung bean starch jelly (cheongpo-muk/청포묵). There is also a traditional technique where radishes are dried in the summer sun to prevent spoilage; they can be rehydrated and eaten throughout the winter months. I have been preparing carrots and parsnips this way. What dehydration does to the vegetables is it collapses their cell structure, so that when they are soaked in water, the texture becomes spongy and crunchy. I fold these rehydrated vegetables and pickled wood ear mushrooms with the mung bean starch jelly, so you have all these textures in your mouth. Some of them really do emulate the texture of cartilage or meat.

Mumallaengi-Muchim

SERVES 8 TO 10

BY SUNNY LEE

VEGETABLES

6 to 8 Persian cucumbers (about 1 pound plus 1 ounce/480 g), halved lengthwise if large, cut into ½-inch (1.25 cm) slices

3¼ teaspoons salt

1 small daikon radish (about 10 ounces/280 g), cut into thin matchsticks

1 tablespoon sugar

1 small white onion, cut into ½-inch (1.25 cm) slices

2 tablespoons Korean chili flakes (gochugaru/고춧가루)

DRESSING

¼ cup (35 g) sesame seeds, toasted

3 tablespoons toasted sesame oil

3 tablespoons Korean chili paste (gochujang/고추장; see page 20)

2 tablespoons apple cider vinegar

2 tablespoons honey

1 tablespoon vegetarian fish sauce or soy sauce

3 garlic cloves, finely chopped

1 teaspoon freshly ground black pepper

"Mumallaengi-muchim (무말랭이 무침) is a traditional Korean banchan of dried daikon marinated in a gochujang-spiked dressing. It highlights one of the many fundamental techniques of Korean food preservation—the annual ritual of drying vegetables in the summer sun, which prevents spoilage and allows them to be eaten throughout the cold winter months. This banchan has a pleasant, chewy texture from the daikon, tender crunch from the cucumbers and onion, and bright spiciness from the dressing. Instead of drying the daikon in the sun, I use salt to quickly extract some of its moisture. It can be enjoyed as a vegetable banchan at a large meal, but I also use it as a topping for salads or chopped up as a sandwich spread. I even find myself snacking on it straight from the fridge."—*Sunny Lee*

1. **For the vegetables,** in a medium bowl, combine the cucumbers and 1 teaspoon of salt. Massage the cucumbers with your hands until they begin to release liquid. Transfer to a colander.
2. Place a large round of parchment paper over the cucumbers and set a weight (canned goods or a heavy mixing bowl) on top.
3. In a separate bowl, toss the daikon together with the remaining 2¼ teaspoons of salt and the sugar.
4. Add the onion to a small bowl and cover with water. Set the cucumber, daikon, and onion aside for 30 minutes.
5. Pour off any exuded liquid from the cucumbers and blot them dry with paper towel. Drain off any exuded liquid from the daikon and drain the onion. Working in batches, wrap them in a clean kitchen towel and squeeze out as much water as possible.
6. Combine the cucumbers, daikon, onion, and chili flakes in a medium bowl. Gently massage the vegetables until they are well-coated and stained bright red.
7. **For the dressing,** in a small bowl, whisk together the sesame seeds, sesame oil, chili paste, apple cider vinegar, honey, vegetarian fish sauce, garlic, and black pepper.
8. Add the dressing to the vegetables and massage everything thoroughly for about 30 seconds. Refrigerate in an airtight container for up to 3 days. Bring to room temperature before serving.

Garden Greens Sambol

SERVES 2

- ¼ block (12 g) dark palm sugar, finely chopped (see page 15)
- 1 green bird's-eye chile, optional
- ½ small red onion, chopped
- 2 tablespoons lime juice
- ½ teaspoon salt
- ½ teaspoon freshly ground black pepper
- 1 cup (90 g) grated coconut (see page 18)
- 1 tomato, chopped
- 3½ cups (140 g) loosely packed, thinly sliced baby romaine or kale

Not to be confused with sambal—an umbrella term for chile condiments in Indonesian and Malay cooking—sambol (සම්බෝල) refers to Sri Lankan side dishes made from raw ingredients. I first learned about this family of dishes when I read Prakash K. Sivanathan's wonderful *Sri Lanka: The Cookbook*. Since then, I've been making sambols with whatever vegetables I have in my fridge or garden, finding them to be the ideal fresh and cooling side dish to serve alongside fiery curries, deep-fried snacks, and rice. Grated coconut lends creamy fattiness to the salads while keeping them fresh and texturally light. This version also takes inspiration from *MasterChef Australia* contestant Savindri Perera, who made a chive sambol with a trickle of melted palm sugar for balance. Given my Singaporean heritage and familiarity with the wonderful pairing of palm sugar and coconut, this combination made perfect sense. Its simplicity is its strength; I've had guests request this recipe even when more extravagant dishes were on the table.

1. Combine the sugar and 1 tablespoon water in a small saucepan and heat until the sugar melts. Alternatively, microwave the mixture in a small bowl on high heat for 30 seconds, or until the sugar melts. Set the syrup aside to cool.
2. Add 1½ teaspoons of the syrup to a medium bowl along with the chile (if using), red onion, lime juice, salt, and black pepper and stir until combined.
3. Add the grated coconut and toss well with your hands, almost massaging everything together. Add more syrup, lime juice, salt, or black pepper to taste. It should taste a little too salty and citrusy; the flavors will balance out once the tomato and greens are added.
4. Add the tomato and romaine and lightly toss to combine with the coconut. Serve.

Soba Salad with Tahini Dressing

SERVES 4

PICKLED DAIKON

⅓ cup (80 ml) Japanese rice vinegar

⅓ cup (65 g) sugar

½ teaspoon salt

1 small daikon radish (about 5 ounces/140 g), cut into ½-inch (1.25 cm) dice

1 tablespoon finely grated beet

NOODLES

10.5 ounces (300 g) dried soba

3 tablespoons soy sauce

3 tablespoons lemon juice

3 tablespoons brown rice syrup or Korean fermented plum syrup (maesil-cheong/매실청; see page 19)

2 tablespoons tahini

5 garlic cloves, finely grated

2 teaspoons Japanese seven-spice seasoning (shichimi togarashi/七味唐辛子; see page 19)

1 large carrot, cut into thin matchsticks

1 large Japanese cucumber, cut into thin matchsticks

ASSEMBLY

A handful of edible flowers, such as pansies, optional

A few shakes of Japanese seven-spice seasoning (shichimi togarashi/七味唐辛子; see page 19)

2 avocados, pitted and thinly sliced

A handful of nori strips (see page 21)

4 eggs, hard-boiled, marinated if desired (see headnote), halved, optional

One of the most popular menu items at a Japanese café I worked at in Melbourne was their soba salad. It was so tasty that I frequently chose it for my lunch. It was there that I learned that a successful soba salad comes down to a few small but pivotal points. The soba has to be cooked until it is just al dente, which can be harder to discern than with pasta. If you think it's slightly underdone, then that's the time to drain it. The noodles must also be thoroughly rinsed so they don't become gummy and starchy as they cool. Finally, treat the noodles like salad leaves; they should never be dripping wet when you toss them with the dressing. If you like, you can steep your peeled hard-boiled eggs overnight in a marinade of one part brown sugar, two parts soy sauce, and six parts water.

1. **For the pickled daikon,** in a saucepan set on high heat, bring ⅓ cup (80 ml) water, the Japanese rice vinegar, sugar, and salt to a simmer.
2. Combine the daikon and beet in a bowl. Pour the simmering liquid over the vegetables, and set them aside to pickle.
3. **For the noodles,** bring a large saucepan of salted water to a boil. Add the dried soba and cook on high heat, stirring occasionally, for 2 minutes or until al dente. Drain the noodles in a colander set in the sink, and rinse under cool running water to quickly stop the cooking process and remove the excess starch. Shake the noodles firmly in the colander and leave in the sink to drain.
4. In the meantime, whisk together the soy sauce, lemon juice, brown rice syrup, tahini, garlic, and Japanese seven-spice seasoning in a large bowl. Add more soy sauce, lemon juice, or brown rice syrup to taste.
5. Transfer the noodles to the bowl with the dressing, along with the carrot and cucumber. Toss well with your hands.
6. **For assembly,** drain the pickled daikon. Divide the noodles between serving bowls. Top with the daikon, edible flowers (if using), Japanese seven-spice seasoning, avocados, nori strips, and eggs (if using). Serve.

Ivy Chen

When a food-loving friend of mine learned that I was writing a vegetarian cookbook, he said that I had to speak to the Taiwanese, as they are well known for their vegetarian cuisine. Ivy Chen is a culinary teacher at Ivy's Kitchen in Taipei and coauthor of *Made in Taiwan: Recipes and Stories from the Island Nation*. With clients that include the Culinary Institute of America and Discovery Channel, her technical cooking ability and respect for heritage shine. To make a vegetarian version of Taiwanese sausage, she tints seitan with red rice wine lees (the residual paste left behind after fermentation), adds water chestnuts to mirror the pork fat in the original, and encases everything in dried tofu skin. By showing that vegetarian cooking can be just as satisfying and dynamic as meat, Chen is carving space for innovation within tradition.

Why are vegetables such a big part of the traditional eating culture of Taiwan?

Taiwan's climate and soil allow for the cultivation of a wide array of vegetables; the richness of our land results in a food culture where vegetables are valued at home and in restaurants.

Taiwan is susceptible to typhoons that devastate crops, so we have honed the craft of preserving vegetables. The older folk who live rurally tend to make their own pickled mustard greens (suān cài/酸菜), preserved radish (cài fǔ/菜脯), and fermented dried mustard greens (méi gān cài/梅干菜).

How does vegetarianism differ in Taiwan from the West?

A distinguishing factor of vegetarianism in Taiwan is that it is associated with moral values such as purity and simplicity; it is not a standalone concept. For instance, it is not uncommon for a Taoist Taiwanese to temporarily adopt a vegetarian diet after they have overcome a hurdle in life to express their gratitude to the heavens. Since it is believed that a vegetarian diet cleanses the body and soul, going vegetarian is considered the greatest honor one could give to the gods. Similarly, eating imitation meat dishes, such as "vegetarian steak" made of mushrooms, is frowned upon by Buddhists in Taiwan. Simply harboring thoughts of eating meat could imply that one is not devout enough.

In Taiwan, is going vegetarian ever regarded as a form of deprivation?

Far from it—it is a pleasure! Taiwan's vegetarian food—from temple cuisine to what is dished up at roadside stalls—is so incredibly delicious that we have a lot of "temporary vegetarians" in the population. I visit vegetarian eateries because they have become so ingrained in our way of life, not because I consciously think of going meatless on any particular day.

While some may be concerned about dietary deficiencies when omitting meat from their diet, there are fewer concerns here as our vegetarian cooking harnesses the knowledge of traditional Chinese medicine. We pay a lot of attention to the concept of nourishing the body in order to strengthen one's life force (yǎng shēng/养生). In the absence of meat, traditional Chinese herbs are added to the diet to boost one's immunity.

What makes Taiwan such a food haven for vegetarian cooks?

In Taiwan, the vegetarian food culture is so developed that vegetarian cooks can find any ingredient they could possibly desire, more so than in other parts of the world. For instance, seitan (miàn jīn/面筋) can be found in many forms anywhere in the country—fresh, deep-fried, puffed, smoked, and more. As Taiwan's food culture is highly influenced by Japan, konnyaku (こんにゃく)—a rubbery, gelatinous Japanese food made from konjac yam—is also beginning to enjoy popularity. It is often shaped into the likeness of prawns and squid, as its firm jelly-like texture allows it to be a good substitute for these seafoods.

Given Taiwan's booming mushroom industry, you will also find dried mushroom stems in vegetarian shops. Cooks typically discard these, but they can be a great meat substitute. To make your own at home, pound each dried mushroom stem gently with a cleaver to flatten it; this fans out the fibers so that it resembles the muscle fibers of a pork fillet. From there, you can add the mushroom stems to your favorite sauces or curries.

Rice Noodle Sheet Rolls

SERVES 3 TO 4

BY IVY CHEN

SAUCE

3 tablespoons soy sauce, preferably made from black soybeans*

1 tablespoon plus 1½ teaspoons light brown sugar

1 tablespoon plus 1½ teaspoons cornstarch

1 teaspoon hot sauce, such as sriracha, optional

FILLING

2 tablespoons oil

½ teaspoon salt

4.25 ounces (120 g) firm tofu (see page 23), cut into ½-inch (1.25 cm) strips

2 king oyster mushrooms (about 4.5 ounces/130 g), cut into thin matchsticks

6 asparagus spears

1 carrot, cut into thin matchsticks

ASSEMBLY

3 nori sheets (see page 21)

3 fresh rice sheets (guǒ zǎi/粿仔; see page 83), trimmed to the size of the nori

1 apple, cored and cut into thin matchsticks

3 tablespoons Kewpie or vegan mayonnaise

"Vegetable dishes in Taiwan employ all the cooking methods that you could possibly think of, while elevating plant-based ingredients through the use of spices and sauces. This Hakka and Japanese-inspired dish of rice noodle sheet rolls (guǒ zǎi juǎn or kué-á-kńg/粿仔捲) features vegetables wrapped in steamed rice sheets and topped with sauce. If you cannot find tofu parcels, use firm tofu—cut it into ½-inch-thick (1 cm) strips before frying."—*Ivy Chen*

1. **For the sauce,** set a saucepan on medium heat and add the soy sauce, ½ cup plus 2 tablespoons (150 ml) water, and the light brown sugar.
2. While the mixture heats up, stir together ¼ cup (60 ml) water and the cornstarch in a small bowl.
3. When the sugar has dissolved, drizzle in the cornstarch slurry, stirring continuously to prevent clumping. Continue cooking for 1 to 2 minutes, or until the mixture thickens into a thin sauce with the consistency of maple syrup. Turn off the heat—the sauce will continue to thicken as it cools—and stir in the hot sauce (if using).
4. **For the filling,** set a skillet over medium heat and add 1 tablespoon of the oil. While the oil heats up, rub ¼ teaspoon of the salt onto the tofu strips. Pan-fry the tofu until it is golden all over, about 1 minute on each side, then remove from the skillet and set aside.
5. Add the remaining 1 tablespoon oil, ¼ teaspoon of salt, and the king oyster mushrooms to the skillet. Stir-fry until the mushrooms turn golden, 3 to 4 minutes, then remove from the heat and set aside.
6. Bring a saucepan of salted water to a boil over high heat. Add the asparagus and carrot and blanch for 30 seconds, or until crisp-tender, then drain and set aside.
7. **For assembly,** place one rice sheet on a sushi mat or cutting board and top with a sheet of nori. Arrange a third of the prepared tofu, mushrooms, asparagus, and carrot, and the apple horizontally across the middle third of the nori. With a spoon, spread a third of the mayonnaise horizontally across the bottom third of the nori.
8. Fold the bottom third of the nori and rice sheet tightly over the vegetables, so that they are in contact with the mayonnaise. Roll tightly away from your body. Repeat with the remaining two rolls.
9. Cut the rolls into 1¼-inch (3 cm) pieces and serve with the sauce.

* Unlike most commercial soy sauces that are made from yellow soybeans and wheat, Taiwanese soy sauce is made exclusively from black soybeans, with a technique brought to Taiwan during the Japanese occupation from 1895 to 1945. This also means that it is a gluten-free product, suitable for those with wheat allergies.

Tomato Salad with Peanuts, Soy, and Cilantro

SERVES 4

- 5 shallots, thinly sliced crosswise
- ¼ cup plus 1 tablespoon (75 ml) oil
- 5 garlic cloves, thinly sliced
- 1 tablespoon plus 1 teaspoon chickpea flour
- 14 ounces (400 g) best-quality cherry tomatoes, halved
- 1 bird's-eye chile, minced
- 3 tablespoons roasted peanuts, chopped
- 2 tablespoons lime juice
- 2 tablespoons soy sauce
- A small handful of cilantro leaves, chopped

In summer, the tomato vines in my garden grow heavy with fruit and we cannot keep up with how fast they ripen. While there's no shortage of tomato salad recipes, this Burmese tomato and peanut salad (kayan jin thee thoke/ ခရမ်းချဉ်သီးသုပ်) is one of the most savory versions I've come across. As it calls for only a few ingredients, the complex flavor is all the more surprising. Chickpea flour might seem like an unconventional salad ingredient but, when toasted, it imparts a subtle nutty aroma and thickens the dressing just enough to make it cling to the tomatoes.

1. Set aside a few slices of the shallots for garnish and add the rest to a saucepan with the oil. Set the saucepan over high heat and fry the shallots, stirring constantly to ensure even cooking and to encourage the shallot rings to separate. When the shallots turn a light golden brown, around 3 to 4 minutes, pour the contents through a fine-mesh strainer set over a small bowl.
2. Return the fragrant oil to the pan and add the garlic. Fry on medium heat until the garlic turns a light golden brown—the color of roasted cashews—2 to 3 minutes. Do not allow the garlic to darken too much or it will taste bitter.
3. Pour the oil and the garlic through the fine-mesh strainer with the shallots set over a bowl. This oil is highly aromatic and can be saved for use in other dishes—we will only use the fried garlic and shallots in this recipe.
4. In a separate dry skillet, toast the chickpea flour on medium heat for about 3 to 4 minutes, stirring constantly. The flour is ready when it darkens in color and smells fragrant.
5. Transfer the toasted flour, along with the fried garlic and shallots, to a large bowl. Add the cherry tomatoes, bird's-eye chile, peanuts, lime juice, soy sauce, and cilantro leaves and toss everything together gently, then transfer the mixture to a serving dish. Separate the reserved shallots into individual rings and scatter them over the tomatoes as a garnish. Serve.

Naengmyeon with Watermelon Dongchimi

SERVES 4

DONGCHIMI

2 small daikon radishes (about 1.3 pounds/580 g), cut into bite-size batons

2 tablespoons plus ¼ teaspoon salt

½ pear, cored

5 garlic cloves

¼ small white onion

One thick coin of ginger

1 green chile, halved

1 green onion, cut into 3-inch (7.5 cm) lengths

A handful of daikon or radish greens

NAENGMYEON

2 tomatoes, roughly chopped

⅓ small watermelon (about 1 pound plus 1.5 ounces/500 g), roughly chopped

13 ounces (370 g) dried naengmyeon (냉면), cooked according to package instructions (see headnote)

¼ cup (70 g) Korean chili paste (gochujang/고추장; see page 20)

¼ cup (60 ml) perilla oil (deulgireum/들기름; see page 21)

1 tablespoon sesame seeds, toasted

2 eggs, hard-boiled and halved, optional

I've always been drawn to acidity. As a kid, impatiently waiting for dumplings to arrive at a restaurant, I would take sips of black vinegar straight from the saucer. I later discovered this was detrimental to my teeth and have since curbed this habit, but my love affair with all things mouth-puckering has continued. Years ago, I was late for dinner at a Korean restaurant, and my friends went ahead and ordered for the table. One of the dishes that arrived was naengmyeon (냉면), or thin, chewy buckwheat noodles served in a slushy kimchi broth. On my first taste of the briny and acidic broth, all I could think about was how to re-create it at home. Luckily, daikon water kimchi—or dongchimi (동치미)—is an easy ferment to make, though it takes over a week to mature, so patience is required. Adding watermelon to dongchimi is definitely not traditional, but it lends refreshing sweetness to the bowl of noodles, making it truly fitting for summertime.

1. **For the dongchimi,** at least a week before planning to serve, toss together the daikon and 1 tablespoon of the salt in a large bowl, then set aside for at least an hour.
2. In a blender, combine the pear, garlic, white onion, ginger, and 5 cups (1.2 L) water and blitz until smooth.
3. Place a fine-mesh strainer over a large jar or container and push the blended mixture through it with a spoon, discarding any unblended bits of pulp.
4. After an hour, drain the released water from the daikon, then add the pieces to the jar along with the green chile, green onion, and 2¼ teaspoons of the salt. Season with salt to taste; the liquid should taste like a seasoned broth—not so salty that you cannot slurp it as is.
5. Seal the jar. Allow the dongchimi to ferment at room temperature, away from direct sunlight, until it tastes pleasantly acidic, almost as if vinegar was added to the brine. This should take 2 days in summer, or about 4 days in the colder months. Store the ferment in the fridge for at least a week before using.
6. **For the naengmyeon,** once the dongchimi has fermented, blend the tomatoes and watermelon until smooth, then pass the fruit juices through a fine-mesh strainer into the jar with the dongchimi, pressing with a spoon to extract as much liquid as possible.
7. Stir in the remaining 1 teaspoon of salt. Place the dongchimi in the freezer for 1 to 2 hours, or until it becomes slushy.
8. Divide the broth and vegetables between serving bowls and top with the cooked naengmyeon, chili paste, perilla oil, sesame seeds, and eggs (if using). Serve.

SAGO DUMPLINGS WITH TEMPEH AND PEANUTS, PAGE 91

Steamed & Blanched

Celery and Black Fungus Salad

SERVES 2 TO 3

- 2 tablespoons small dried black fungus (see page 15)
- 10.5 ounces (300 g) celery stalks, or a mix of stems and leaves
- ⅓ cup (40 g) raw peanuts, with or without skin
- 3 tablespoons oil
- ¾ cup (15 g) cilantro stems and leaves, cut into 1-inch (2.5 cm) lengths
- 1 tablespoon plus 1½ teaspoons chili crisp (see page 14)
- 1 tablespoon vegetarian oyster sauce or mushroom stir-fry sauce
- 1½ teaspoons Chinkiang black vinegar (see page 14)
- 1½ teaspoons soy sauce
- A pinch of sugar

Celery is one of those vegetables that I find difficult to love, but my mind was changed on one of my mother's visits. For dinner one night, she decided to make an appetizer with celery. I assumed that she was going to slice the celery thinly on a diagonal and was startled when she left it in long batons. She proceeded to blanch them, which tamed the assertive pungency that I hate, while retaining their crispness. I finished most of the celery that night. This is her recipe—my only contribution being the precise measurements—and I guarantee that if you avoid using old, stringy stalks of celery, even the pickiest eaters will enjoy this salad.

1. In a bowl, cover the dried black fungus with warm water and set aside to soak for 15 minutes, or until fully hydrated.
2. Cut the celery crosswise into 2½-inch (6 cm) lengths, then cut the stems lengthwise into ½-inch (1.25 cm) thick batons.
3. Line a dish with paper towel. Add the peanuts and oil to a small saucepan and stir-fry on medium heat. When the skins begin to peel or the skinless peanuts turn golden, about 4 minutes. Using a slotted spoon, transfer them to the prepared dish.
4. Bring a pot of lightly salted water to a boil. While waiting, in a large bowl, stir together the cilantro, chili crisp, vegetarian oyster sauce, black vinegar, soy sauce, and sugar.
5. Tear the hydrated black fungus into bite-size pieces if needed. When the water comes to a boil, add the black fungus and celery to the pot.
6. Blanch for 1 minute, or until the celery is crisp-tender. There will be a slight color change when the celery is cooked, but the best way to know when it is perfectly done is to taste a baton.
7. With a spider skimmer, transfer the black fungus and celery to a large bowl of cold water to stop the cooking. Drain in a colander set in the sink, shaking it firmly to remove excess water.
8. Add the black fungus, celery, and fried peanuts to the dressing. Toss thoroughly and season with salt and pepper to taste before serving.

Steamed Eggplant with Preserved Mustard Stem, Garlic, and Soy

SERVES 3 TO 4

¼ cup (60 ml) oil

12 garlic cloves (about 1 head), chopped

2 tablespoons plus 1½ teaspoons soy sauce

2¼ teaspoons sugar

1 globe eggplant, stem removed, peeled, and cut into batons roughly ½ inch (1.25 cm) thick and 2¾ inches (7 cm) long

1 tablespoon plus 1½ teaspoons cornstarch

3 ounces (85 g) preserved mustard stem strips (zhà cài/榨菜; see page 21)

1 green onion, thinly sliced

Cooked rice or congee, for serving

Can we talk about how underrated steaming is as a cooking technique? I have seen so many recipes for charred, fried, deep-fried or roast eggplant, but relatively few for steamed eggplant. It surprises me that not many people are attuned to how suited this vegetable is for steaming. Here, the gentle cooking technique coaxes out a creaminess in the eggplant that utterly beguiles, while the marinated mustard stem strips and garlicky dressing bring big flavors to the table.

1. In a saucepan set on low heat, combine the oil and garlic. Cook, stirring occasionally, until the garlic just begins to turn golden, about 4 minutes. Turn off the heat and stir in the soy sauce and sugar.
2. Place the eggplant in a large mixing bowl. Add the garlic mixture and cornstarch and toss everything together gently with your hands, then place in a heat-safe dish. Top the eggplant with the preserved mustard stem strips.
3. Prepare a steaming setup by placing a trivet in a wok or large saucepan. Fill with enough water to come up just below the level of the trivet. Cover with a lid and set on high heat. When the water comes to a boil, place the dish on the trivet. Cover with the lid again and steam on medium heat for 15 minutes, or until the eggplant turns translucent and custardy tender.
4. Scatter the green onion slices on top, and serve immediately with steamed rice or congee.

Vasunthara

Vasunthara's food is colorful. Think: sago appalam (அப்பளம்) stained magenta with beet, a jade swirl of cilantro chutney, or podi (பொடி) the color of marigolds. Growing up in Singapore with ancestral roots in South India, Vasunthara lived with her maternal grandmother, who prepared mainly vegetarian meals. Now, Vasunthara is a private dining chef and culinary teacher who feels strongly about showcasing the best of Indian home cooking. As she says, "If you have something dull in color like bitter gourd, then you will need something vibrant to balance it, like carrot or beet. It is always a celebration this way."

How do Indians view vegetables?

When we look at vegetables, we think of abundance. We are in a tropical or subtropical area where a lot of vegetables and fruits grow. There is such mind-blowing variety and you will never get bored because there are so many flavors and textures. Westerners might not have the same bounty that we have access to, which might explain the association of meatless cuisine with deprivation. But, in the South of India, the range of produce grown at different times and places makes it a joy to eat vegetables.

In particular, I think the way lentils are treated in Indian food is amazing. They keep in your cupboard forever, and are very affordable, filling, and protein-rich. They can take on so many flavors and be cooked in so many different ways. It may be just a few dollars for a whole bag of lentils, but you can eat like a king if you know how to cook them.

What is meatless cuisine to South Indians?

South Indian Tamil-Brahmin vegetarian cooking is considered a cuisine on its own. It employs ingredients that are hardly used in meat-based cooking, such as asafoetida and gingelly oil (Indian sesame oil) to enhance vegetal flavors. In this way, meatless cuisine in South India was developed to stand on its own, rather than being adapted from meat-based cooking. This is what makes it so unique and delicious.

What is the key to cooking vegetables deliciously?

It's the little things that make a huge difference. When you grind your own spices using an Indian blender or spice mill, you will realize that the flavor is completely different from store-bought ground spices. Freshly ground asafoetida from whole blocks, in particular, is life-changing because it gives food a boost of umami.

Indian food is also all about layering and the key is tempering (thalippu/தாளிப்பு), which means to roast spices in fat. In South Indian vegetarian cooking, this is usually gingelly, coconut, or peanut oil. Because of alarmist health reporting, society has vilified fat and forgotten that oil is a crucial flavoring tool. The truth is, a wok (kadai/कड़ाही) or tadka pan allows you to bloom spices in less oil compared to a flat pan. I believe that spending money on just a few really good cooking tools will transform your cooking.

What are some ways Indians enjoy their vegetables?

A basic stir-fry is what we call poriyal (பொரியல). After blooming your spices, you add minced onions and cut vegetables and sauté on high heat. If you cook dal separately and add that to the poriyal, you have the more substantial kootu (கூட்டு). If you add grated coconut to the poriyal in roughly the same ratio as the vegetables, the dish becomes a refreshing Keralan thoran (தோரன்). There is yet another variation in Tamil cooking—masiyal (மசியல்)—where greens or tubers are mashed until they form a gravy, like creamed spinach without the cream.

Another great way to use vegetables is in chutneys. All parts of a vegetable (peel, flesh, seeds) can be ground to make these. This goes back to the Indian cooking ethos of stretching whatever you have—it is not that we have very little, but it is more a mindset of making the most of what we have.

Chayote Paruppu Poriyal

SERVES 2 TO 3

BY VASUNTHARA

- 2 teaspoons gingelly oil (Indian sesame oil) or other oil
- ½ teaspoon black mustard seeds
- 10 curry leaves (see page 15)
- 1 dried red chile, torn in two
- A pinch of asafoetida (hing/हींग; see page 14)
- 1 green chile, finely chopped
- 1 chayote or zucchini, cored, cut into ½-inch (1.25 cm) dice
- ½ teaspoon salt
- 3 tablespoons split mung beans (moong dal/मूंग दाल), soaked in water for 10 minutes, then drained
- 2 tablespoons grated coconut (see page 18)
- 2 teaspoons lemon juice
- A pinch of jaggery (unrefined cane sugar) or dark brown sugar

"Chayote paruppu poriyal (சௌசௌ பருப்பு பொரியல்) is a refreshing vegetable dish. You can reduce the amount of mung beans if you prefer more of a juicy bite from the chayote. If your chayote is naturally sweet, you might not need the jaggery."—*Vasunthara*

1. Add the oil to a skillet and set it on medium heat, then add the black mustard seeds and wait for them to splutter, around 30 seconds. Stir in the curry leaves, dried red chile, and asafoetida.
2. Cook until the leaves crackle, about 10 seconds, then add the green chile. Sauté for a few seconds to release the chile's fragrance, then add the chayote and sauté for 1 minute, until softened slightly, before adding the salt, mung beans, and ¼ cup (60 ml) water.
3. Turn the heat to medium-low and immediately cover the pan with a lid. Allow the mung beans and chayote to steam for 10 to 15 minutes or until they are cooked through. The texture of the moong dal and chayote should be firm yet yielding.
4. Once the chayote and mung beans are cooked, mix in the grated coconut. Switch off the heat and season with salt to taste, then mix in the lemon juice and jaggery. Serve.

Steamed Okra with Sambal and Red Onion

SERVES 4

SAMBAL

10 dried red chiles, halved crosswise

½ cup (120 ml) oil

1½ small red onions, roughly chopped

5 garlic cloves

One ½-inch (1.25 cm) piece of galangal (10 g; see page 17), roughly chopped

One 1½-inch (4 cm) piece of turmeric root (10 g), roughly chopped

1 stalk of lemongrass, bottom half only (see page 20), minced

2 tablespoons tamarind concentrate (see page 22)

2 tablespoons sugar

1 teaspoon salt

OKRA

12 ounces (340 g) okra, ends trimmed

¼ red onion, thinly sliced

Sambal is in my blood. It can be used in so many ways—as a condiment to have on the side, as an ingredient in stir-fries, or as a topping for steamed and roasted dishes. If you are new to sambal-making, you might be tempted to cut down on the oil in this recipe, but I urge you to resist—you will need sufficient oil to fry the sambal thoroughly. What you are looking for is for the aromatics to lose their raw, pungent edge and to become nuanced and harmonious in flavor. I have also noticed that it is uncommon in the Western world to eat raw onion, but the subtle crispness and freshness that it adds to fiery sambal dishes is thoroughly enjoyed in Southeast Asia. If okra is unavailable, spears of asparagus or eggplant batons are also fabulous prepared this way.

1. **For the sambal,** place the dried red chiles in a medium bowl. Cover with boiling water and set aside to soak for 30 minutes. Transfer the chiles to a separate bowl with a slotted spoon, leaving the seeds behind. Rinse with water and repeat the soaking once more to flush out as many seeds as possible; this reduces the heat of the dried chiles.
2. In a blender, grind the chiles, oil, red onion, garlic, galangal, turmeric, and lemongrass to a smooth paste.
3. Transfer the paste to a saucepan. Cook on medium-low heat, stirring frequently, for 15 to 20 minutes. The paste should transform from a creamy-looking mixture to a deep terra cotta–colored lumpy paste.
4. When the sambal is ready, turn off the heat and stir in tamarind concentrate, sugar, and salt. Add more tamarind concentrate, sugar, or salt to taste. The sambal should be strongly seasoned and delicious on its own. You will have about 0.6 pound (290 g) sambal, but will require only half of it for this recipe; the rest can be stored in an airtight container in the refrigerator for up to 3 days or in the freezer for up to 2 months.
5. **For the okra,** prepare a steaming setup by placing a trivet in a wok or large saucepan. Fill with enough water to come up just below the level of the trivet. Cover with a lid and set on high heat. When the water comes to a boil, arrange the okra on a heat-safe serving dish and place this on the trivet. Cover with the lid again and steam on high heat for 7 to 10 minutes, or until the okra is fork-tender. Remove from the steamer and tip the plate carefully over the sink to drain any liquid that has accumulated.
6. Spoon the sambal over the okra and top with the red onion. Serve.

1
2
3
4

Chayote and Glass Noodle Dumplings

SERVES 4

- 1½ chayote (about 12 ounces/ 340 g), cut into thin matchsticks
- 1 teaspoon salt
- ¼ cup plus 2 tablespoons (90 ml) oil
- 1 small bundle (50 g) dried glass noodles (see page 15), roughly cut up with scissors
- 6 dried shiitake mushrooms (see page 16), soaked in boiling water until soft and finely diced
- 3 tablespoons finely chopped preserved radish (cài fǔ/菜脯; see page 21), rinsed, drained, and squeezed dry
- 1 tablespoon plus 1½ teaspoons soy sauce
- ½ teaspoon sugar
- ½ teaspoon toasted sesame oil
- ¼ teaspoon ground white pepper
- ¼ cup plus 3 tablespoons (50 g) tapioca starch
- 1 tablespoon Chinkiang black vinegar (see page 14)
- A handful of cilantro leaves, chopped
- 2 tablespoons chili crisp (see page 14)

If you enjoy dim sum, or little bites of food to "touch the heart," you'll love these Hakka dumplings. Known as daikon balls (luó bo wán/萝卜丸), they traditionally contain pork but are so named for the way the meat plays second fiddle to the vegetables. When a wave of Hakkas (a people from southern China) migrated to Mauritius between the late 1800s and mid-1900s, daikon was substituted with chayote, which was abundant in their new home. Today, chayote dumplings are a Sino-Mauritian specialty known as "boulette chouchou." If chayote is unavailable, you can use zucchini or daikon.

1. In a large bowl, toss together the chayote and salt. Set aside.
2. Place a wok or large saucepan on medium-low heat and add the oil and dried glass noodles. Stir-fry the noodles, breaking them up further with your spatula as you go, until they lose their transparent appearance and turn golden brown and puffy, about 4 minutes. ①
3. Line a dish with paper towel. Transfer the contents of the wok to a fine-mesh strainer set over a bowl. Shake a few times to allow excess oil to drip off, then transfer the noodles to the prepared dish. With another piece of paper towel, dab the glass noodles thoroughly to remove excess grease, then place in a large mixing bowl.
4. Wipe the wok with paper towel and return 1 tablespoon of the oil to it, along with the soaked shiitake mushrooms and preserved radish. Stir-fry on medium heat until fragrant, about 2 minutes, before transferring them to the bowl with the glass noodles.
5. Place the salted chayote on a large, clean kitchen towel. Gather the sides of the towel and wring well to squeeze out excess moisture. Add the chayote to the glass noodle mixture, along with the 1 tablespoon of soy sauce, the sugar, sesame oil, and white pepper. ②
6. Add more soy sauce or sugar to taste. When you are happy with the way that it tastes, add the tapioca starch. Mix the starch with the rest of the ingredients thoroughly with your hands. Like tart dough, it should appear too loose to form a ball, but hold together when compacted with your hands. ③ If needed, you can add a little more tapioca starch if the mixture is not holding together well, but avoid being overly generous or the dumplings will end up being too chewy.
7. Form 2-tablespoon portions of the mixture into balls that weigh roughly 1 ounce (30 g) each, pressing well between your hands to compact the ingredients together. Place the dumplings on a heat-safe dish, roughly 1 inch (2.5 cm) apart.
8. Prepare a steaming setup by placing a trivet in a wok or large saucepan. Fill with enough water to come up just below the level of the trivet. Cover with a lid and set on high heat. When the water comes to a boil, place the dish on the trivet. Cover with the lid again and steam on high heat for 10 minutes or until the dumplings turn translucent. ④
9. Allow to cool slightly, then drizzle with the remaining 1½ teaspoons of soy sauce and black vinegar and scatter with the cilantro leaves and chili crisp. Serve.

Maori Murota

When I first came across Maori Murota's culinary creations on social media, they drew me in because of how vibrant and inviting they looked; it was only later that I realized that many of her dishes are vegan. Murota, author of *Tokyo Cult Recipes* and *Japanese Home Cooking*, attributes this to her childhood in Tokyo. Raised by a mother who was intentional about preparing well-balanced meals, she ate vegetables of all tastes and textures as a child. It was out of a desire to leave a better world behind for her daughter that she started adopting a largely plant-based diet.

Have meat and dairy always been a large part of the food culture of Japan?

Traditionally, the Japanese do not have a culture of eating meat. Japan is an island, so it was far more common for its people to rely on seafood. The terrain was also not conducive to rearing livestock, so it was used for agriculture.

Buddhism also had an influence, most prominently in the form of shojin ryori (精進料理), or temple cuisine. This was developed by monks who refrain from killing animals and indulging in luxury food. They eat only simple and humble foods, but they have developed techniques to make them delicious. An example of this is a dashi made with dried shiitake and grilled soybeans for smoky flavor. Shojin ryori, which literally means "devotion food," exemplifies respect and gratitude for nature's bounty and seasons. With the rise of Zen Buddhism, this way of eating spread across Japan in the thirteenth century.

At the end of the nineteenth century, the Japanese first came into contact with Westerners and felt that they had to adopt a diet of meat and dairy to improve their physiques. Western culture was put on a pedestal and wealthy Japanese even adopted Western dress.

After World War II, the Americans introduced Japanese people to ingredients like powdered milk and encouraged a Western diet. While children would previously eat rice and pickles, the Americans offered them bread, canned meat stews, and packets of milk as school lunches. It drastically changed the way Japanese people ate.

Every time I visit Japan, I am bowled over by the quality of the produce. Why are vegetables and fruits there so good?

Japanese people look for the best-quality ingredients all the time and this can be a double-edged sword. When we seek perfection in, say, a melon, what happens when a melon is not perfect? The bar for ingredients is set so high that anything that does not meet the mark is discarded. The pursuit of perfect produce is ultimately unsustainable, and I find that this is sometimes at odds with the spirit of Japanese cooking.

What do you think is the true spirit of Japanese cooking, and how is it aligned with sustainability?

My grandmother lived in the countryside and, every year during school vacations, I would go to live with her. Like others in the countryside, we would have food-related activities tied to the seasons. In winter, we would prepare pickles and miso. In autumn, we busied ourselves with hanging persimmons for hoshigaki (干し柿). We were truly self-sufficient. If we did not prepare food in the spring, summer, or autumn, we would have nothing to eat in winter.

My grandmother never threw anything away in the kitchen. Many traditional Japanese recipes make use of the skin of a carrot or leaves of a root vegetable. For example, we would boil turnip leaves and squeeze out excess moisture before chopping and mixing them into rice. Otherwise, we would make pickles. To me, the true spirit of Japanese cooking lies in frugality—the sense that everything from nature is precious.

1
2
3
4

Whole Tomato Rice

SERVES 2 TO 3

INSPIRED BY MAORI MUROTA

DASHI

2 large dried shiitake mushrooms (see page 16)

One 2-inch (5 cm) piece of kombu (see page 19)

RICE

1½ cups plus 2 tablespoons (320 g) Japanese or Korean short-grain rice, rinsed thoroughly and drained

1 best-quality tomato

1 teaspoon salt

2 teaspoons perilla oil (deulgireum/들기름; see page 21)

"As Japanese, we are sensitive to the subtle changes in nature. We have three expressions for seasonal foods. *Hashiri* (走り), or ingredients at the start of the season, includes little sprouts of herbs, vegetables and shoots. *Shun* (旬) refers to ingredients at their peak; the best moment to enjoy them. *Nagori* (名残) is the end of the peak; the last chance to eat them till next year. Each phase does not last long; it might be a few weeks, sometimes mere days. It is all about appreciating nature, cherishing what it gives us and seizing the fleeting moment. This is a wonderful and simple dish that is perfect for summer."—*Maori Murota*

1. **For the dashi,** the night before you intend to serve, combine the dried shiitake mushrooms, kombu, and 2½ cups (600 ml) water in a bowl. Leave to soak overnight in the refrigerator.
2. The next day, strain the contents of the bowl and reserve the dashi. Squeeze the mushrooms to expel excess liquid, then snip off any tough stems with scissors and thinly slice the caps. Thinly slice the kombu.
3. **For the rice,** add the short-grain rice to a rice cooker and bury the tomato in the center. (See page 3 for instructions on cooking rice without a rice cooker.) Scatter the mushrooms and kombu around the tomato, along with the salt and perilla oil.
4. Pour 1¾ cups plus 2 tablespoons (450 ml) of the dashi into the rice cooker, saving the rest for another use, ① and allow the rice to cook. ②
5. When all of the liquid has been absorbed and the rice is tender, ③ crush the tomato gently with a spatula and mix it into the rice before serving. ④

Watercress Noodles with Split Pea Fritters

SERVES 4

NOODLES

2.25 ounces (60 g) watercress leaves and tender stems

2¼ cups (300 g) all-purpose flour

½ teaspoon salt

3 tablespoons oil

FRITTERS

Oil, for deep-frying

½ cup (95 g) split chickpeas (chana dal/चना दाल), soaked overnight

¼ cup (45 g) rice flour

2 tablespoons plus 1½ teaspoons self-rising flour

¼ teaspoon salt

DRESSING

¼ cup (60 ml) soy sauce

3 tablespoons Chinkiang black vinegar (see page 14)

1 tablespoon plus 1½ teaspoons vegetarian oyster sauce or mushroom stir-fry sauce

1 tablespoon toasted sesame oil

TOPPINGS

2 green onions, thinly sliced

5 garlic cloves, finely chopped

1 tablespoon plus 1½ teaspoons Korean chili flakes (gochugaru/고춧가루)

1 teaspoon ground Sichuan pepper (see page 22)

1 teaspoon sugar

BROCCOLINI

10.5 ounces (300 g) broccolini, cut into 2-inch (5 cm) lengths

There are likely as many different noodle shapes and sizes in Chinese cuisine as there are in Italian, and what makes them so habit-forming is their pleasant chew. I used to treat myself to biang biang noodles, also known as yóu pō chě miàn (油泼扯面)—wide Chinese noodles finished with Sichuan peppercorn–spiked chili oil—near my apartment in Melbourne, but the dish was so heavy on the noodles, I felt guilty about consuming it on a regular basis. That gave me reason to make my own, and I was surprised that all it took was all-purpose flour, water, salt, and a little patience. I use puréed watercress in my dough for added nutrition, which turns the noodles a vivid green when cooked, and top the dish with Burmese split pea fritters (pe kyaw/ပဲကြော်) for crunch. This is also a fun recipe for a night with friends—make all the components and dough the night before, set a pot on the stove, and get everyone involved in pulling, blanching, and finishing the noodles.

1. **For the noodles,** swish the watercress in a large bowl of water to remove any dirt. You might have to repeat this a few times if the watercress is very dirty. Once cleaned, lift the watercress from the bowl and place it directly in a saucepan set on high heat. Stir-fry for 1 to 2 minutes, or until the watercress wilts.
2. Blend the wilted watercress to a fine paste with ¼ cup plus 3 tablespoons (100 ml) water, then transfer the purée to a large bowl and add the flour and salt.
3. Combine everything with a wooden spoon until the liquid is absorbed, then firmly knead the mixture in the bowl until the dough is completely homogenous, 3 to 5 minutes. While the dough might look a little dry initially, it should have no dry spots at the end of the kneading. Cover the bowl and allow the dough to rest for 30 minutes.
4. Cut the rested dough into 8 pieces, each weighing about 2 ounces (55 g). Shape each into a ball, then roll into a sausage-like log between your palms—it should not stick to your hands. Drizzle with the oil and roll the logs to coat them thoroughly, then cover and allow them to rest for at least 3 hours at room temperature.
5. **For the fritters,** fill a wok or large saucepan with 2 inches (5 cm) of oil and set it on high heat. Allow the oil to heat to 320°F (160°C).

RECIPE CONTINUED →

6. While the oil heats, drain the split chickpeas. Rinse thoroughly with water and drain well, then add to a large bowl with the rice flour, self-rising flour, salt, and ½ cup plus 2 tablespoons (150 ml) water. Mix everything together until you obtain a batter that is as thin and watery as milk.
7. Gently add a scant ¼ cup (50 ml) of the mixture to the hot oil, keeping the ladle close to the oil's surface to minimize splattering and help maintain the fritters' shape. Aim to get a mix of batter and chickpeas. Within seconds, bubbles should begin to stream from the batter. With tongs or a wooden spatula, gently dislodge the fritter from the bottom of the pan. Repeat the process, dropping ladlefuls of the mixture into the oil until the entire surface of the pan is covered.
8. Line a dish with paper towel. Fry the fritters until golden brown and crispy, 3 to 5 minutes. Using tongs, transfer them to the prepared dish, and carefully set the oil aside to cool. The fritters can be prepared several days in advance, cooled, and stored in airtight containers at room temperature.
9. **For the dressing,** stir together the soy sauce, black vinegar, vegetarian oyster sauce, and sesame oil in a large mixing bowl.
10. **For the toppings,** assemble the green onions, garlic, chili flakes, Sichuan pepper, and sugar in a separate small dish.
11. **For the broccolini,** bring a pot of salted water to a rolling boil and add the broccolini. Fill a bowl with cold water. Blanch the broccolini for 2 minutes or until just tender. Using a spider skimmer, transfer the broccolini from the pot to the bowl of cold water to stop the cooking. Drain and set aside. Do not remove the pot of water from the heat.

12. With your fingers, pat a piece of noodle dough into an oval measuring roughly 4 by 8½ inches (10 by 22 cm). The dough should be cooperative so this should not take much strength. Cut the oval into four 1-inch (2.5 cm) thick strands. Stretch the strands out further with your hands, smacking them on the counter gently to help elongate them.

13. When the noodles are stretched as long as they can be without breaking, roughly 21 inches (54 cm) in length, drop them into the pot of boiling water. Cook the noodles on high heat for 1 minute, or until tender but chewy.

14. Remove the noodles from the pot with tongs and place them in the bowl with the dressing. Repeat the shaping with the remaining dough, boiling the noodles as soon as they are shaped; the stretched noodles are sticky and will clump if left uncooked.

15. When all the noodles have been cooked and added to the bowl, toss them gently to coat with the dressing, then tip the assembled toppings on top of the dressed noodles without mixing them in.

16. Set a saucepan on high heat and add ¼ cup (60 ml) of the leftover deep-frying oil. When the oil begins to smoke, pour it directly over the toppings—the oil should splutter furiously. ①

17. Toss everything together briskly to coat the noodles in the oil. ② Taste a small piece of noodle and add more soy sauce, sugar, or vinegar to taste. Add the blanched broccolini and gently distribute it throughout the noodles. ③

18. Divide everything between serving dishes or a large platter and scatter with the broken-up split pea fritters. ④ Serve immediately.

Mushroom Rice Rolls with Bean Sprout Salad

SERVES 4 TO 6

RICE SHEETS

¼ cup (45 g) rice flour

⅓ cup (45 g) tapioca starch

2 teaspoons oil, plus more for brushing

¼ teaspoon salt

FILLING

1 pound (450 g) shiitake mushrooms, stems removed, roughly chopped

1 tablespoon oil

3 garlic cloves, chopped

⅔ cup (160 ml) boiling water

1 tablespoon plus 1½ teaspoons soy sauce

1 teaspoon sugar

½ teaspoon toasted sesame oil

¼ teaspoon freshly ground black pepper

DRESSING

2 tablespoons plus 1½ teaspoons soy sauce

1 tablespoon plus 1½ teaspoons sugar

1 teaspoon toasted sesame oil

SALAD

7 ounces (200 g) bean sprouts

A handful of mint leaves, roughly chopped

A handful of cilantro leaves, roughly chopped

A handful of fried shallots (see page 17)

No trip to Singapore is complete without going to the hawker center. The experience for me begins the moment I get in line. It is a treat to watch seasoned hawkers blend sauces, blanch noodles, or simmer dumplings to order. My favorite is when a hawker pours a thin batter onto muslin cloth in a steamer and nimbly maneuvers the steamed rice sheets into rolls, before dousing them in a house-made dressing. Steamed rice rolls are no stranger to other parts of Asia. There are endless variations of chéung fán (肠粉) in Hong Kong, where the dish originated. In Vietnam it is known as bánh cuốn and is enjoyed with nước chấm (a Vietnamese dipping sauce). Making steamed rice sheets can be challenging and takes patience if you are new to it, but the results are worth it. If making them from scratch is too intimidating, feel free to substitute ready-made rice sheets from the Asian grocer instead.

1. **For the rice sheets,** in a large bowl, whisk together the rice flour, tapioca starch, oil, salt, and 1 cup (240 ml) water. Allow the batter to rest for 1 hour at room temperature.
2. **For the filling,** while the batter rests, place the shiitake mushrooms in a food processor and pulse until the mushrooms are diced to the size of peas. If you prefer, you can chop the mushrooms by hand.
3. Add the mushrooms to a large saucepan set on high heat along with the oil. Cook, stirring infrequently, until the mushrooms wilt significantly and begin to brown in places, 4 to 5 minutes. Add the garlic, soy sauce, sugar, sesame oil, and black pepper.
4. Cook for 1 to 2 minutes to release the fragrance of the garlic, then turn off the heat. Add more soy sauce or sugar to taste, then set the mushrooms aside.
5. **For the dressing,** stir together the boiling water, soy sauce, sugar, and sesame oil in a medium bowl.
6. **For the salad,** prepare a steaming setup by placing a trivet in a wok or large saucepan. Fill with enough water to come up just below the level of the trivet. Cover with a lid and set on high heat. When the water comes to a boil, place the bean sprouts on a plate and set it on the trivet. Cover with the lid again and steam for 1 minute, or until the bean sprouts are cooked but still crisp.

RECIPE CONTINUED →

7. To make the rice sheets, brush the base of a 9-inch (23 cm) springform pan lightly with oil. Place the empty pan in the steamer and allow it to preheat, uncovered, until it is hot to the touch.

8. Give the batter a thorough stir with a ladle, then add approximately a scant ¼ cup (50 ml) of the batter to the pan. Tilt the pan gently, using oven mitts if necessary, so that the batter sets in an even layer across the base. This will take a few seconds.

9. Cover the steamer and steam the rice sheet for 2 minutes on high heat, or until it is translucent and set to the touch.

10. Remove the pan from the steamer and unclip the ring. Place about 3 tablespoons of the mushroom filling in a line across the center of the rice sheet. ① Loosen the edges of the sheet with a spatula, then use your fingers to pull the sheet over the filling on all four sides to enclose it. ②③ Gently turn the roll over so that it sits seam side down and set aside. ④ Repeat the steaming and filling process until all the batter and filling have been used up.

11. Transfer the rolls to a serving dish. Top them with the bean sprouts, mint leaves, cilantro leaves, and fried shallots. Drizzle liberally with the dressing before serving.

3

4

Sonoko Sakai

Sonoko Sakai is the author of *Japanese Home Cooking: Simple Meals, Authentic Flavors*, which won the prestigious IACP International Cookbook Award, and *Wafu Cooking: Everyday Recipes with Japanese Style*. Sakai's cooking philosophy is about using the freshest seasonal ingredients and allowing them to speak for themselves. For this reason, she takes time to make yuzu kosho with yuzu and peppers from her garden, and hangs persimmons to dry come autumn. Even the smallest gifts from nature are not taken for granted, as she harvests shungiku flowers for tea. She explains, "My favorite pastime is working in the garden and coming back to the kitchen with something I grew. Then, going back to the garden with kitchen scraps and getting my hands dirty again. The cycle of cooking begins and ends in the garden." Very fitting for someone whose name means "garden child."

What is your philosophy on eating and cooking vegetables?

I like eating vegetables and wild edible plants, particularly at the height of their seasons (shun/旬). When I was younger, spring was always heralded with the harvest of wild bamboo from the forest. Digging the young shoots up from the ground and parboiling them with rice bran to rid the bitterness before cooking them with rice was a lot of work, but always rewarding. As I grew older, I learned about the shun (the peak) of many vegetables, fruits, grains, seaweed, and more. Nature is always moving and I have learned to pay attention to that constant movement.

Also, when we think of vegetables, we think of land foods, but I would encourage people to incorporate sea vegetables into their cooking and diets as well for their nutritional benefits.

What ingredient do you reach for the most to add flavor to your vegetable dishes?

Miso. For a soothing vegetarian breakfast, you can do a cold brew with kombu the night before. Bring it to a boil the next morning, and add sliced vegetables, veggie scraps from the fridge, and cubes of soft tofu. Cook until everything is warmed through. Dissolve some miso into the dashi before sprinkling with sliced green onions and Japanese seven-spice seasoning (shichimi togarashi/七味唐辛子). It's ready in no time.

Miso is also a versatile seasoning that finds its way into so many of my dishes: thinned with vinegar and oil to make a nutty dressing, smeared on rice balls or added to pasta sauce for a punch of umami.

What does miso mean to you?

My mother used to make miso by packing soybeans, rice that had been inoculated with a beneficial mold called "koji-kin" (麹菌), and sea salt into a crock. She would leave the miso to ferment in our basement for six months to two years, and the result was a hauntingly delicious living food.

We have a Japanese phrase, "temae miso" (手前味噌), or "my homemade miso," which is used when you want to show off something you are proud of, but don't want to be boastful. It can be anything you nurtured with your hands. Miso is mine.

How does fresh produce inspire and inform you?

My apprenticeship with Chef Takashi Hosokawa, a master of soba and tempura in Tokyo, left a lasting mark on me. He sourced the best seasonal vegetables for making tempura and would be tasting the vegetables throughout the day. I once saw him get mad when he was dissatisfied with the crunch of a carrot that had just arrived from a farm in Kyoto.

Now, when I see asparagus at the farmers market in springtime, or carrots growing in my garden, I get inspired to make kakiage (かき揚げ). An "all-in-one" tempura, this was my mother's way to get her five children to eat more vegetables and a clever way to get rid of scraps from the fridge. The deep-frying seals the moisture, flavor, and nutrients of the vegetables inside that crispy crust. You can taste sweetness that a boiled vegetable just can't deliver. Onions, especially, turn magically sweet when deep-fried. When you have wonderful vegetables, the cooking is easy—it is all about respecting the natural ingredient.

1
2
3
4

Chilled Ohitashi Heirloom Tomatoes

SERVES 4

*BY SONOKO SAKAI**

TOMATOES

1 tablespoon dried soybeans

One 3-inch (7.5 cm) piece of kombu (see page 19)

2 large dried shiitake mushrooms (see page 16)

One 2½-inch (6 cm) piece of dried gourd shavings (kanpyō/かんぴょう), cut in half, optional

2 tablespoons soy sauce

1 tablespoon mirin

1 teaspoon salt

1 pound (450 g) heirloom tomatoes

ASSEMBLY

A handful of shiso leaves (see page 22) or basil, thinly sliced

1½ teaspoons sesame seeds, toasted

A few cracks of freshly ground black pepper

"Ohitashi (お浸し) is a dish in which vegetables are briefly blanched and infused in savory dashi to enhance their natural flavors. The tomatoes are blanched to remove the skin and allow the dashi to penetrate into their flesh. This is an incredibly versatile dish; instead of tomatoes, you can use blanched asparagus, green beans, cabbage, spinach, sprouts, okra, mushrooms, mizuna, bitter melon, chrysanthemum leaves, cabbage, corn—you name it."—*Sonoko Sakai*

1. **For the tomatoes,** place a medium saucepan on high heat and add the dried soybeans. Allow the soybeans to cook, shaking occasionally, for 3 to 4 minutes or until lightly toasted.
2. Turn off the heat and add the kombu, dried shiitake mushrooms, dried gourd shavings (if using), and 3 cups (720 ml) water to the pan. Cover the pan and leave the mixture overnight at room temperature.
3. The following day, put the pan over medium heat and bring to a gentle simmer. Simmer for 1 minute, then lower the heat and simmer uncovered for a further 20 minutes.
4. Strain the dashi into a small saucepan. Discard the solids or save them for another round of dashi. Add the soy sauce, mirin, and salt. Bring to a boil over medium heat, then remove from the heat and let cool. Season with salt to taste. The dashi should be drinkable like soup.
5. Bring a medium pot of water to a boil over high heat. Score a cross about 1⁄16-inch (1.5 mm) deep across the bottom of the heirloom tomatoes, then drop them into the boiling water. When you see their skin start to crack and peel, within about 30 seconds, remove them from the water with a slotted spoon and immediately transfer to a bowl of ice water.
6. When the tomatoes are cool enough to handle, peel the skin, trying not to scar the surface of the tomatoes. ① Cut them into bite-size wedges and place in a medium serving bowl.
7. Pour the dressing over the tomatoes, cover, and let them marinate for 30 minutes to 1 hour in the refrigerator. ②
8. **For assembly,** garnish the tomatoes with the shiso leaves, sesame seeds, and black pepper. ③

* Adapted from *Japanese Home Cooking: Simple Meals, Authentic Flavors* by Sonoko Sakai, copyright © 2019. Published by Roost Books.

Sago Dumplings with Tempeh and Peanuts

MAKES ABOUT 24 DUMPLINGS

DUMPLINGS

1 cup plus 1 tablespoon (160 g) sago, the smallest you can find

¼ cup plus 1 tablespoon (75 ml) oil

5 garlic cloves, chopped

½ small red onion, finely diced

¾ cup (120 g) finely chopped tempeh (see page 22)

3.25 ounces (90 g) dark palm sugar (see page 15), roughly chopped

⅓ cup (40 g) roasted peanuts, finely chopped

2 tablespoons soy sauce

1 ounce (30 g) ginger flower petals (see page 18) or 3 makrut lime leaves (see page 20), finely chopped

ASSEMBLY

A handful of cilantro leaves

1 bird's-eye chile, thinly sliced

1 small head of lettuce, leaves separated

Part of the joys of making these dumplings—known as saku sai moo (สาคูไส้หมู) in Thailand or sakoo yat sai (ສະກູຍັດໄສ້) in Laos—is watching their transformation as they steam. Instead of a dough wrapper, the filling is encased in a compact layer of sago, which is used in much the same way as tapioca pearls. When steamed, the sago turns translucent, with a jewel-like sheen. The chewy exterior conceals a sticky, caramelized mixture of chopped tempeh and peanuts. I perfume the filling with chopped ginger flower petals, which have a zippy, citrus-forward flavor that balances the richness. If ginger flower petals are unavailable, makrut lime leaves make a delicious alternative.

1. **For the dumplings,** add the sago to a bowl and cover with a liberal amount of water. Soak for 25 minutes before draining. Set aside.
2. Add the oil and garlic to a saucepan set on high heat. Fry the garlic, stirring frequently. When it turns lightly golden, 2 to 3 minutes, strain through a fine-mesh strainer set over a bowl.
3. Return 2 tablespoons of the garlic oil to the saucepan and set it on high heat. Reserve the rest of the garlic oil. Add the red onion to the pan and fry until lightly golden, around 2 minutes.
4. Add another tablespoon of garlic oil and the tempeh and fry for 1 minute for it to lightly brown, then add the palm sugar and ¼ cup (60 ml) water.
5. Stir the pan briskly to deglaze it and encourage the sugar to melt. Add the peanuts, soy sauce, and ginger flower petals. Cook until the mixture sticks together in a single mass. Err on the side of overcooking the mixture; you will not be able to form it into individual balls if the filling is undercooked.
6. Spread the mixture out on a dish and place it in the freezer for 20 minutes or until it cools down and firms up.
7. Divide the mixture into 1-tablespoon portions weighing roughly 0.3 ounce (10 g), and roll each into a ball.
8. Sprinkle some sago on your palm, place the ball on top, and sprinkle more sago over it. As if you are coating something in breadcrumbs, move the ball back and forth between your palms, closing your fist lightly with each pass, until the filling is covered in a thin layer of sago. Repeat until all of the filling is used up.
9. Space the dumplings 1 inch (2.5 cm) apart on an oiled heat-safe dish. Prepare a steaming setup by placing a trivet in a wok or large saucepan. Fill with enough water to come up just below the level of the trivet. Cover with a lid and set on high heat. When the water comes to a boil, place the dish with the dumplings on the trivet. Cover with the lid again and steam on high heat for 8 to 10 minutes, or until they turn translucent.
10. **For assembly,** brush the dumplings with the reserved garlic oil and sprinkle the fried garlic over them. Top with the cilantro leaves and bird's-eye chile. Wrap the warm dumplings individually in the lettuce leaves and enjoy.

Egg Tofu with Mapo Mushroom Sauce

SERVES 4

MAPO SAUCE

3 tablespoons chili oil (see page 14)

One 1-inch (2.5 cm) piece of ginger (10 g), finely chopped

1½ red chiles, finely chopped

4 garlic cloves, finely chopped

9 ounces (250 g) king oyster mushrooms, diced

1 tablespoon plus 1 teaspoon fermented broad bean paste (dòu bàn jiàng/豆瓣酱; see page 16)

2 teaspoons fermented black beans (dòu chǐ/豆豉; see page 16), rinsed, drained, and finely chopped

1 tablespoon plus 1½ teaspoons Shaoxing wine

1 teaspoon toasted sesame oil

¾ teaspoon dark soy sauce

2 teaspoons cornstarch

1 tablespoon sugar

1 teaspoon soy sauce

EGG TOFU

1½ cups plus 1 tablespoon (375 ml) soymilk

5 eggs

2 teaspoons salt

ASSEMBLY

A small handful of cilantro leaves

1 green onion, thinly sliced

Cooked rice, for serving

One thing that surprised me when I moved to Melbourne was how obsessed people were with mapo tofu (má pó dòu fǔ/麻婆豆腐). My colleagues raved about this classic Sichuan dish of braised tofu and minced pork all the time, and mapo tofu jaffles (toasted sandwiches), mapo tofu pies, mapo tofu lasagnas, and the like proliferated across the city. I caught on to the craze because, what's not to like? This recipe is inspired by chef Dan Hong's version in his cookbook *Mr. Hong: Outrageously Delicious Recipes from the Chef Behind Mr. Wong and Ms. G's*, where he presents the tofu as a silken steamed egg custard. Genius. For a vegan alternative, cut silken tofu into slices and steam them until they are warm and quivering. Pour off excess liquid and top with the mapo sauce and herbs. Whether you go with egg tofu or silken tofu, cooked rice is a delicious accompaniment.

1. **For the mapo sauce,** in a saucepan set on high heat, combine the chili oil, ginger, red chiles, and garlic.
2. Sauté for 1 to 2 minutes to release the fragrance of the aromatics, then add the king oyster mushrooms. Cook for 3 to 4 minutes, stirring occasionally, until the mushrooms wilt and shrink in size.
3. Add the fermented broad bean paste and fermented black beans and fry for another minute, then add the Shaoxing wine, sesame oil, dark soy sauce, and ¾ cup (180 ml) water.
4. Bring the mixture to a boil on high heat. Meanwhile, in a small bowl, stir together the cornstarch and 2 tablespoons water.
5. Add the slurry to the pan, stirring, until the liquid thickens, then add the sugar and soy sauce. Add more sugar or soy sauce to taste, then set the sauce aside.
6. **For the egg tofu,** heat the soymilk in a microwave or saucepan until it is as warm as a baby's bath. This will help the soymilk incorporate more evenly with the other ingredients and allows the tofu to steam and set smoothly. Pour into a large bowl, and whisk together with the eggs and salt.
7. To remove any stray strands of unbeaten egg, strain the mixture into a casserole dish that is large enough to accommodate the liquid comfortably. Skim off any foam from the surface with a spoon and cover the dish tightly with foil.
8. Prepare a steaming setup by placing a trivet in a wok or large saucepan. Fill with enough water to come up just below the level of the trivet. Cover with a lid and set on high heat. When the water comes to a boil, place the casserole dish on the trivet. Cover with the lid again and steam on low heat for 20 to 25 minutes or until the surface of the custard feels set to the touch.
9. **For assembly,** spoon the mapo sauce over the custard and scatter with the cilantro leaves and green onion. Serve with the rice.

RENGHAN REVEYA, PAGE 115

Simmered

Beet Curry with Coconut Sambol

SERVES 3 TO 4

CURRY

2 tablespoons oil

1 teaspoon black mustard seeds

1 small red onion, roughly chopped

2 garlic cloves, minced

1½ green chiles, chopped

1 pandan leaf (see page 20), knotted

5 small beets (14 ounces/400 g; see headnote), cut into ½-inch (1.25 cm) dice

1 teaspoon Kashmiri chili powder

1 teaspoon ground coriander

1 teaspoon ground cumin

1 teaspoon ground turmeric

½ teaspoon ground cinnamon

1 teaspoon salt

¾ cup (180 ml) coconut cream (see page 14)

SAMBOL

5 black peppercorns

2 dried red chiles, roughly torn

1 heaping cup (100 g) grated coconut (see page 18)

2 large garlic cloves, chopped

¼ small red onion, chopped

½ small tomato, chopped

1 tablespoon plus 1½ teaspoons lime juice

½ teaspoon salt

ASSEMBLY

Cooked rice, for serving

A small handful of cilantro leaves

A small handful of roasted fava beans, optional

When I was cooking at Candlenut in Singapore, staff meals were taken very seriously. The kitchen prepared two meals a day for the entire staff—one before lunch service, and another before dinner. Each kitchen member was assigned to cook at least one meal a week and, as someone whose eyes hadn't yet been opened to the richness of vegetable cooking, I always hoped that mine wouldn't coincide with any vegetarians working that day. Eventually, my shift collided with a vegetarian colleague from India, and rather than prepare a separate plate of food, I fully embraced vegetarianism for that meal. I made a Sri Lankan–inspired beet curry, cashew curry, and hoppers (Sri Lankan crepes), which my colleague later told me reminded her of home. It surprised me how well the earthy flavor of beets works in curry, and this dish has since become a staple at home. I recommend making this curry only with fresh beets; canned or vacuum-sealed beets tend to be overly tender and have their character sucked out of them.

1. **For the curry,** set a medium-sized pot or a wok on high heat and add the oil and black mustard seeds. Wait for the seeds to pop slightly, around 15 seconds, before adding the red onion.
2. Fry for 1 to 2 minutes, until the onion begins to brown, then add the garlic, green chiles, and pandan leaf. When the garlic smells fragrant, around 10 seconds, add the beets, chili powder, coriander, cumin, turmeric, and cinnamon.
3. Fry for about 3 minutes to release their fragrance, then add the salt and 1¾ cups (420 ml) water. Bring the mixture to a boil, then turn the heat down to low. Simmer, covered, for 20 minutes or until the beets are tender.
4. **For the sambol,** toast the black peppercorns and dried red chiles in a dry saucepan for 2 to 3 minutes on medium high heat until fragrant, shaking frequently.
5. Transfer to a mortar or spice grinder and grind to a coarse powder, then transfer to a large bowl along with the grated coconut, garlic, red onion, tomato, lime juice, and salt.
6. Massage everything with your hands, really squeezing the mixture to color the coconut red and to release the juices from the tomatoes. Season with salt or add more lime juice to taste. The resulting sambol should be delicious on its own. Set aside.
7. When the beets are tender, stir in the coconut cream. Bring the curry to a boil on high heat, then take it off the heat and remove the pandan leaf. Season with salt to taste.
8. **For assembly,** spoon the sambol and beet curry over hot rice and scatter with the cilantro leaves and roasted fava beans (if using).

Butternut Squash Kootu with Spiced Chickpeas

SERVES 4

KOOTU

½ butternut squash (about 1 pound/450 g), diced

1 large tomato, chopped

½ cup (100 g) split mung beans (moong dal/मूंग दाल) or red lentils, rinsed and drained

1½ teaspoons salt

1½ teaspoons ghee (see page 18) or coconut oil

4 dried red chiles

1 teaspoon cumin seeds

½ cup (45 g) grated coconut (see page 18)

CHICKPEAS

One 14-ounce (400 g) can of chickpeas, drained, rinsed, then drained again

3 teaspoons ghee (see page 18) or coconut oil

1 tablespoon plus 1½ teaspoons meat curry powder (see headnote)

½ teaspoon salt

YOGURT

¼ cup (60 ml) yogurt or coconut cream (see page 14)

½ teaspoon salt

TEMPERED SPICES

2 tablespoons ghee (see page 18) or coconut oil

2 teaspoons black mustard seeds

5 dried red chiles

A handful of curry leaves (see page 15)

1 teaspoon Kashmiri chili powder

This dish began as a recipe for kootu (கூட்டு)—a lentil and vegetable stew—shared with me by Manasa Sitaram. I was publishing an indie zine on Deepavali food in Singapore and she contributed a recipe from her mom, Latha. I was immediately struck by how complex it tasted with just a handful of ingredients while remaining entirely vegetarian! It became my go-to dish at that time because it uses pantry ingredients and is endlessly variable. This version is gussied up with spiced chickpeas and a tangy drizzle of yogurt, which cuts through the richness of the ghee. If you are new to tempering spices, this is a great entry point. Meat curry powder, sometimes also labeled as meat masala, is available at Southeast Asian and Indian grocers.

1. **For the kootu,** combine the butternut squash, tomato, mung beans, salt, and 1⅔ cups (400 ml) water in a medium pot set on high heat.
2. When the water boils, cover the pot and turn the heat down to low. Allow the kootu to simmer for 40 minutes, stirring from time to time, until it thickens to a porridge-like consistency and the squash is completely tender.
3. In a saucepan, combine the ghee, dried red chiles, and cumin seeds. Fry on low heat for 1 minute or until the seeds are fragrant.
4. Transfer the spices to a blender with the grated coconut and ¼ cup (60 ml) water and grind into a paste. Add this to the pot with the mung beans and stir well. Season with salt to taste.
5. **For the chickpeas,** add the chickpeas to a dry saucepan on high heat and allow them to cook for a minute to evaporate some of their moisture. Add the ghee, meat curry powder, and salt and cook for 1 to 2 minutes to melt the ghee, release the fragrance of the masala, and coat the chickpeas well in the fragrant fat.
6. Turn off the heat and taste. Season with salt to taste, then set aside.
7. **For the yogurt,** in a small bowl, stir together the yogurt, salt, and about 2 tablespoons water, adjusting the amount of water as needed to obtain a sauce with the consistency of coconut milk.
8. When the kootu is ready, season with salt to taste. Transfer it to a serving bowl. Drizzle the thinned yogurt over the kootu and spoon the chickpeas on top.
9. **For the tempered spices,** add the ghee and black mustard seeds to a pan set on medium heat. When the seeds pop, around 15 seconds, carefully add the dried red chiles and curry leaves, which will splutter slightly. When the leaves take on a glassy appearance, about 20 seconds, turn off the heat and add the chili powder. Swirl to bloom the chili powder in the fat, then pour everything over the kootu and serve immediately.

Gayan Pieris

Gayan Pieris is the executive chef of Many Little Bar & Dining and Polperro Wines in Mornington Peninsula, Australia. He grew up in Sri Lanka and recalls picking mushrooms from under mounds of rice hay and taking them home to be cooked with strong spices. This memory, along with many others, would later serve as inspiration for dishes on his menu, which celebrates Sri Lankan traditions and flavors. About putting together a plant-based degustation that promises as much pleasure as its omnivore counterpart, Pieris says, "I don't try to disguise the vegetables to make them look like meat, and one cannot say either one is better than the other."

Sri Lankan food appears to be very vegetable-forward. Why are vegetables so highly prized there?

No cuisine is divorced from culture and Sri Lanka is no exception. Buddhism, which became intertwined with Sri Lankan culture over 2,500 years ago, promotes values of nonviolence and compassion. While not all Buddhists are strictly vegetarian, the religion encourages plant-based diets, which influences the culinary traditions of the island. Ayurveda, the holistic medicine of Sri Lanka where vegetables and spices are thought of to have healing properties, has also shaped the cuisine into one that prioritizes fresh and seasonal plant-based ingredients.

The way we structure a meal in Sri Lanka is very different from the approach we see in the West. In Western cuisine, you have your starch, vegetables, and meat. The animal protein is the star, and everything else is there to fill you up. In Sri Lanka, rice is the star, and all our other dishes are built around it. We have saucy and dry curries, tempered vegetable preparations, salads and chutneys. In this way, you can build a solid, proper Sri Lankan meal without the need for animal protein.

What was your relationship with vegetables like growing up in Sri Lanka?

Agriculture is the main economic activity in Sri Lanka, so almost everyone has their own farm. My parents were rice farmers and in our backyard we had bananas, custard apples, pennywort, wing beans, snake beans, and so on. We were able to grow these with minimal maintenance since we were in the tropics—the land was so fertile. As children, our job was to pick whatever we wanted to eat for lunch after coming home from school. Because of that, eating vegetables was a lot of fun. We never craved meat because everything was so fresh and there was such variety to choose from.

What does "meat substitute" mean to you?

Sometimes, when there is a protein source, the easiest way for Westerners to wrap their heads around it is to label it a meat substitute. This indicates that something is a good replacement for meat in terms of protein and texture. Jackfruit is one such ingredient. It served us well as a nation when we experienced massive starvation on multiple occasions, such as when Sri Lanka faced inflation, droughts, and widespread food shortages. Sri Lankans were able to remain fed thanks to the jackfruit trees grown in backyards. For that reason, we call it "rice tree" (bath gasa/ බත්ගස) out of reverence.

We have eight to ten different preparations for young jackfruit, depending on the stage of ripeness it is at. Super-young jackfruit, harvested at roughly a quarter of its lifetime, is often pounded using a pestle and mortar with coconut and black pepper and stir-fried. When it is riper, we boil it with salt and turmeric, pound it, then toss it with raw ingredients to create a salad called kos mallum (කොස් මැල්ලුම). As the fruit ripens further, we prepare it in the form of a sour curry called polos ambula (පොළොස් ඇඹුල).

What can we learn from Sri Lanka's approach to vegetables?

People find vegetables boring because they are eating them in the same way every day. How many times can you have the same vegetable as a salad? However, if you learn to enjoy it as a stir-fry, then a salad, and then a curry, the variation keeps things interesting.

Polos Ambula

SERVES 4

INSPIRED BY GAYAN PIERIS

- 8 red chiles (3 ounces/85 g), seeded if desired, roughly cut
- 2 tablespoons plus 1½ teaspoons coconut oil
- ½ teaspoon black mustard seeds
- ½ teaspoon cumin seeds
- ¼ teaspoon fenugreek seeds
- 5 garlic cloves, chopped
- 1 small red onion, chopped
- 15 curry leaves (see page 15)
- 1 pandan leaf (see page 20), knotted
- ½ teaspoon ground turmeric
- 3 tablespoons Sri Lankan roasted curry powder (see headnote)
- Two 20-ounce (565 g) cans of young jackfruit, drained
- 1⅔ cups (400 ml) coconut cream (see page 14)
- 1 tablespoon tamarind concentrate (see page 22)
- 1 tablespoon salt
- 1 teaspoon sugar
- Cooked rice, for serving

"Polos ambula (පොලොස් ඇඹුල), or young jackfruit curry, is a great showcase of Sri Lankan techniques. The roasted curry powder—the key flavoring agent of this dish that can be found at Sri Lankan grocers—is made by deeply roasting spices before grinding, so it tastes incredibly different from your typical curry powder. We add the spices to young jackfruit along with water and coconut milk, and cook the curry until the fat from the coconut begins to separate. We also add pieces of char-grilled coconut flesh for another layer of texture that is akin to cartilage."
—*Gayan Pieris*

1. In a blender or spice grinder, grind the red chiles to a smooth paste.
2. Add the coconut oil, black mustard seeds, cumin seeds, and fenugreek seeds to a medium pot set on high heat. When the mustard seeds pop and the cumin and fenugreek seeds turn a shade darker, 1 to 2 minutes, add the garlic, red onion, curry leaves, and pandan.
3. Sauté the aromatics for 10 seconds before adding the ground chili paste. Turn the heat to medium low, and continue frying for 2 minutes before adding the turmeric and Sri Lankan roasted curry powder.
4. Cook for 30 seconds to bloom the spices, then add the jackfruit, coconut cream, tamarind concentrate, salt, sugar, and 1¼ cups (300 ml) water. Bear in mind that the curry will be reduced and taste more seasoned at the end. Stir until everything is combined before covering with a lid.
5. Turn the heat to low and simmer for 1 hour, stirring frequently toward the end of cooking to prevent scorching.
6. When the curry is ready, a thick layer of red oil will split from the coconut cream. Season with more tamarind, salt, or sugar to taste if desired. Remove the pandan leaf and serve with rice.

Buddha's Delight

SERVES 6

9 dried shiitake mushrooms (see page 16)

2 cups (480 ml) boiling water

3 dried tofu sticks (about 2.5 ounces/70 g; fǔ zhú/腐竹; see page 16)

¼ cup (25 g) dried lily buds (jīn zhēn huā/金针花), optional

½ small bundle (25 g) dried glass noodles (see page 15)

¼ cup (20 g) small dried black fungus (see page 15)

A small handful dried black moss (fà cài/发菜), optional

3 tablespoons oil

¼ cup (60 g) red fermented tofu (hóng fǔ rǔ/红腐乳; see page 22)

1 tablespoon toasted sesame oil

1 tablespoon vegetarian oyster sauce or mushroom stir-fry sauce

1½ teaspoons soy sauce

½ teaspoon salt

½ teaspoon sugar

¾ green cabbage (1 pound plus 1.5 ounces/500 g), roughly cut into 2- to 3-inch (5 to 7.5 cm) pieces

1 large carrot, cut into ⅓-inch (8 mm) slices

A handful of cilantro leaves

Cooked rice, for serving

Ground red chiles, optional

Commonly known in the West as Buddha's Delight, in Singapore this dish is known as chap chye (杂菜), which is Hokkien for "mixed vegetables." Almost every Singaporean, regardless of race or background, encounters it in some way while growing up—whether as a no-frills side at rice hawker stalls, as part of a home-cooked meal, or as an elaborate braise reserved for Lunar New Year. Of all the dishes in this book, this one means the most to me. It has become my go-to side when hosting a Chinese feast, as it pairs remarkably well with rice. Each ingredient that goes into the dish has meaning and symbolism. The cabbage—which is pau chye in Hokkien (包菜), "pau" meaning "to encircle or surround"—signifies one's hopes for close ties. The dried lily buds and dried black moss are symbolic of wealth and prosperity, but can be omitted if you can't find them. Be sure to age the chap chye for at least a day in the fridge—the flavor vastly improves with time.

1. Soak the dried shiitake mushrooms in the boiling water for 30 minutes, or until softened. Soak the tofu sticks, dried lily buds (if using), dried glass noodles, dried black fungus, and dried black moss (if using) individually in room temperature water for 30 minutes, or until softened.
2. When the ingredients are fully hydrated, drain them separately, reserving the mushroom soaking liquid.
3. Trim and discard the mushroom stems, then halve or quarter the caps as necessary to create bite-size pieces. Squeeze the lily buds to remove excess water, then tie each into a knot to prevent them from fraying during cooking. Tear the black fungus into bite-size pieces, discarding any hard bits. Snip the tofu sticks into 2-inch (5 cm) lengths.
4. Add the oil to a large saucepan or wok and set it on low heat. In a small bowl, mash the red fermented tofu well with a fork. Add the tofu to the oil and stir-fry on low heat for 1 to 2 minutes to release the paste's fragrance. Add the dried mushrooms, black fungus, and lily buds. Turn the heat to high and stir-fry the mixture for 2 to 3 minutes to release the fragrance of the mushrooms.
5. Measure the soaking liquid from the shiitake mushrooms and top it up with water as needed to yield 1 quart (1 L). Add the mushroom water to the saucepan, along with the sesame oil, vegetarian oyster sauce, soy sauce, salt, and sugar. Stir everything well and taste the liquid—it should be well-seasoned. Season with salt or add more sugar to taste.
6. Add the tofu sticks to the saucepan, along with the green cabbage and carrot. Bring everything up to a boil on high heat. Cook, uncovered, until the cabbage wilts, stirring occasionally, for 5 to 10 minutes. There should not be much liquid in the wok—more like a flavorful gravy than a soup.

RECIPE CONTINUED →

7. Add the drained black moss and simmer, covered, until the cabbage is very tender. This will take 15 to 20 minutes.
8. Add the drained glass noodles and allow the braise to cook for 2 to 3 minutes, or until the noodles are tender.
9. Season with salt or add more sugar to taste. Cool the braise and store it in your refrigerator for a day or two to allow the flavors to develop.
10. Reheat before topping with the cilantro leaves. Serve with rice and, if desired, ground red chiles.

1

Tofu and Chive Dumplings with Peanut Sauce

SERVES 4 TO 6

DUMPLINGS

8.5 ounces (240 g) extra-firm tofu (see page 23)

3 ounces (85 g) garlic chives (see page 17), trimmed and thinly sliced

2 tablespoons cornstarch

¾ teaspoon salt

One 7-ounce (200 g) packet of square wonton wrappers or gyoza wrappers

ASSEMBLY

3 tablespoons natural peanut butter

2 tablespoons brown rice syrup or honey

2 tablespoons soy sauce

2 garlic cloves, finely grated

3 tablespoons chili crisp (see page 14)

1 teaspoon sesame seeds, toasted

A small handful of cilantro leaves

On the first day of Lunar New Year this year, I wasn't feeling up to preparing a grand feast, especially since we didn't have guests visiting. However, I still wanted something special on the table, so I turned to dumplings with a tofu and chive filling—one of the simplest fillings you can make, but also one of the most classic and enduring. People tend to stress out over the wrapping, but my method produces rustic rather than precisely pleated dumplings, making the shaping more therapeutic than a chore. Despite this, the resulting dumplings don't lack grace when cooked. In fact, they remind me of goldfish with plump bodies and flowing tails. When it comes to the chili crisp, any will work, but I recommend one with a Sichuan peppercorn–forward flavor for this recipe; you need something punchy for a filling so pure.

1. **For the dumplings,** wrap the tofu in a clean kitchen towel. Squeeze well to mash the tofu into a paste and expel excess liquid.
2. Transfer the tofu to a large bowl and add the garlic chives, cornstarch, and salt. Mix everything together with your hands, almost kneading the mixture, until the chives are evenly distributed and the mixture forms moist clumps that hold together.
3. Add a few tablespoons water to a small bowl or saucer. Lay one wrapper on your non-dominant hand with its tip facing you, so that it looks like a diamond. Place a heaping teaspoon of the filling onto the center. ① Run a moistened finger along the top two sides of the wrapper, ② then fold the bottom corner over the filling; it should resemble a triangle. ③ With your nondominant thumb and index finger, gather the wrapper toward the center and squeeze to form a "waist." ④ Repeat until all the filling has been used up.
4. Fill a medium pot with water and bring it to a rolling boil on high heat. Working in two batches, add the dumplings to the pot and give them a stir so that they don't stick to the bottom. Turn the heat down to medium-low and simmer for 3 minutes, or until the wrappers become tender and translucent. With a slotted spoon or spider skimmer, lift the dumplings from the pot and shake off excess moisture before transferring them to a large platter.
5. **For assembly,** in a medium bowl, stir together the peanut butter, brown rice syrup, soy sauce, and garlic.
6. Drizzle the peanut sauce over the dumplings, followed by the chili crisp. Sprinkle with the sesame seeds and cilantro leaves before serving. ⑤

2
3
4

5

Minal Patel

The restaurant Prashad came to my attention when it finished second in the reality television program *Ramsay's Best Restaurant* in 2010, beating 12,000 restaurants in Britain. How did Prashad do it? Honest, flawless vegetarian cooking. You know that a restaurant is special when Gordon Ramsay, the chef who famously said that his biggest nightmare was his children turning vegetarian, vouches for it. At the helm of Prashad is Minal Patel, who has been its executive chef since 2005. Hailing from Gujarat in India, Patel adds her unique twist to traditional family recipes. Her efforts and commitment to culinary excellence were recognized when Prashad received a Bib Gourmand in the *Michelin Guide* in 2014, and every year since.

What does vegetarianism mean to the Gujarati people and how does it affect their diet?

Vegetarianism in India comes from living within the guidelines of the Hindu religion. Within Gujarat, and the Gujarati community, the ethos goes even deeper than the food. We aim to live life without creating hurt or pain to any being that can feel. Vegetarianism has been a core part of our culture for generations because of that ethos. This is also why our vegetarian cuisine is so well-developed and balanced.

Back in the days when village life meant no access to doctors and medicine, home remedies and Vedic principles were used to treat ailments, and this has spilled over into the food we eat. Gujarati food is known for its delicate and balanced dishes, packed with feel-good ingredients.

What role did vegetables play in your family?

Gujarat has a huge farming community and we love to eat what we grow. You could find black-eyed beans, bottle gourd, okra, and onions in my family's backyard; there was never a shortage of textures and flavors to cook with. These seasonal vegetables not only played an important role in keeping my family healthy, but also kept food costs to a minimum. The weather in the United Kingdom means that I am not able to grow all of my own ingredients, but I still adhere to cooking with the seasons.

What advice would you give someone who wants to eat more plants and less meat?

My message to anyone wanting to improve their vegetarian cooking is to open your spice box and just be free! Find your own balance and explore how spices can work together to lift your dish. Also, select produce of the best quality and always go for fresh ingredients whenever you can; they make a world of difference. There is no compromise when it comes to garlic, ginger, and chiles. Those ready-prepped pastes just won't bring the same depth of flavor.

What is the key to preparing a vegetarian dish that would please the staunchest meat lover?

When you're cooking meat-free food for a carnivore, people are naturally drawn to meat substitutes. But for me, if a vegetable dish is done right, there's no need for a substitute. I focus on creating well-balanced, well-seasoned dishes. If it has the wow factor, no one will think it's missing meat. Ingredients like eggplant, potato, and lentils work really well to make a dish feel substantial. When cooking for dedicated meat lovers, I reach for a well-flavored paneer and pair it with an onion base and plenty of my house-blend garam masala.

Chickpea flour is popular in plant-based circles, but has been a staple of Gujarati cooking for a long time. What are your favorite ways to use this ingredient?

Chickpea flour, also known as besan (बेसन), is one of my go-to ingredients because it is really versatile. I use it in a batter for vegetable fritters (pakora/पकोड़ा) and various types of Bombay mixes. In fact, my favorite snack to munch on the sofa is a bowl of Bombay mix with a cup of ginger chai. I also use besan to make dhokla (ढोकला), a steamed savory cake. This may sound unusual, but when we served it at Prashad, there were queues out of the door and down the road every weekend.

Patel
ed

Renghan Reveya

SERVES 4

*BY MINAL PATEL**

STUFFING

- 1¼ cups (150 g) raw peanuts, with or without skin
- Scant 2 tablespoons (25 g) jaggery (unrefined cane sugar) or dark brown sugar
- 1 tomato, finely chopped
- 3 tablespoons ground coriander
- 2 teaspoons ground turmeric
- 1¼ teaspoons salt
- 1 teaspoon cumin seeds
- ¼ teaspoon asafoetida (hing/हींग; see page 14)
- 1½ cups (30 g) cilantro leaves and tender stems, finely chopped
- ½ cup plus 2 tablespoons (150 ml) oil
- One 1½-inch (4 cm) piece of ginger (15 g), finely grated
- 3 teaspoons Kashmiri chili powder

EGGPLANTS

- 14 baby round eggplants or 6 Lebanese eggplants (1.75 pounds/800 g)
- 1½ cups (360 ml) boiling water

"Renghan reveya (રીંગણ રવૈયા), or eggplant satay, is a Gujarati recipe and a favorite among my family—especially my father. It's a really unique dish to the rest of the world, but it's something we would cook all the time in India. Eggplant is a staple in every Gujarati household; we call it the king of vegetables. In this dish, baby eggplants are cooked whole in the sauce, so it looks beautiful. This recipe is vegan and free of gluten, onion, and garlic."—*Minal Patel*

1. **For the stuffing,** pulse the peanuts and jaggery in a blender to form a semi-fine powder. Tip the rubble into a medium bowl and add the tomato, coriander, turmeric, salt, cumin seeds, and asafoetida.
2. Mix everything together with your hands, working the spices into the tomato flesh with your fingertips. Leave to rest for a few minutes to allow the spices to infuse, then stir in the cilantro, oil, ginger, and chili powder.
3. **For the eggplants,** if using baby round eggplants, slice each eggplant into quarters from the bottom, leaving each attached at the stem. If using Lebanese eggplants, cut off the stems and cut them crosswise into 2-inch (5 cm) pieces. Quarter each piece lengthwise, without slicing all the way through, to form slits. To stuff the eggplants, gently pull the quarters apart with your fingers and fill with a generous quantity of the stuffing. Be sure to spread it right to the end of the incisions but take care not to overfill, or the eggplants may split apart completely—part of the beauty of this dish is to serve them whole.
4. Arrange the filled eggplants in a large, deep saucepan and spoon any remaining stuffing around them. Cook, covered, on low heat for 5 minutes.
5. Pour in the boiling water, taking care to pour around and not over the eggplants, so as not to wash away the stuffing. Cover the pan and bring the mixture to a boil on high heat, then lower the heat to a simmer and cook for 25 minutes, or until a knife tip slides easily into the eggplant.
6. Turn off the heat and let rest, covered, for at least 20 minutes to allow the flavors to infuse and the oil to release from the sauce.
7. Reheat on medium heat, stirring gently, until piping hot. Serve the eggplants with a good helping of the thick sauce.

* Adapted from *Prashad: Indian Vegetarian Cooking* by Kaushy Patel, copyright © 2012. Published by Saltyard.

Cauliflower Laab

SERVES 3 TO 4

- 3 tablespoons glutinous rice
- 9 small dried red chiles
- ⅔ large cauliflower (14 ounces/ 400 g), chopped
- 4 shallots, thinly sliced
- 3 tablespoons vegetarian fish sauce or soy sauce
- 2 makrut lime leaves (see page 20), thinly sliced
- 1 tablespoon plus 1½ teaspoons lime juice
- 1 large tomato, finely diced
- Cooked rice, for serving

I cringe when I hear people talk about "cauliflower rice" because cauliflower simply does not share the same sticky, slightly glutinous quality of freshly steamed rice. That said, cauliflower rice is stupendous as a laab (ลาบ or ລາບ). In fact, when I have a head of cauliflower in the fridge and can't think of what to cook for dinner, I make laab because it is so simple and quick. While laab traditionally refers to a salad of ground meat, vegan versions abound all over Thailand and Laos, as the dish is more about the exuberant mix of herbs, chile, lime juice, and toasted rice powder than it is about the meat. Do not skip toasting and grinding your own dried chiles and glutinous rice—it is the key to a good laab.

1. Toast the glutinous rice in a dry skillet set on medium-low heat, shaking occasionally. When the rice turns golden and smells like popcorn, 4 to 5 minutes, transfer it to a spice grinder or blender. Pulse until you get a slightly coarse powder; you want to retain some texture. Tip the powder out onto a dish and set aside.
2. In the same skillet, on medium-low heat, toast the dried red chiles. When the chiles smell fragrant and deepen in color, 2 to 3 minutes, set 4 or 5 aside for garnish. Grind the rest to coarse flakes in the spice grinder or blender.
3. In a medium pot set on high heat, combine the cauliflower and ¼ cup plus 3 tablespoons (100 ml) water. Cook the cauliflower until it turns slightly translucent and tender, about 3 minutes, stirring occasionally.
4. Turn off the heat. Add the chile flakes, shallots, vegetarian fish sauce, lime leaves, lime juice, and tomato. Toss everything together and add more vegetarian fish sauce or lime juice to taste.
5. Add the toasted glutinous rice powder to taste, then transfer the mixture to a serving dish. Garnish with the reserved dried chiles and serve with rice.

Tempeh Chili Pan Mee with Thai Basil

SERVES 3 TO 4

NOODLES AND TOPPINGS

4 eggs, optional

9 ounces (250 g) bok choy or other leafy green, cut into 2¾-inch (7 cm) lengths

14 ounces (400 g) fresh wheat noodles (lā miàn/拉面)

1 tablespoon oil

¼ cup (60 ml) chili crisp (see page 14)

SAUCE

2 tablespoons oil

15 ounces (425 g) tempeh (see page 22), finely chopped by hand or in a food processor

8 garlic cloves

2½ red chiles, roughly chopped

3 tablespoons Shaoxing wine

2 tablespoons vegetarian oyster sauce or mushroom stir-fry sauce

2 tablespoons kecap manis (see page 19)

1 tablespoon plus 1½ teaspoons soy sauce

1 tablespoon cornstarch

1 tablespoon dark soy sauce

1½ teaspoons Chinkiang black vinegar (see page 14)

1 cup (20 g) Thai basil leaves (see page 23)

This dish came to be because I was craving a bowl of chili pan mee—a popular Malaysian Chinese dish of freshly made wheat noodles topped with savory minced pork and poached egg—but didn't have meat in my fridge. I chopped up tempeh and was impressed by how much its nubbly texture and the way that it browns resembles ground pork; even my husband Wex was fooled when he tasted it. Before tucking in, it is important to break into the yolk and give everything a good mix so that the rich sauce coats every single noodle.

1. **For the noodles and toppings,** set a big pot of salted water on high heat. Line a dish with paper towel. When the water reaches a simmer, crack in the eggs (if using). Poach the eggs to your desired doneness, then gently remove them from the water using a slotted spoon and transfer them to the prepared dish. I like my eggs runny, verging on jammy—this takes about 1 minute. With a fine-mesh strainer, remove any remnants of egg from the water in the pot.
2. Bring the water up to a boil and add the bok choy. Once cooked—this should take around 1 minute—remove the greens with a spider skimmer and set aside.
3. Bring the water back up to a boil and add the fresh wheat noodles. Boil according to package instructions, or until tender. Drain the contents of the pot through a colander set in the sink. Rinse the noodles thoroughly in cold running water to stop the cooking before tossing with the oil.
4. **For the sauce,** add the oil and tempeh to a large saucepan or wok set on high heat. Fry for 5 minutes, stirring only occasionally to encourage the tempeh to brown.
5. Meanwhile, in a spice grinder or small blender, pulse the garlic and red chiles until a chunky paste forms.
6. When the tempeh is mostly browned, add the garlic and chili paste to the pan. Stir-fry for around 1 minute to release the fragrance, then turn the heat to low.
7. Stir together the Shaoxing wine, vegetarian oyster sauce, kecap manis, soy sauce, cornstarch, dark soy sauce, black vinegar, and 2 cups (480 ml) water in a bowl. Add the mixture to the saucepan and bring it to a simmer on high heat. Continue to cook until the sauce thickens to a gravy-like consistency, about 2 minutes, then add the Thai basil leaves. Cook for another minute, or until the basil wilts, then turn off the heat.
8. Divide the noodles among serving bowls. Top each bowl with the tempeh sauce, a poached egg (if using), cooked bok choy, and chili crisp, and serve.

Jihee Shin

Jihee Shin is a Melbourne-based professional chef and founder of Sarap Catering. Her passion for kimchi began when she was a young girl helping out at her family's restaurant and participating in the Korean tradition of gimjang (김장), where large quantities of kimchi are prepared for consumption throughout the cold months. At home, her mother fermented her own doenjang (된장), fish sauce, and soy sauce in large crocks. With these memories, life experiences, and a passion for sharing Korean ferments, Shin started Ji Kimchi, her kimchi business, in 2018.

Can you tell me about the traditional Korean diet?

In Korea, our meals consist of rice, soup, and banchan (반찬). The latter is a category of small dishes that are mostly made with vegetables. Korea is largely mountainous, so the amount of land suitable for rearing livestock is limited. This, together with the influence of Buddhism, resulted in plants being a large part of the traditional Korean diet. It was only in recent times, with growing affluence and the development of the livestock industry, that heavy meat consumption became the norm.

I turned vegetarian for a year and a half for health reasons and it wasn't difficult because of the range of banchan and the varied ways of enjoying vegetables in Korea. Now, when I visit home, most of the items on my to-eat list are vegetables, such as the sweet potato stem banchan that my mother makes, or steamed squash leaves when they are in season.

Kimchi is perhaps the most popular banchan of all. What memories do you have of it growing up?

For twelve years, my family owned a Korean restaurant selling seolleongtang (설렁탕). This is a nourishing beef bone broth, typically served with daikon radish kimchi (kkakdugi/깍두기) and Napa cabbage kimchi (baechu kimchi/배추김치). Though Mom made these kimchi throughout the year, the mass production, a practice known as gimjang (김장), would begin in winter when cabbage and radish were in season.

We would order close to a thousand heads of cabbage and, because the space inside the restaurant wasn't big enough to make all that kimchi, the preparation had to be done outside. We used to bury big crocks of kimchi underground, though with the advent of kimchi fridges, people don't do this anymore. A fridge dedicated to kimchi might seem excessive to some, but to Koreans, it is essential.

Can any vegetable be made into kimchi?

Koreans grow up with a fixed concept of what kimchi is, but for others, there are no boundaries. It's really wonderful to see people all over the world making kimchi with vegetables local to them. I have grown to enjoy making kimchi with seasonal ingredients from the farmers markets such as baby leek and fennel. The rule of thumb is, if a vegetable is sturdy, like fennel, it is better to ferment it for a long period. However, if you are working with something more delicate, like cilantro, it might be better suited for geotjeori (겉절이), a fresh vegetable kimchi that is more reminiscent of a salad.

What style of kimchi do you make for Ji Kimchi?

In addition to the traditional cabbage and radish kimchi, I also make vegan kimchi. To replace the fish sauce and fermented shrimp, I use an umami stock of kombu, shiitake mushrooms, and vegetables for depth of flavor.

My favorite type of kimchi is clean and fresh. Outside of Korea, people tend to think that kimchi has to be sour and spicy. That does not have to be the case, as there are different styles of kimchi in Korea. We don't use much fish sauce in the region where I come from. We keep it minimal and use seasonings such as chili powder, garlic, and ginger sparingly. The result is kimchi that is well-balanced and not too strong.

Tofu Kimchi

SERVES 2 TO 3

INSPIRED BY JIHEE SHIN

6 dried shiitake mushrooms (see page 16)

1¼ cups (300 ml) boiling water

1½ teaspoons oil

3 garlic cloves, minced

⅔ cup (140 g) vegan Napa cabbage kimchi (baechu kimchi/ 배추김치); see page 37)

½ small brown onion, thinly sliced

1 tablespoon Korean chile flakes (gochugaru/고춧w가루)

1 tablespoon sake

1 tablespoon soy sauce

1½ teaspoons perilla oil (deulgireum/들기름; see page 21)

½ teaspoon sugar

½ green onion, thinly sliced

12.25 ounces (350 g) firm tofu (see page 23), cut into 1¼-inch (3 cm) squares

1½ teaspoons sesame seeds, toasted

Cooked rice, for serving, optional

"I sell my kimchi quite young, to be eaten as is. For kimchi that is sour or stronger in flavor, the best way to enjoy it is cooked in kimchi pancakes or in a stew. I particularly love the stem of cooked kimchi as it has a meaty and juicy mouthfeel."—*Jihee Shin*

1. In a medium bowl, cover the dried shiitake mushrooms with the boiling water. Leave the mushrooms to soak for 30 minutes, or until fully rehydrated, then strain and reserve the soaking liquid. Snip off the tough stems with scissors and discard. Slice the caps finely and set aside.
2. Combine the oil and garlic in a saucepan and set it on high heat. Fry for 30 seconds, or until the garlic is fragrant, before adding the mushrooms. Fry for a further minute, then add the mushroom soaking liquid, kimchi, brown onion, Korean chile flakes, sake, soy sauce, perilla oil, and sugar.
3. Cook on low heat until the liquid evaporates, 5 to 10 minutes, stirring occasionally. Add more soy sauce or sugar to taste. Turn off heat and stir in the green onion.
4. For the tofu, set a medium saucepan of water on high heat. Once boiling, add the tofu and cook for 2 minutes to heat it through.
5. Drain the tofu and place it on one side of a serving dish. Place some of the kimchi next to it. Sprinkle with the toasted sesame seeds.
6. To enjoy, pick up a bit of tofu and kimchi and eat them together. This dish is great on its own as a snack with drinks, or with rice for a meal.

Mushroom Ramen with Fermented Tofu Broth

SERVES 4

CHILE OIL

¼ cup plus 1 tablespoon (75 ml) oil

3 garlic cloves, finely grated

1 tablespoon plus 1½ teaspoons Korean chili flakes (gochugaru/고춧가루)

1 teaspoon Kashmiri chili powder

SEAWEED SEASONING

¼ cup plus 1 tablespoon (75 ml) soy sauce

3 tablespoons mirin

2 tablespoons sake

1 tablespoon sugar

4 nori sheets (see page 21), roughly torn

MUSHROOMS

¼ cup (60 ml) oil

14 ounces (400 g) oyster mushrooms, torn or cut into large pieces

½ teaspoon salt

BROTH

⅔ cup (160 g) red fermented tofu (hóng fǔ rǔ/红腐乳; see page 22)

½ cup (120 g) natural peanut butter

1½ teaspoons toasted sesame oil

1 tablespoon plus 1½ teaspoons soy sauce

ASSEMBLY

12.75 ounces (360 g) dried ramen noodles, cooked in salted water according to package instructions until al dente

10.5 ounces (300 g) bok choy or other leafy greens, blanched

A handful of thinly sliced green onion

2 eggs, hard-boiled and halved, optional

A few shakes of Japanese seven-spice seasoning (shichimi togarashi/七味唐辛子; see page 19)

Traditional ramen is never a quick dish to make because many hours go into simmering chicken or pork bones to yield a rich broth. My simplified and very untraditional version cuts to the chase by dissolving red fermented tofu (hóng fǔ rǔ/红腐乳) and peanut butter into hot water to impart deep umami and creamy richness. Still, my favorite part of this dish is the seaweed seasoning—that stuff makes anything taste good. Drizzle it over avocado toast with a dusting of shichimi togarashi (七味唐辛子) for breakfast, or shake it up in a jar with chili oil and a splash of vinegar for a kickass salad dressing.

1. **For the chile oil,** set a small saucepan on high heat and add the oil. As the oil heats up, combine the garlic, chili flakes, and chili powder in a small bowl. When the oil just begins to smoke, pour it over the aromatics and set the bowl aside.
2. **For the seaweed seasoning,** in the same saucepan, combine the soy sauce, mirin, sake, sugar, nori, and 2 tablespoons water. Bring the mixture to a boil on high heat, then transfer to a blender. Blend until a loose paste forms, being careful not to burn yourself. Set aside.
3. **For the mushrooms,** add the oil and oyster mushrooms to a wide pot set on high heat. Do not stir the mushrooms as they cook so that they caramelize deeply. This will take 4 to 5 minutes.
4. **For the broth,** mash together the red fermented tofu, peanut butter, and sesame oil in a large bowl. Gradually stir in the soy sauce and 6¾ cups (1.6 L) water.
5. When the mushrooms appear shrunken and their undersides have browned nicely, give them a stir. Cook for 2 to 3 minutes to brown further, then add the salt. Remove the mushrooms from the pot and set aside.
6. Set a fine-mesh-strainer over the pot, and pour the tofu and peanut butter liquid through it, squashing any clumps with a spoon. Bring the broth to a boil. Add more soy sauce to taste.
7. **For assembly,** divide the broth and cooked ramen noodles between serving bowls. Top with the mushrooms, bok choy, green onion, and eggs (if using). Drizzle with the chile oil and seaweed seasoning and sprinkle with the Japanese seven-spice seasoning. Serve.

Tempered Beans with Tomato Casarecce

SERVES 6

BREAD CRUMBS

¼ cup (60 ml) melted coconut oil

¾ cup (50 g) panko

PASTA

¼ cup (60 ml) melted coconut oil

3 sprigs of curry leaves, stripped from the stems (see page 15)

2 small red onions, chopped

7 garlic cloves, minced

1½ teaspoons ground coriander

1½ teaspoons ground cumin

1 teaspoon Kashmiri chili powder

1 teaspoon ground turmeric

¾ teaspoon freshly ground black pepper

¼ cup plus 2 tablespoons (90 ml) coconut cream (see page 14)

2 tablespoons tomato paste

2 teaspoons salt

1 pound (450 g) green beans, trimmed and thinly sliced on the diagonal

8 ounces (225 g) cherry tomatoes, halved

10.5 ounces (300 g) dried casarecce or other short pasta shapes

A handful of cilantro leaves, thinly sliced

My husband's colleagues often glance over at his lunchbox, especially on days when he packs leftovers from our dinner the evening before. On multiple occasions, he has brought pasta dishes cooked with ingredients that aren't classically Italian, drawing skepticism from his Italian colleagues. However, as Singaporeans, we have grown up with such a diverse mix of cultures that it is second nature for us to blend elements of different cuisines to achieve delicious results. This pasta dish features beans and tomatoes, a classic combination in both Asian and Western cuisines. Inspired by Sri Lankan and Indian tempered bean dishes, it begins with tempering the spices and aromatics in coconut oil. While it might seem fussy, thinly slicing the green beans on the diagonal—so that the knife is nearly parallel to the bean—creates the most delicate crunch, which is an absolute pleasure to eat.

1. **For the bread crumbs,** combine the coconut oil and panko in a saucepan set on low heat. Stir-fry for 5 minutes, or until the panko is evenly golden and crispy.
2. **For the pasta,** bring a medium pot of salted water to a boil on high heat.
3. Meanwhile, in a large saucepan set on medium heat, combine the coconut oil and curry leaves. When the curry leaves splutter, about 15 seconds, add the red onions and garlic. Fry, stirring occasionally, for 4 minutes or until the onion turns translucent.
4. Stir in the coriander, cumin, chili powder, turmeric, and black pepper. Stir-fry for 30 seconds to bloom the spices. Add the coconut cream, tomato paste, salt, and 1½ cups (360 ml) water to form a sauce.
5. Add the pasta to the boiling water and cook on high heat according to package instructions or until al dente.
6. Add the green beans to the sauce and cook on medium-low heat, stirring occasionally, for 7 minutes or until the green beans are tender and the sauce has thickened. Add the cherry tomatoes and cook for 2 minutes, or until the tomatoes begin to burst.
7. With a slotted spoon or spider skimmer, transfer the pasta to the sauce, allowing some pasta water to drip into the saucepan. Stir to combine and simmer for 30 seconds, or until the sauce clings to the pasta.
8. Divide the pasta among serving dishes and sprinkle with the toasted bread crumbs and cilantro leaves.

EE-FU NOODLES WITH BRAISED SHIITAKE MUSHROOMS, PAGE 149

Fried

Tteokbokki with Soybean Sprouts and Garlic Chives

SERVES 4

½ cup (120 ml) oil

1 pound plus 1.5 ounces (500 g) frozen Korean rice cakes (tteokbokki/떡볶이), defrosted

3 tablespoons finely chopped preserved radish (cài fǔ/菜脯; see page 21), rinsed, drained, and squeezed dry

3 garlic cloves, chopped

¼ cup (60 ml) kecap manis (see page 19)

3 tablespoons soy sauce

1½ teaspoons sambal, plus more if desired, store-bought or homemade (see page 71)

4 eggs, beaten

5.25 ounces (150 g) soybean sprouts

2 ounces (55 g) garlic chives (see page 17), cut into 2-inch (5 cm) lengths

When I was living in Australia, I was pleasantly surprised to learn that there was another Singaporean living close to me in Daylesford, which despite being a tourist destination for its mineral springs, is a town of roughly 3,000 people. She shared that when her parents moved from Singapore decades ago, they deeply missed fried carrot cake—a beloved hawker dish made by stir-frying cubes of daikon radish (known as "white carrot" to the Chinese) rice cake with garlic, eggs, preserved radish, and a sweet-savory sauce. Without access to these rice cakes, they improvised by using snipped-up crumpets from the supermarket as a substitute. I've found that Korean rice cakes (tteokbokki/떡볶이) work wonderfully with the sauce as well. Frying the tteokbokki beforehand helps the sauce cling to the blistered crust beautifully.

1. Heat the oil to 400°F (200°C) in a wok or large saucepan. Line a dish with paper towels. Working in batches, add the tteokbokki to the pan. Fry the rice cakes, turning them from time to time, until their exteriors blister and crisp but do not brown, about 3 minutes. Using a spider skimmer or slotted spoon, transfer them to the prepared dish. Repeat until all of the rice cakes are fried. Pour most of the oil into a small bowl to reserve for later, leaving behind about a tablespoon.
2. Set the wok on low heat and add the preserved radish and garlic. Gently fry for 1 minute or until fragrant, then add the kecap manis, soy sauce, sambal, and ¼ cup (60 ml) water.
3. Stir well and bring to a boil on high heat. Add the fried tteokbokki and toss well to coat.
4. Continue to cook until the sauce is completely absorbed, then push the tteokbokki to one side of the wok and add 1 tablespoon of the reserved oil to the space created. Add the eggs and scramble until they form curds, then toss them with the rice cakes. Add the soybean sprouts and garlic chives.
5. Stir-fry the mixture until the vegetables wilt, 1 to 2 minutes. Turn off the heat and serve immediately with more sambal on the side if desired.

Stir-Fried Glass Noodles with Cilantro and White Pepper

SERVES 4

MUSHROOMS

3 dried shiitake mushrooms (see page 16)

¾ cup plus 2 tablespoons (200 ml) boiling water

AROMATICS

8 garlic cloves

½ teaspoon white peppercorns

2 cilantro roots (see headnote), scraped with a knife to clean

NOODLES

3 tablespoons oil

8 ounces (225 g) shiitake mushrooms, cut into ½-inch (1.25 cm) slices

One 1½-inch (4 cm) piece of ginger (15 g), thinly sliced

1 bird's-eye chile, thinly sliced

1 large carrot, cut into thin matchsticks

1 bell pepper, seeded and thinly sliced

2 tablespoons Shaoxing wine

2 tablespoons soy sauce

1 tablespoon dark soy sauce

1 tablespoon vegetarian oyster sauce or mushroom stir-fry sauce

1½ teaspoons toasted sesame oil

3 small bundles (150 g) dried glass noodles (see page 15)

1 cup (100 g) bean sprouts

A generous squeeze of lime juice

If I had to pick one type of noodle to eat for the rest of my life, it would be glass noodles. Despite what my friends think, I am not immune to laziness in the kitchen. Glass noodles take only minutes to cook and are tremendously versatile. Toss them with a cold, sharp dressing for a quick salad on a hot day or add them to a pot of broth at the very last minute. This dish, a riff on Thai claypot glass noodles, goong ob woon sen (กุ้งอบวุ้นเส้น), is defined by the belly-warming heat of white pepper and pungent fragrance of cilantro roots. Cilantro is often sold with roots intact at Asian supermarkets, but if this is not available to you, a handful of roughly chopped cilantro leaves tossed through the noodles at the end works too.

1. **For the mushrooms,** in a bowl, cover the dried shiitake mushrooms with the boiling water and set aside to soak for 30 minutes.
2. **For the aromatics,** pulse the garlic, white peppercorns, and cilantro roots in a blender or pound with a mortar and pestle to make a coarse paste.
3. When the shiitake mushrooms have softened, trim off any tough stems and slice the caps thinly. Set the mushrooms aside, reserving the soaking liquid.
4. **For the noodles,** add the oil to a wok or large saucepan set on high heat. When the oil begins to shimmer, add the fresh shiitake mushrooms. Allow to cook, without stirring, until the undersides of the mushrooms are well-browned, about 5 minutes.
5. Give them a quick toss, then add the aromatic paste, rehydrated shiitake mushrooms, ginger, and bird's-eye chile. Fry for 1 minute or until the aromatics are fragrant, then add the carrot and bell pepper.
6. Meanwhile, in a medium bowl, combine the reserved mushroom soaking liquid with the Shaoxing wine, soy sauce, dark soy sauce, vegetarian oyster sauce, sesame oil, and 1⅔ cups (400 ml) water. Add the liquid to the mushroom mixture in the wok.
7. Bring to a boil and add the glass noodles. It might seem as though there is too little liquid for the noodles—this is to be expected. Cover the wok, and cook on low heat for 5 minutes.
8. Remove the lid and give the noodles a good stir. Add more soy sauce to taste. Turn off the heat and stir in the bean sprouts and lime juice. Serve.

Cathy Erway

Cathy Erway is a James Beard Award and IACP Award–winning food writer, and what I love about her work is that it shines a spotlight on Asian pantry ingredients for a global audience. In her articles for *The New York Times* and *TASTE*, she extols the virtues of fermented tofu, which she calls "vegetables' best friend," and five spice–braised firm tofu (dòu fu gān/豆腐干), which "plays well against any crisp vegetable." She is also the author of *The Food of Taiwan: Recipes from the Beautiful Island* and coauthor of *Win Son Presents A Taiwanese American Cookbook*.

What are your experiences with vegetarian food in Taiwan?

My grandfather passed away when I was in my early twenties and my family visits his ashes at a Buddhist temple during Tomb Sweeping Day (qīng míng jié/清明节). One of the highlights of the festival is the vegetarian meal served at the temple's cafeteria. It's always a buffet of four or so dishes that are prepared simply and quickly—a combination of vegetables in light sauces that coat your rice and plant-based proteins, such as wheat gluten (miàn jīn/面筋) and tofu, which are shaped to resemble meat or seafood. It's more like home-cooking than restaurant-eating, but I just love how it makes the most out of all these ingredients. Vegetarians definitely don't suffer in Taiwan.

What underrated meat substitute should people be eating more of?

Seitan. Also known as wheat gluten, this food dates back to ancient times in China. Like tofu, it can be made and prepared in a variety of ways. Some traditional forms include mock duck, a vegetarian roast duck analogue that's been soaked in a sweet, hoisin-based sauce and textured to resemble a duck's skin. Fried seitan has a bubbly texture and is ideal for retaining sauces. Seitan can also be leavened and baked until puffy.

I'm not sure why wheat gluten-making hasn't caught on like bread-baking. It's much easier than making bread—the first steps of kneading the dough are really similar—but there's no baking required and there are endless possibilities for shaping, flavoring, and using your wheat gluten. You can make your own faux chicken slices and use them in a stir-fry with broccoli, or even prepare wheat gluten like chicken nuggets. It's a great alternative if you don't have the time to run out to the store to grab tofu.

Wheat gluten also has a quality to it, called Q, that Taiwanese people love. Can you tell me more about it?

Taiwanese eaters are almost as concerned with texture as they are with taste. Hence we find examples of rather tasteless elements in dishes that only add textural appeal.

Q texture, which is springy and bouncy, features commonly in rice-based noodles and dumpling skins. There's a lot to chew on (physically, that is), so you could have a vegetable noodle dish without meat and be totally satisfied.

What ingredients would a Taiwanese pantry have that can boost vegetarian dishes?

Fermented black beans (dòu chǐ/豆豉) are like little pellets of umami. They're commonly tossed into stir-fries or simply sautéed vegetables. I've also blended them into a Caesar-inspired dressing that I make with lots of garlic.

Another tasty ingredient that packs a big punch is fermented tofu cubes (fǔ rǔ/腐乳). Growing up, a jar of this was always in the back of the refrigerator. It comes in a few varieties, one being red fermented tofu (hóng fǔ rǔ/红腐乳), deep red from the addition of fermented red rice yeast. This is the kind of fermented tofu that is added to long-simmered red-braised Chinese stews. The off-white fermented tofu, swimming in a brine seasoned with sesame oil and sometimes chili flakes, is often included in a battalion of condiments to serve with a bowl of morning congee. Dissolve a little of this into a sautéed leafy green like spinach, and the sauce will become slightly milky and super tasty.

Dried Radish Omelet

SERVES 4

*BY CATHY ERWAY**

¼ cup (30 g) finely chopped preserved radish (cài fŭ/菜脯; see page 21)

6 eggs

¼ teaspoon salt

¼ teaspoon ground white pepper

2 tablespoons oil

"Cài fŭ dàn (菜脯蛋), a famous Taiwanese Hakka dish, is an omelet studded with little salty pieces of sun-dried radish. It's so delicious. The radish can be found at Asian grocers but, even if you don't have this ingredient, I've found that making an omelet with whatever pickles or preserves I have around is equally satisfying. I sometimes pickle peppers in the late summer, dice them up, and cook them in the same manner as below. It's all done cooking in just a few seconds and is great served with rice. Pickle omelet!"—*Cathy Erway*

1. Rinse the preserved radish in cold water, then squeeze to drain and pat dry with paper towel. (For less salty pieces, the chopped dried radish can also be soaked in water for 5 to 10 minutes before draining and drying.)
2. In a bowl, whisk together the eggs, salt, white pepper, and 2 tablespoons water.
3. Add the oil to a large skillet or wok set on medium-high heat. When the oil is very hot, stir in the dried radish and cook, stirring, for about 30 seconds.
4. Pour in the beaten eggs. As the edges begin to cook, scrape them toward the center of the pan to create ruffles of gently cooked egg in a tall, round heap. Loosen the edges of the omelet with a spatula.
5. Once the eggs are almost thoroughly set on top and the underside of the omelet is golden brown, about 3 minutes, carefully flip the entire omelet over.
6. Cook on the opposite side until lightly browned, about 1 more minute. Transfer to a serving dish and serve immediately.

* Adapted from *The Food of Taiwan: Recipes from the Beautiful Island* by Cathy Erway, copyright © 2015. Published by Houghton Mifflin Harcourt.

Mushroom Adobo Spaghetti

SERVES 3 TO 4

- 9 ounces (250 g) dried spaghetti
- 3 tablespoons oil
- 10 garlic cloves, chopped
- 2 dried bay leaves
- 1½ teaspoons chopped ginger
- 1 small red onion, chopped
- 12.25 ounces (350 g) pine mushrooms or oyster mushrooms, cut or torn into bite-size chunks
- ¼ cup (60 ml) apple cider vinegar or cane vinegar
- 3 tablespoons kecap manis (see page 19)
- 3 tablespoons soy sauce
- 2 small tomatoes, chopped
- 2 green onions, thinly sliced
- A few cracks of freshly ground black pepper

When my husband and I lived in Daylesford, Australia, years ago, there was a patch of pine forest near our home. On days of alternating sun and rain, pine mushrooms would emerge from the fallen needles and we loved foraging for them each autumn. These mushrooms grow in such abundance that we often returned home with more than we could eat. Mushroom adobo pasta was our go-to because it is a simple dish that relies on the marriage of a few basic ingredients, nearly all of which you can obtain from the supermarket. While European cooking typically emphasizes sweating onions before adding the garlic to prevent it from burning, in Filipino cooking, this order is often reversed, as it is the careful browning of garlic that lends dishes their characteristic fragrance. If you want to go the extra mile, look for cane vinegar, the traditional souring agent for adobo, at Filipino grocers. The Datu Puti brand is popular.

1. Bring a pot of salted water to a boil on high heat, then add the spaghetti and cook according to package instructions until al dente.
2. While the pasta cooks, add the oil and garlic to a large saucepan or wok. Fry on high heat, constantly stirring, until the garlic begins to brown, about 1 minute. Add the bay leaves, ginger, and red onion and stir-fry until the onion turns translucent, 2 to 3 minutes.
3. Add the pine mushrooms. Fry for 3 to 4 minutes until they no longer look raw, then add the apple cider vinegar, kecap manis, and soy sauce and ⅓ cup (80 ml) water.
4. Allow everything to simmer on low heat for 2 to 3 minutes, so that the mushrooms can absorb the seasonings, then taste the liquid and add more vinegar, soy sauce, or kecap manis to taste.
5. Once the pasta is cooked, transfer it straight to the saucepan using tongs. Toss well and cook on high heat until most of the liquid has been absorbed, about a minute.
6. Turn off the heat and stir in the tomatoes, green onions, and black pepper. Discard the bay leaves. Taste the pasta and add more soy sauce or vinegar, if desired, before serving.

Savory Turmeric Cakes with Seeni Sambol

MAKES 18 MINI MUFFINS OR 10 MINI PANCAKES

SEENI SAMBOL

2 tablespoons coconut oil

2 cardamom pods

2 cloves

1 sprig of curry leaves, stripped from the stems (see page 15)

1 pandan leaf (see page 20), knotted

1 cinnamon stick

2 small red onions, thinly sliced

½ teaspoon Korean chili flakes (gochugaru/고춧가루)

½ teaspoon salt

2 tablespoons dark brown sugar or granulated dark palm sugar (see page 15)

2 tablespoons tamarind concentrate (see page 22)

BATTER

½ cup plus 2 tablespoons (100 g) all-purpose flour

⅓ cup (80 ml) coconut cream (see page 14)

1 egg

1 tablespoon oil

¾ teaspoon ground turmeric

½ teaspoon meat curry powder (see headnote, page 99)

¼ teaspoon salt

ASSEMBLY

Oil, for brushing

1 red chile, thinly sliced

2 green onions, thinly sliced

Kuih bakar berlauk is a popular Malay snack in Singapore, where I grew up. Traditionally, each bite-size morsel is made by pouring a turmeric-and-coconut-milk batter into a pan with flower-shaped hollows and sprinkling over a savory filling. Cooked on the stove, the little treats turn out so tender and moist that they are almost custardy, with the fillings picturesquely engulfed by the yellow "cake." While the traditional version is topped with minced beef, my take uses seeni sambol (සීනි සම්බෝල), a Sri Lankan caramelized onion relish scented with spices. The traditional brass molds are hard to come by, particularly outside of Asia, but one can also use a stovetop pan with hollows like a takoyaki maker or poffertjespan, or mini muffin pans for baking. Topped with chile and green onion, these turmeric cakes are perfect as a midday snack or picnic food.

1. **For the seeni sambol,** heat the coconut oil in a saucepan on high heat. Add the cardamom pods, cloves, curry leaves, pandan leaf, and cinnamon stick.
2. When the curry leaves splutter, about 15 seconds, add the red onions, chili flakes, and salt. Once the onion wilts and softens, about 3 minutes, add the brown sugar and tamarind.
3. Increase the heat to high and cook, stirring constantly, until the onion turns brown and slightly jammy, around 5 minutes. Remove from the heat.
4. **For the batter,** whisk together the flour, coconut cream, egg, oil, turmeric, meat curry powder, salt, and ⅔ cup (160 ml) water in a bowl to form a smooth batter.
5. **For assembly,** you can make these cakes on the stovetop with a mini pancake pan or bake them in a mini muffin pan. Either way, brush the cavities of the pan with oil.
6. Fill the cavities three-quarters full with batter. Add a generous teaspoon of the seeni sambol, followed by a slice of red chile and a pinch of green onion.
7. If cooking on the stovetop, cover the pan and cook the cakes on low heat for 2 minutes or until the tops are set. Increase the heat to medium and cook uncovered for 3 minutes, or until the sides are browned and a toothpick emerges cleanly. If cooking in the oven, preheat the oven to 375°F (190°C), then once hot, bake the cakes for 10 minutes. Remove the cakes from the pan with a toothpick and serve warm or at room temperature.

Cathie Carpio

Cathie Carpio is a food and beverage consultant based in the Philippines who has been documenting Mindanaoan food culture since 2017. The plant-based dishes she prepares with Filipino techniques and ingredients are exactly the kind that I want to eat. She cooks green beans with Maranao palapa (a native green onion condiment) and amps up the flavor of job's tears (a locally cultivated grain) and grilled vegetables with smoked coconut cream. Carpio believes that Filipino cuisine has much to teach us about getting flavor into our vegetables. "Don't let the meat-centric cuisines deter you from exploring," she says.

Growing up, what was your relationship with vegetables like?

I gravitated to chicken and fish growing up, but my grandmother played an important role in fostering an appreciation for vegetables. We live in the province of Batangas, where bulanglang, a dish where fresh vegetables are boiled in hugas bigas (rice-washing water), is popular. As a soup, bulanglang tastes gingery and is slightly thick in consistency. The vegetables in the soup vary with the seasons, so you could have sitaw (green beans), kalabasa (squash), or patani (lima beans) depending on the time of the year.

Watching my grandmother in the kitchen familiarized me with Filipino preservation and fermentation practices. She used to make atsara—a condiment of grated green papaya, carrots, garlic, ginger, and onions—all pickled in lightly sweetened vinegar. It was delicious when paired with rich meat or vegetable dishes. She also used to make large batches of burong mustasa (pickled mustard greens), which went brilliantly with braised or fried fish. I learned early on that preserved vegetables could accentuate the enjoyment of a meal.

What is the Filipino approach to vegetables?

There is an emphasis on using ingredients that are abundant in the region. Bulanglang appears to be a simple dish, but it is a lesson in how Batangueño cuisine banks on what is in season and what is local.

An ingredient that grows plentifully in our province is kamias (a sour fruit, also known as bilimbi). Tamarind is the most popular souring agent in the Filipino sour soup sinigang, but I grew up using fresh kamias for acidity. We also use a lot of dried kamias in braised dishes. It is about appreciating what is local and maximizing its use.

People tend to characterize Filipino food as centered around meat. How accurate is this?

Dishes like pork lechon (roasted pig) and pork adobo (a style of cooking where meat or vegetables are braised in vinegar, salt, garlic, pepper, and soy) are given the spotlight in the media, so our vegetable dishes tend to be neglected.

In recent years, there has been a movement of turning traditional Filipino dishes vegetarian or vegan. I have tried this with some of my favorite dishes, and the key to successfully accomplishing this is to retain traditional flavors and textures. In dishes where fish sauce is typically used, savoriness can be added with tahure (fermented tofu) or tausi (fermented soybeans).

What is an ingredient that you appreciate more since changing the way you cook traditional meals?

Coconut. As I grew older and more open to exploring non-meat dishes, I began to appreciate vegetables cooked in coconut cream. The separation of oil from a coconut-based dish makes it irresistible. Kulawong talong, grilled eggplant with coconut cream extracted from charred coconut flesh, is one of these dishes—one that I enjoy often.

The uses of coconut in the Philippines go far beyond coconut cream–based dishes. Grated coconut can be used to make a variety of condiments and braises. For example, Maranao palapa—a pounded native green onion, ginger, and chile condiment— includes toasted grated coconut, while Tausug cuisine uses burned coconut pounded with aromatics to create a base paste for braises.

Quail Egg Bhejo* with Palapa

SERVES 4 TO 6

INSPIRED BY CATHIE CARPIO

PALAPA

4.25 ounces (120 g) sakurab, white part only, or green onion or leek whites

One 3-inch (8 cm) piece of ginger (30 g), thinly sliced

3 green chiles, seeded if desired, roughly cut

¼ cup plus 1 tablespoon (75 ml) oil

½ teaspoon ground turmeric

1 teaspoon sugar

½ teaspoon salt

EGG BHEJO

40 hard-boiled quail eggs, fresh or from a can, halved lengthwise

A handful of cilantro leaves, roughly chopped

A handful of fried shallots (see page 17), roughly chopped

½ small red onion, finely diced

A big pinch of flaky sea salt

Juice of a wedge of lime

A pinch of Kashmiri chili powder

"I dream of seeing palapa in every Filipino household and beyond. Sakurab has a distinctive earthiness, but green onions or leeks can be used as an alternative. Only use the white part of the sakurab, green onions, or leeks in this recipe, as the green portion alters the taste."—*Cathie Carpio*

1. **For the palapa,** add the sakurab, ginger, and green chiles to a food processor or blender and pulse to make a coarsely ground paste. Alternatively, you can do this with a mortar and pestle.
2. Transfer the paste to a saucepan set on low heat. Add the oil and turmeric and cook for 5 to 10 minutes, stirring continuously, or until very fragrant and the bright green color turns brownish. Turn off the heat and season with the sugar and salt.
3. **For the egg bhejo,** place the quail eggs, cut side up, on a cutting board and use your fingers to smear the cut side of each egg half with a small amount (roughly the size of a chickpea) of palapa.
4. Top half of the egg halves with the cilantro, fried shallots, and red onion, and sprinkle with the flaky sea salt and lime juice.
5. Place an egg half with just the palapa on it over an egg half with the additional toppings. With your fingers, press the egg halves gently together to seal, then transfer to a serving platter. Sit the egg on its side so that the exposed filling faces up. Repeat with the rest of the eggs. Season with the chili powder. Serve.

* *Egg bhejo* ((முட்டை பீஜோ) is a Burmese-Indian street snack of hard-boiled eggs traditionally stuffed with a spicy, tangy mixture of fried onions and garlic.

Bánh Xèo with Mushrooms, Corn, and Bean Sprouts

MAKES 7 CREPES

BATTER

⅔ cup (85 g) rice flour

⅓ cup plus 1 teaspoon (85 ml) coconut cream (see page 14)

¼ cup plus 2 tablespoons (40 g) cornstarch

1 tablespoon plus 1 teaspoon oil

1½ teaspoons ground turmeric

¾ teaspoon salt

¼ cup plus 2 tablespoons (90 ml) sparkling water

DIPPING SAUCE

2 tablespoons lime juice

2 tablespoons vegetarian fish sauce or soy sauce

1 tablespoon apple cider vinegar

1 tablespoon sugar

2 garlic cloves, finely chopped

1 bird's-eye chile, finely chopped

BÁNH XÈO

¾ cup plus 2 tablespoons (200 ml) oil

½ cup (90 g) fresh or frozen corn kernels

7 cremini or button mushrooms, cut into ¼-inch (6 mm) slices

1 cup (100 g) bean sprouts

1 small head of lettuce, leaves separated

A handful of cilantro or mint leaves

One of my favorite things to order at Vietnamese restaurants is bánh xèo, whisper-thin savory crepes. Bánh is a loose term denoting bread, while xèo imitates the sizzling sound the batter makes as it hits the greased pan. Served with fresh greens and a dipping sauce, it is an ideal hot weather dish, being both intensely flavorful yet light and refreshing. Despite looking very much like an omelet, bánh xèo contains no eggs and derives its color from turmeric. The batter is also gluten-free, relying on rice flour for structure. The key to these crepes is the consistency of the batter; it should be on the thin side, forming such a delicate layer that you doubt it will ever crisp up. Minutes later, the sides begin to curl and a lacy shell forms, ready to be filled.

1. **For the batter,** whisk together the rice flour, coconut cream, cornstarch, oil, turmeric, salt, and ⅔ cup (160 ml) water in a medium bowl. Cover and leave the batter to rest for at least 1 hour at room temperature, or ideally overnight in the refrigerator.
2. **For the dipping sauce,** while the batter rests, stir together the lime juice, vegetarian fish sauce, apple cider vinegar, sugar, garlic, and bird's-eye chile in a medium bowl. Taste the dressing and season with more vegetarian fish sauce, vinegar, or sugar if desired. It should taste balanced and light. Set aside.
3. When the batter is rested, whisk in the sparkling water until smooth.
4. **For the bánh xèo,** set an 11-inch (28 cm) skillet on high heat. Add 1 tablespoon oil and a handful of corn and mushrooms; don't be too generous with the toppings as these will break up the batter in the pan and make the bánh xèo more prone to falling apart.
5. Once fried, about 1 minute, arrange the ingredients evenly around the pan. Add a ladleful of batter; it should sizzle and bubble immediately upon contact with the pan. Allow the batter to more or less bind the toppings in place before you pick up the pan and swirl to distribute the batter. The key is to get the batter as thin as possible.
6. Scatter over a handful of bean sprouts and drizzle a tablespoon of oil around the circumference of the bánh xèo. Cover the pan and allow the bean sprouts to steam for 2 minutes, or until they wilt slightly and the bánh xèo begins to brown on the underside and turn lacy.
7. With a spatula, fold the crepe in half and move it to the center of the pan. Fry for another 1 to 2 minutes on each side until the crepe is nicely browned and very crispy, then transfer to a platter. Repeat until all of the batter has been used up. You will produce roughly 7 crepes.
8. Transfer the crepes to serving plates. Serve with the dipping sauce, lettuce leaves, and cilantro.

Ee-Fu Noodles with Braised Shiitake Mushrooms

SERVES 2 TO 3

BRAISED MUSHROOMS

8 dried shiitake mushrooms (see page 16)

3 thick coins of ginger

2 green onions, cut roughly into shorter lengths

1 tablespoon plus 1½ teaspoons sugar

1 tablespoon plus 1½ teaspoons soy sauce

1 tablespoon plus 1½ teaspoons vegetarian oyster sauce or mushroom stir-fry sauce

1 tablespoon dark soy sauce

1½ teaspoons toasted sesame oil

NOODLES

5.5 ounces (160 g) ee-fu noodles (yī fǔ miàn/伊府面; see headnote)

1 tablespoon plus 1½ teaspoons oil

1 package (5 ounces/150 g) brown shimeji mushrooms, trimmed and separated

3.5 ounces (100 g) garlic chives (see page 17), cut into 2-inch (5 cm) lengths

These noodles are typically served as a main course at a traditional Singaporean Chinese wedding banquet, possibly because the noodles' length symbolizes a long marriage. While this dish appears vegetarian at first glance, Chinese cooks are prone to adding chicken stock or a dash of dried fish powder to amp up the flavor. I turn to dried shiitake mushrooms instead, drawing inspiration from bak chor mee (肉脞面). This is a hawker dish from Singapore, where the mushrooms are braised until they become plump. Meanwhile, the mushrooms' umami seeps into the braising liquid, which, when cooked with the noodles, infuses them with incredible intensity. Ee-fu noodles (yī fǔ miàn/伊府面)—which might also be labeled as "yi mein," "yee mein," "longevity noodles," or "yifu noodles"—are nonnegotiable in this dish. Because these noodles are deep-fried, they have a richness of flavor even before being cooked with additional ingredients—an invaluable trait in a dish like this. You will find them sold in large circular plastic packages at Chinese or Southeast Asian grocers.

1. **For the braised mushrooms,** combine the dried shiitake mushrooms, ginger, green onions, sugar, soy sauce, vegetarian oyster sauce, dark soy sauce, sesame oil, and 1¼ cups (300 ml) water in a saucepan. Bring everything to a boil on high heat, then turn the heat to low. Simmer, covered, for 10 minutes, or until the mushrooms are tender.
2. **For the noodles,** while the mushrooms braise, fill a medium saucepan with water and bring to a boil on high heat. Add the noodles and cook on high heat for 2 minutes, or until the noodles are loosened and tender but still retain a bite.
3. Drain the noodles in a colander and rinse to remove excess starch. Leave them in the colander to drain in the sink.
4. Once the mushrooms are tender, remove them from the saucepan and set aside in a small bowl until cool enough to handle.
5. Squeeze the mushrooms into the saucepan to catch the excess braising liquid, then thinly slice them. Reserve the braising liquid.
6. Heat the oil in a wok or large saucepan on high heat and add the shimeji mushrooms. Fry for 3 minutes or until lightly browned.
7. Add the braised mushrooms and strain the braising liquid into the wok; discard the debris in the strainer. Bring the liquid to a boil.
8. Add the blanched noodles and cook on high heat, stirring the noodles frequently to allow them to absorb all the braising liquid evenly. Cook for 3 minutes, or until the liquid in the wok evaporates, then taste the noodles. If they are not tender enough for your liking, add a splash of water and continue cooking for a little longer.
9. Add the garlic chives and cook on high heat for 2 minutes, tossing until they wilt. Serve.

Julie Kleeman and Yeshi Jampa

Curious about what Tibetan food culture could contribute to the lexicon of vegetable cookery, I instantly thought of Julie Kleeman and Yeshi Jampa. Jampa grew up in Tibet learning to cook nomadic food. He met Kleeman—the editor of the *Oxford Chinese Dictionary*—in India, where he lived after the age of nineteen. They are now married with two children and live in Oxford, UK. Their award-winning restaurant and food stall, Taste Tibet, features a wide range of vegan dishes, and their cookbook *Taste Tibet: Family Recipes from the Himalayas* offers plenty of inspiration. I spoke with Julie about their approach to vegetable cooking.

How does the environment, lifestyle, and religion dictate the diet of Tibetans?

For nomads, the consumption of meat is unavoidable. Most of Tibet is too high in altitude for agriculture, so nomadic people depend on meat and dairy for survival. Due to their Buddhist practice, Tibetans aspire to limit the loss of life. As a result, they tend to bypass smaller animals such as goats and chickens in favor of the yak—the largest beast on the plateau. Yaks thrive at high altitudes and provide nomads with valuable dairy products (notably butter and yogurt). Many families slaughter only one yak a year, in the late autumn, and its meat is preserved for consumption over the course of winter and beyond.

In the valleys of Tibet, some farmers enjoy two growing seasons a year and more fresh produce than local people know what to do with. Hardy vegetables and fruits are typically harvested in the autumn. Root vegetables, mustard, and cabbage have their roots cut off and are stored in caves, which prevents them from perishing in the frost and allows them to last right through the barren wintertime when vegetables are scarce.

With the relocation of many nomadic people into towns and cities, vegetarianism is becoming more common and brings Tibetans more in line with their Buddhist practice.

What are some plants that thrive at high altitude?

Barley is one of the few cereal crops that can survive on the high, arid, and harsh Tibetan Plateau, and is turned into roasted barley flour (tsampa/རྩམ་པ), which is nutty in flavor and high in fiber and protein. For a nutritious and filling meal, tsampa is mixed by hand in a bowl with butter and boiling water, then rolled or squeezed into small balls to eat. Some nomads enjoy it up to three times a day on the Plateau.

How do plants play a role in Tibetan medicine?

Tibetans have become experts in the art of healing by identifying the potency of specific foods and drinks for treating different ailments. They understand certain foods to be "hot" in nature (tomatoes or garlic, for example): These generate heat in the body. Some plants are perceived to be "cooling" (cucumber or spinach, for example): These cleanse the body. "Neutral" foods include potatoes and mushrooms, which keep the body in balance. All these types of foods are represented across the Tibetan dinner table, so that the range of dietary needs can be met. The result is a diet that doesn't favor one food group to the exclusion of another, or operate according to the protein or carbohydrate content of a meal.

What do you think is the key to cooking vegetables?

The trick is to preserve their natural buoyancy and innate nutritional value: This means not overcooking them. Stir-frying gives you control over how much bite you leave in the vegetable and usually produces the best results. A key factor is how much oil to use: Root vegetables tend to need more, and green vegetables less. Green vegetables can cook quickly and must be carefully watched so that they do not wilt. Seasoning is also key—don't be scared to use salt! This helps to bring out a vegetable's natural flavor and can also remove bitterness.

TASTE
TIBET

Stir-Fried Sweetheart Cabbage

SERVES 2 TO 4

*BY JULIE KLEEMAN AND YESHI JAMPA**

- 3 tablespoons oil
- 2 dried red chiles
- ½ teaspoon crushed Sichuan peppercorns (see page 22)
- 3 garlic cloves, roughly chopped
- One 1-inch (2.5 cm) piece of ginger (10 g), unpeeled, thinly sliced
- 1 large sweetheart cabbage or any other green cabbage, shredded into bite-size pieces
- 1 tablespoon plus 1½ teaspoons Chinkiang black vinegar (see page 14)
- 2 teaspoons soy sauce
- 1 teaspoon sugar
- ½ teaspoon salt
- Cooked basmati rice or Tibetan flatbread (balep/བག་ལེབ), for serving

"In many parts of Tibet where few vegetables flourish, cabbage can be grown in large quantities, harvested in the autumn, and made to last right through winter. It is used across a range of dishes during this time. The following recipe is one where the cabbage takes center stage."—*Julie Kleeman and Yeshi Jampa*

1. Add the oil to a wok placed over high heat and heat until it starts to smoke. Add the red chiles and Sichuan peppercorns. Swirl the spices until they brown, about 20 seconds.
2. Quickly add the garlic and ginger and stir-fry for about 1 minute to release their fragrance. Add the cabbage and keep stirring and cooking for another 2 minutes.
3. In a small bowl, mix together the black vinegar, soy sauce, sugar, and salt. Add to the wok and cook for a further 2 minutes, or until the cabbage is cooked but maintains a light crunch.
4. Serve with the basmati rice or Tibetan flatbread.

* Adapted from *Taste Tibet: Family Recipes from the Himalayas* by Julie Kleeman and Yeshi Jampa, copyright © 2022. Published by Murdoch Books.

Egg Bhurji with Peas

SERVES 2

EGG BHURJI

¼ cup (60 g) ghee (see page 18)

1½ tomatoes, chopped

1½ green chiles, chopped

1 small red onion, chopped

2 tablespoons pav bhaji masala (पाव भाजी मसाला; see headnote)

½ teaspoon salt

3.5 ounces (100 g) peas or fava beans, fresh or frozen

4 eggs, beaten

ASSEMBLY

¼ small red onion, chopped

A small handful of cilantro leaves, chopped

1 tablespoon ghee (see page 18)

2 brioche burger buns, split in half

2 lime wedges

I don't often eat breakfast, but when I do, it is always on the weekend when it is worth making something a little special. Egg bhurji (एग भुजी), or Indian scrambled eggs, is perfect for two. The spice blend that you use is crucial because it sculpts the flavor profile of the dish. While you can use garam masala, I love egg bhurji made with pav bhaji masala (पाव भाजी मसाला), the spice blend for the popular mashed vegetable curry served with soft bread rolls. This is typically sold in small cardboard boxes at Indian grocers. The punch of flavor also comes from cooking down a generous amount of tomatoes, so use the ripest ones you can find.

1. **For the egg bhurji,** add the ghee, tomatoes, green chiles, and red onion to a saucepan set on high heat. Cook, stirring frequently, until the tomatoes break down, the liquid has completely evaporated, and the onions are tender. This will take 3 to 4 minutes.
2. Add the pav bhaji masala and salt and cook for another minute before adding the peas. Stir-fry the mixture until the peas are tender, 2 to 3 minutes.
3. Add the eggs, and scramble briskly. As soon as they begin to thicken and turn creamy, 1 to 2 minutes, turn off the heat. Season with salt to taste.
4. **For assembly,** divide the eggs between two serving plates and sprinkle with the red onion and cilantro. Set a clean skillet on high heat and add the ghee and brioche buns, cut side down. Fry until golden brown and crispy on the underside, 2 to 3 minutes. Serve the eggs with the toasted buns and lime wedges.

Fig and Brie Hotteok

MAKES 6 HOTTEOK

DOUGH

2 tablespoons plus 1½ teaspoons olive oil

1 tablespoon sugar

One 2¼-teaspoon (7 g) envelope of active dry yeast

1 teaspoon salt

2¼ cups plus 2 tablespoons (300 g) bread flour

FILLING

⅔ cup (60 g) walnuts

3 tablespoons dark brown sugar

1½ teaspoons all-purpose flour

½ teaspoon salt

2 large figs, stems trimmed, cut into 6 pieces each

2 tablespoons olive oil

5.25 ounces (150 g) rindless brie, cut into 6 pieces

FRYING

Oil, for shallow-frying

Sesame seeds, for sprinkling

Some people think the best way to enjoy fruit is to eat it raw, but I believe certain fruits are best cooked. One of my favorite dishes to prepare at my first restaurant job was a baked-to-order flatbread with figs and blue cheese. The sight of the caramelized, collapsed fruit and gooey cheese was enough to make anyone go weak in the knees. These filled Korean pancakes (hotteok/호떡), inspired by that memory, perfectly tread the fine line between savory and sweet, and go brilliantly with a salad with balsamic dressing.

1. **For the dough,** combine the olive oil, sugar, yeast, salt, and 1 cup plus 1 tablespoon (250 ml) warm water in a large bowl, then stir in the bread flour until thoroughly combined. The mixture should form a very wet dough. Resist adding more flour. Cover and allow the dough to rest for an hour, or until it has more than doubled in size and jiggles like Jell-O when the bowl is shaken.
2. **For the filling,** while the dough rests, toast the walnuts in a saucepan set on high heat, shaking the pan frequently, for 2 to 3 minutes, or until the walnuts are fragrant and crisp. Tip the walnuts onto a cutting board and leave them until they are cool enough to handle, then chop them roughly and transfer to a small bowl. Stir in the dark brown sugar, all-purpose flour, and salt, and set the mixture aside.
3. In a small bowl, gently toss the figs in the olive oil.
4. When the dough has risen, stir it thoroughly with a wooden spoon to degas it. With oiled hands, divide it into 6 pieces weighing approximately 3.5 ounces (100 g) each.
5. **For the frying,** set a large saucepan on low heat and fill with ⅓-inch (8 mm) of oil. As the oil heats up, transfer a piece of dough to an oiled surface and flatten it gently with your fingers. Top it with 2 pieces of fig, 1 piece of brie, and a heaping spoonful of the nut mixture. Gently bring the sides of the dough together to completely envelop and conceal the filling, pinching the ends together to seal the package.
6. When the oil shimmers gently, place the filled dough, seam side down, in the pan. You should hear light sizzling noises immediately; if not, remove the dough and wait a little longer.
7. Line a dish with paper towel. While the hotteok cooks, sprinkle the top with the sesame seeds. When the underside turns golden brown, about 3 minutes, flip the hotteok. With a weight or a flat-bottomed pot, press down on the dough gently to flatten it slightly. Remove the weight and allow the hotteok to continue cooking.
8. When the second side of the hotteok turns golden brown, about 2 more minutes, remove it from the pan and transfer to the prepared dish. Repeat with the rest of the dough. Serve the hotteok warm or hot.

FRIED CAULIFLOWER WITH GOCHUJANG GLAZE, PAGE 179

Deep-Fried

1

2

Hot Butter Mushrooms

SERVES 3 TO 4

MUSHROOMS

Oil, for deep-frying

10.5 ounces (300 g) king oyster mushrooms or oyster mushrooms

¼ cup plus 2 tablespoons (40 g) cornstarch

1½ teaspoons Kashmiri chili powder

1 teaspoon salt

1 teaspoon ground turmeric

¾ teaspoons baking powder

¾ teaspoon freshly ground black pepper

STIR-FRY

2 tablespoons unsalted butter or coconut oil

2 garlic cloves, chopped

One 1-inch (2.5 cm) piece of ginger (10 g), chopped

½ bell pepper, seeded and thinly sliced

½ small red onion, thinly sliced

2 green onions, halved lengthwise and cut into 2-inch (5 cm) lengths

1½ teaspoons Kashmiri chili powder

2 tablespoons kecap manis (see page 19)

2 tablespoons ketchup

Heaping ½ cup (90 g) roasted cashews

This dish has been greatly appreciated by everyone I've cooked it for, and it's no surprise—the ingredient list is so eclectic that there's bound to be something for everyone to enjoy. When I first cooked the dish that inspired this creation—Sri Lankan hot butter cuttlefish (හොට් බටර් කට්ල්ෆිෂ්)—at home, it captivated me; it tasted nothing like how I had imagined, the combination of ginger, bell pepper, and cashews bringing Chinese stir-fries to mind. It all made sense when I learned that this dish is closely associated with Sri Lankan Chinese cuisine, influenced by dishes such as salt and pepper calamari. Later, when I began substituting mushrooms for the calamari and teaching the dish at my cooking classes in the Netherlands, it was a hit with my students. I've experimented with an assortment of mushrooms in this dish, but king oyster mushrooms and oyster mushrooms are the best—once battered and fried, they provide a satisfying chew that makes you forget that this dish is entirely vegetarian.

1. **For the mushrooms,** fill a wok or large saucepan with 2 inches (5 cm) of oil and set it on high heat. Allow the oil to heat to 400°F (200°C).
2. While the oil heats, cut the mushrooms lengthwise into ⅓-inch (8 mm) thick pieces with a knife. Place in a large container with the cornstarch, chili powder, salt, turmeric, baking powder, and black pepper. ① Cover and shake well to coat the mushrooms thoroughly.
3. Line a dish with paper towel. Working in batches to avoid overcrowding, carefully add the mushrooms to the hot oil. Deep-fry, stirring frequently, until golden brown, crispy, and shrunken, about 3 minutes. Using a slotted spoon or spider skimmer, transfer the mushrooms to the prepared dish.
4. **For the stir-fry,** pour off the oil from the wok and wipe it clean with a paper towel. Add the unsalted butter, garlic, and ginger, and fry on medium heat until the butter melts and the mixture smells fragrant, around 30 seconds.
5. Add the bell pepper, red onion, and green onions. Cook for 1 minute, or until the green onions soften.
6. Add the chili powder and fry for 30 seconds, then stir in the kecap manis and ketchup. Add the fried mushrooms and toss thoroughly to coat in the sauce. Season with salt or add more kecap manis or ketchup to taste.
7. Add the roasted cashews and mix thoroughly. ② Turn off the heat and serve immediately.

Tofu Nanban

SERVES 4

SAUCE

2 eggs

3 tablespoons plus 1½ teaspoons Kewpie mayonnaise

1 tablespoon plus 1½ teaspoons lemon juice

1 Japanese cucumber, seeded and diced

A pinch of salt

TOFU

Oil, deep-frying

¼ cup plus 2 tablespoons (75 g) sugar

3 tablespoons plus 1½ teaspoons Japanese rice vinegar or apple cider vinegar

3 tablespoons soy sauce

1 pound (450 g) firm tofu (see page 23), cut into ⅔-inch (1.5 cm) slices

½ teaspoon salt

½ teaspoon freshly ground black pepper

All-purpose flour, for dredging

2 eggs, beaten

ASSEMBLY

1 small head of lettuce, leaves separated, optional

A few shakes of Japanese seven-spice seasoning (shichimi togarashi/七味唐辛子; see page 19)

As someone who began cooking European food before developing an interest in Asian cooking, learning about Asian culinary techniques has often involved unlearning Western conventions. For instance, in Asia, the purpose of deep-frying is not always to create a crispy bite in the finished dish; it can also serve as an intermediate, rather than final, step. I first became aware of this when an East Timorese friend gifted me some incredible braised pork belly where the rind had the gelatinous, chewy texture of sea cucumber. Her secret was deep-frying the pork belly so that it puffed up and blistered before adding it to the braising liquid; when softened, the rind had a wonderful wrinkly texture that absorbed flavors superbly. Just as with that pork belly, here, deep-frying slices of tofu transforms them into sponges for the sweet-sour soy marinade. If you're not a fan of tofu, this recipe is just as delicious with starchy vegetables, such as pumpkin or sweet potato—simply dip thin slices in water before coating in flour and deep-frying.

1. **For the sauce,** bring a saucepan of water to a boil on high heat and add the eggs. Lower the heat to bring the water to a simmer, and hard-boil the eggs. Depending on their size, this could take 7 to 8 minutes. Once cooked, run them under tap water to cool.
2. Peel and finely chop the eggs and transfer them to a bowl. Stir in the Kewpie mayonnaise, lemon juice, Japanese cucumber, and salt. Set the sauce aside.
3. **For the tofu,** fill a wok or large saucepan with 2 inches (5 cm) of oil and set it on high heat. Allow the oil to heat to 400°F (200°C). In a large bowl, combine the sugar, Japanese rice vinegar, and soy sauce to make the soy marinade.
4. Season the tofu with the salt and black pepper, then line up shallow bowls of the flour and beaten egg. Coat the slices in the flour, working carefully to prevent the tofu from breaking. Pat off any excess flour, then dip the tofu in the egg wash.
5. Carefully place the dredged tofu in the hot oil—the egg coating should puff up immediately. Repeat until the wok is filled; fry the tofu in batches to avoid overcrowding. Cook, flipping the pieces occasionally so that they fry evenly, until golden brown on all sides, 2 to 3 minutes.
6. Using tongs, transfer the fried tofu one at a time to the soy marinade, and turn the tofu so that it absorbs the marinade on all sides. Place the tofu on a serving dish.
7. **For assembly,** place the freshly fried tofu on a lettuce leaf (if using), spoon on some of the sauce, and sprinkle with the Japanese seven-spice seasoning.

Andrea Quynhgiao Nguyen

Andrea Quynhgiao Nguyen is a James Beard Award–winning author whose work includes *Asian Tofu: Discover the Best, Make Your Own, and Cook It at Home*. Her latest acclaimed cookbook, *Ever-Green Vietnamese: Fresh Recipes Starring Plants from Land and Sea*, offers flavorful, doable takes on traditional Vietnamese plant-based cooking. Based in California, she is the publisher of vietworldkitchen.com and the popular newsletter *Pass the Fish Sauce*.

What led you to write your vegetable-centric latest cookbook *Ever-Green Vietnamese*?

I changed my diet after I turned fifty and had health problems related to eating too many things that shouldn't be eaten together and in large quantities. I felt physically awful and was extremely stressed due to a hectic career schedule. My doctors didn't see any medical issue, but I realized that if I changed my diet, I could heal myself and alter my lifestyle for the long haul.

I've loved vegetables all my life because they're part of the Viet eating experience. Cue all the fresh herbs and lettuces! But despite my love for fresh produce, I didn't prioritize it enough. Like many refugee immigrants in America, my family changed our diet after we fled Vietnam. The traditional Viet diet is low in animal protein, but in America, meat is plentiful and affordable. So are processed foods. In many regards, my journey to eating a plant-forward diet is about rediscovering my heritage.

What do you think is the key to cooking vegetables?

Sourcing the freshest vegetables is key. That may simply involve talking to your produce vendor to explore what's best when. Shop at farmers markets! Garden if you've got space and want hyper-local veggies.

Aside from fresh produce, you're a huge advocate for homemade soymilk and tofu. Why?

They are delicious, easy, and fun to make. People adore freshly made cheese and yogurt, so why not tofu? In Asia, we have small vendors who sell freshly made soymilk and tofu daily—akin to the neighborhood bakery. If you don't live in that situation but want that fresh experience, you can make the milk from soybeans and coagulate it into tofu. The magical transformation from beans to curds thrills me every time.

I use soymilk lees (okara), leftover from soymilk- and tofu-making, for croquettes, doughnuts, and cookies. You may also use it as a binder in place of bread in meatballs. It's got plenty of fiber.

What are some of your favorite tofu products?

Aside from tofu, I enjoy tofu skin; both fresh and tender (eat it like sashimi), and dried as sticks (simmer them in broth). Tofu skin is fabulous for dim sum treats, too. Pressed tofu is terrific for bánh mì and dumpling fillings. Fermented tofu is a wonderful seasoning that I advocate for in *Ever-Green Vietnamese*. It has many uses, not just for stir-frying water spinach.

How do you think the perception of tofu differs in the West compared to Asia?

To understand and appreciate any food, a cook should consider how it's prepared and enjoyed by people who know it best—the people for whom the food is a staple.

Tofu is mostly seen as a meat substitute in the West. However, many Asian dishes combine tofu with meat or seafood. Mapo tofu is a great example of how a little meat with lots of tofu can be spectacular. And deep-fried tofu isn't just a meat stand-in. It's wondrous in its own right.

People respect how much Italians revere pasta, so why shouldn't they offer the same consideration for Asians and tofu?

Lemongrass Tofu with Chiles

SERVES 4

*BY ANDREA QUYNHGIAO NGUYEN**

1 pound (450 g) firm tofu (see page 23)

1 teaspoon plus a generous pinch of salt

2 cups (480 ml) boiling water

2 tablespoons oil, plus more for deep-frying

3 shallots, finely chopped

1 stalk of lemongrass, bottom half only (see page 20), finely chopped

1 bird's-eye chile, finely chopped

½ red bell pepper, seeded and diagonally cut into ¼-inch (6 mm) strips

12 green beans or asparagus, cut on steep diagonals to match the bell pepper strips

2 teaspoons Madras curry powder

½ teaspoon sugar

¼ cup (60 ml) coconut milk

1½ teaspoons vegetarian fish sauce or soy sauce

A small handful of cilantro leaves

"I first had this southern Vietnamese dish (Đậu Hũ Xào Sả Ớt) on Phú Quốc island. Under a spot of shade gazing out at the ocean about thirty feet away, I enjoyed this tofu, a bowl of rice, and a glass of beer on ice. It was one of the best meals I'd ever had, and I was eager to replicate it at home. I still prepare this dish and use soy sauce in lieu of fish sauce for strict vegetarian diners."
—Andrea Quynhgiao Nguyen

1. Cut the tofu lengthwise into two pieces, then slice crosswise into squares roughly 2 to 3 inches (5 to 7.5 cm) wide and ½ to ¾ inch (1.25 to 2 cm) thick. Cut each square into 2 triangles then transfer to a shallow bowl.
2. Line a dish with kitchen towel or a double layer of paper towel. In a separate bowl, combine 1 teaspoon of the salt with the boiling water, then pour it over the tofu. Set aside for 15 minutes, then pour off the water. Transfer the tofu to the prepared dish. Let it drain for about 15 minutes.
3. Line a dish with paper towel. Fill a wok or large saucepan with 2 inches (5 cm) of oil and set it on high heat. Allow the oil to heat to 375°F (190°C).
4. Blot excess water from the tofu triangles, then slide them into the oil in batches of 5 or 6. Stirring gently with chopsticks or a spider skimmer, fry the tofu for 2 minutes, or until crispy and golden. Carefully remove them from the oil using a slotted spoon or spider skimmer and transfer them to the prepared dish. Return the oil to 375°F (190°C) before frying another batch.
5. Add 2 tablespoons of the oil and the shallots, lemongrass, and bird's-eye chile to a wok or large skillet set on high heat, and stir-fry for about 1 minute, until fragrant. Add the red bell pepper, green beans, and a generous pinch of salt, and stir-fry for about 2 minutes, or until the vegetables have slightly softened.
6. Add the tofu, then sprinkle in the Madras curry powder and sugar. Stir-fry for about 45 seconds, then add the coconut milk, vegetarian fish sauce, and ¼ cup (60 ml) water and cook for 2 to 3 minutes more, stirring until there is little liquid visible.
7. Transfer to a serving plate and sprinkle with the cilantro leaves. Serve.

* Adapted from *Asian Tofu: Discover the Best, Make Your Own, and Cook It at Home* by Andrea Quynhgiao Nguyen, copyright © 2012. Published by Ten Speed Press.

Eggplant Croquettes with Cilantro Mayonnaise

SERVES 2 TO 3

CROQUETTES

- 2 globe eggplants (about 2 pounds/900 g)
- 1 tablespoon plus 1½ teaspoons salt
- Oil, for deep-frying
- 7 garlic cloves, chopped
- One 2-inch (5 cm) piece of ginger (20 g), chopped
- 1 red chile, chopped
- 1 tablespoon plus 1½ teaspoons yellow bean paste (tau cheo/豆酱; see page 23)
- 1 tablespoon Chinkiang black vinegar (see page 14)
- 1 tablespoon dark soy sauce
- 2½ teaspoons sugar
- All-purpose flour, for dredging
- 1 egg, beaten
- Panko, for crumbing

MAYONNAISE

- ½ cup (115 g) mayonnaise
- A handful of cilantro leaves

When I was working at Carlton Wine Room in Melbourne, croquettes were one of the biggest hits on the menu. Whole pork shoulders would be roasted, pulled, and mixed with the pan juices. The gelatin in the juices allowed the meat to set firm when the mixture was chilled, making it a dream to slice and crumb. Now that I'm living in the Netherlands, I've been exposed to another way of making croquettes. Bitterballen, or minced beef croquettes, use béchamel as a binder. When dreaming up vegetarian croquettes, it occurred to me that eggplant would be terrific, as it turns so buttery and soft after being deep-fried. Sure enough, when mashed, it formed a cohesive paste that could be molded into quenelles between two spoons. If making these for entertaining, you can crumb the croquettes and keep them in your refrigerator for up to 3 days, and deep-fry them when your guests arrive.

1. **For the croquettes,** cut the eggplants into ½-inch (1.25 cm) thick rounds, then cut the rounds into ½-inch (1.25 cm) thick batons. Toss with the salt and set aside for 30 minutes so that the eggplant can release water.
2. Working in batches, wrap the eggplant pieces in a clean kitchen towel and squeeze over the sink to expel excess moisture.
3. Line a dish with paper towel. Fill a wok or large saucepan with 2 inches (5 cm) of oil and set it on high heat. Allow the oil to heat to 400°F (200°C). Working in batches, deep-fry the eggplant for 4 minutes or until golden and tender. Using a slotted spoon or spider skimmer, transfer the eggplant to the prepared dish.
4. Transfer 2 tablespoons of the leftover oil into a saucepan over low heat and add the garlic, ginger, and chile. Stir-fry for 1 minute, or until fragrant, then add the eggplant, yellow bean paste, black vinegar, dark soy sauce, and sugar.
5. Stir-fry the mixture over low heat for 5 minutes while coarsely mashing the eggplant with a wooden spoon. The mixture should be a silky, cohesive mass with some texture. Season with salt or add more sugar to taste. Transfer to a bowl to cool completely.
6. Line up three shallow bowls of the flour, beaten egg, and panko. With two tablespoons, form quenelles (rounded oblongs) of the eggplant mixture and roll one at a time in the flour, then place in the beaten egg and roll to coat evenly. Carefully transfer to the panko and coat well, pressing the panko onto the quenelles so that each is thoroughly coated. At this point, the croquettes can be put in an air-tight container, with parchment between each layer, and chilled for up to 3 days.
7. Heat 2 inches (5 cm) of oil in a wok or large saucepan to 400°F (200°C) and deep-fry the croquettes for 2 minutes, or until golden brown all over.
8. **For the mayonnaise,** blend the mayonnaise and cilantro in a small blender until smooth. Scrape this into a small bowl and serve alongside the croquettes.

Spinach Leaf Chaat

SERVES 4

DATE CHUTNEY

7 Medjool dates, pitted

¼ cup (60 ml) tamarind concentrate (see page 22)

½ teaspoon Kashmiri chili powder

½ teaspoon ground cumin

½ teaspoon salt

2 tablespoons lemon juice

HERB CHUTNEY

1 cup (20 g) cilantro leaves and tender stems, roughly chopped

1 cup (20 g) mint leaves

1 green chile, minced

1 tablespoon finely grated ginger

½ teaspoon ground cumin

½ teaspoon salt

SPINACH

Oil, for deep-frying

20 spinach leaves, roughly 3 inches (7.5 cm) in length

½ cup (75 g) chickpea flour

1½ teaspoons ground turmeric

YOGURT

¼ cup (60 ml) yogurt or coconut cream (see page 14)

½ teaspoon salt

ASSEMBLY

A handful of pomegranate seeds

A handful of crispy gram flour noodles (sev/सेव; see page 14)

Spinach leaves are not an obvious choice for battering and deep-frying, but you'll be convinced when you cook them in the style of palak patta chaat (पालक पत्ता चाट), a popular Indian street food where crispy fried spinach leaves turn into a vehicle for shoveling chutneys, yogurt, and pomegranate into your mouth. Whether you choose to serve these as dainty, individually assembled canapés or a spectacular family-style pile, this is perfect picking food and fantastic for parties.

1. **For the date chutney,** the night before you plan to serve, soak the dates in just enough boiling water to cover. The next day, strain the dates and place them in a small blender with ½ cup (120 ml) of the soaking liquid, the seedless tamarind concentrate, chili powder, cumin, and salt. Blend until the mixture is completely smooth before transferring it to a squeeze bottle or small bowl.
2. **For the herb chutney,** rinse the blender and add the cilantro, mint, green chile, ginger, cumin, salt, and ¼ cup (60 ml) water. Blend until the mixture is completely smooth before transferring to a small bowl.
3. **For the spinach,** fill a wok or large saucepan with 2 inches (5 cm) of oil and set it on high heat. Allow the oil to heat to 325°F (165°C). Meanwhile, rinse the spinach well and pat dry with paper towel.
4. In a medium bowl, whisk together the chickpea flour, turmeric, a pinch of salt, and ¼ cup plus 2 tablespoons (90 ml) water until no lumps remain.
5. Line a dish with paper towel. One at a time, dip the spinach leaves into the batter, then run them along the side of the bowl to remove any excess. Lower them carefully into the oil. Repeat until the surface of the oil is covered with spinach leaves—do not crowd the pan.
6. Fry for 2 to 3 minutes, or until the leaves are crispy and the batter turns a shade darker. Using a slotted spoon, transfer the leaves to the prepared dish.
7. **For the yogurt,** combine the yogurt and salt in a small bowl, along with just enough water to obtain the consistency of thick coconut milk.
8. **For assembly,** if you want to serve this dish canapé-style, spoon 1 to 2 teaspoons of herb chutney onto each spinach leaf, followed by the same amount of yogurt and date chutney. Sprinkle with the pomegranate seeds and crispy gram flour noodles. Alternatively, if serving family-style, arrange the spinach leaves on a large platter and spoon over the toppings decoratively. Serve immediately.

R. G. Enriquez-Diez

R. G. Enriquez-Diez grew up in Bacoor Cavite, Philippines, and never thought that she would eventually give up an omnivorous diet—she loved meat too much and thought vegetables were boring. When she moved to the United States at 15, her homesickness was quenched by fatty sinigang and tocino (cured pork shoulder). A nutrition class in her college years made her reconsider her diet, and eventually, she became vegan. Torn between her lifestyle and her heritage, she learned to veganize her favorite dishes while retaining their Filipino essence. *Astig Vegan*, her website, has since been featured in the *San Francisco Chronicle* and *CNN Philippines.*

What's the Filipino relationship with meat like?

Historically speaking, the early Filipinos relied on native vegetables, fruits, fish, and fowl, reserving meat for big occasions like weddings. It wasn't until the Spaniards colonized the country that the Filipinos developed a zest for meat.

These days, more Filipinos in the Philippines are recognizing the benefits of plant-based food. Still, gatherings with loved ones can be trying. I have to think about whether there will be food for me at the event, how I will feel when I see them feast on meat, and how to defuse loaded conversations—among other ordeals. Hopefully, with more access to Filipino vegan cuisine and awareness, this will become less of a struggle.

What are some examples of traditional plant-based dishes in the Philippines?

There are many dishes in the Philippines where the star is a vegetable. These tend to be coconut milk–based, such as jackfruit in coconut milk (ginataang langka), squash and long beans in coconut milk (ginataang kalabasa at sitaw), taro leaves in coconut milk (laing), spicy green beans in coconut milk (gising gising), and cotton fruit in coconut milk (sinantolan). These are usually cooked with shrimp paste or fish sauce so they are not entirely vegan, but you can easily remove these seasonings to make them plant-based, and people won't be thrown off that there is no chicken or beef.

For traditional vegan desserts, I'd look to bananas fried in lumpia wrapper (turon), rice balls with tapioca pearls in coconut milk (ginataang bilo-bilo), or kakanin. The latter is an umbrella term for rice treats such as sticky rice wrapped in aromatic leaves (suman).

What is your approach to making vegan versions of Filipino dishes?

It begins with studying the original forms of the dishes. For example, with kare-kare (a peanut stew), there is an old-school method and a new way to make it. A lot of Filipinos use peanut butter to make the stew these days, but the traditional way is to roast peanuts and rice, then grind them. I have adopted this method in the preparation of my vegan kare-kare and find that it lends the dish greater complexity and depth of flavor.

Filipino food is often stereotyped as having a lot of animal products in it, so for a dish to be completely vegan and still remind me of home is exciting.

What do you think the world can learn from the Philippines about cooking vegetables deliciously?

The Philippines have been colonized many times, by many cultures, which influences the way we cook. This is why it is hard to name a distinctively Filipino technique or ingredient. That said, I notice that we Filipinos use way more garlic than other cultures. We also fry our garlic before adding onions, as opposed to other cuisines.

Another unique feature of Filipino food culture is that acidity plays a big role and we have a wide range of souring agents at our disposal. We use sour fruits like kamias (bilimbi), as well as different kinds of vinegars like coconut, nipa, and spiced vinegar. All these acidic ingredients produce a more complex, multidimensional flavor in the final dish.

Astig
VEGAN

Ginataang Munggo

SERVES 8

INSPIRED BY R. G. ENRIQUEZ-DIEZ

MUNG BEANS

2 cups (400 g) dried mung beans

TOFU

Oil, for deep-frying

10.5 ounces (300 g) extra-firm tofu (see page 23), cut into ½-inch (1.25 cm) cubes

STEW

2 tablespoons oil

6 garlic cloves, chopped

One 1½-inch (4 cm) piece of ginger (15 g), minced

1 small red onion, chopped

2 large tomatoes, chopped

2 tablespoons salt

4½ cups (135 g) loosely packed baby spinach

1¼ cups (300 ml) coconut cream (see page 14)

Cooked rice, for serving

"Cooking mung beans in coconut milk is a new discovery for me. My late aunt-in-law, who lived in the southern part of the Philippines, would cook her ginataang with mung beans, coconut milk, ginger, and tomatoes, and it was such a lovely flavor combination!"—*R. G. Enriquez-Diez*

1. **For the mung beans,** add the dried mung beans and 6 ⅓ cups (1.5 L) water to a medium pot set on high heat. Bring to a boil, then turn the heat to low. Simmer, covered, for 40 minutes or until the beans split from their skins and are tender to the point of being mushy.
2. **For the tofu,** fill a wok or large saucepan with 2 inches (5 cm) of oil and set it on high heat. Line a dish with paper towel. Allow the oil to heat to 400°F (200°C). Using a spider skimmer, carefully add the extra-firm tofu. Fry for 3 to 4 minutes, or until lightly golden. Remove the cubes from the pan using the spider skimmer or a slotted spoon and transfer them to the prepared dish.
3. **For the stew,** add the oil and garlic to a large pot set on high heat. Fry, stirring continuously, for 1 minute, or until the garlic turns the color of roasted cashews. Add the ginger and red onion, and continue to cook on high heat, stirring, until the onion turns soft and translucent, around 3 minutes. Add the tomatoes, and fry until they are broken down to mush, about 5 minutes.
4. Add the mung beans and cooking liquid, fried tofu, salt, and 3 cups (720 ml) water. Bring to a boil and simmer uncovered for 5 to 10 minutes to allow the mung beans to continue breaking down and the tofu to absorb the flavors of the stew.
5. Add the spinach and cook for 1 minute on high heat, or until the leaves wilt, then stir in the coconut cream and turn off the heat.
6. Serve the stew with rice. Any leftovers can be stored in your refrigerator for up to 2 days.

Thai Corn Fritters with Roasted Rice Dressing

SERVES 3 TO 4

FRITTERS

Oil, for deep-frying

1½ cups (360 g) drained canned corn kernels

1 egg

1½ teaspoons vegan Thai red curry paste

¼ cup (45 g) rice flour

3 makrut lime leaves (see page 20), thinly sliced

1 teaspoon salt

½ teaspoon baking powder

DRESSING

1 tablespoon glutinous rice

¼ cup (30 g) chopped onion

3 tablespoons sugar

2 tablespoons lime juice

2 tablespoons vegetarian fish sauce or soy sauce

1 tablespoon chopped cilantro

1 tablespoon chopped mint

½ teaspoons Korean chili flakes (gochugaru/고춧가루)

Fritters from Asia tend to be featherlight because they are bound with rice flour rather than all-purpose flour. Being gluten-free, rice flour promises fritters that are never dense or heavy. What also makes these a treat is the fact that they are double-fried. Double-frying is a technique I first learned about when I was working the fryer section at a restaurant, and a service staff member emptied a bag of chicken wings that she had bought for lunch into the fryer to "refresh" them. In Korea, no one would bat an eyelid at this, as double-frying is standard procedure. The first fry serves to set the crust, while the second fry eradicates excess moisture that has migrated to the surface from the interior, thus restoring crispiness. For these Thai corn fritters, a touch of store-bought red curry paste and a sprinkling of lime leaves is all that is needed to subtly amp up the umami and impart a heady perfume.

1. **For the fritters,** fill a wok or large saucepan with 2 inches (5 cm) of oil and set it on high heat. Allow the oil to heat to 400°F (200°C).
2. While the oil heats up, transfer a scant ½ cup (100 g) drained canned corn kernels to a small blender along with the egg and red curry paste. Blend until a smooth paste is formed.
3. Scrape this into a medium bowl and stir in the remaining corn kernels, rice flour, lime leaves, salt, and baking powder. The corn kernels should look like they are coated in a red-tinted mayonnaise, somewhat similar to mac and cheese before baking.
4. Working in batches to avoid overcrowding, carefully drop in tablespoonfuls of the mixture from just above the surface of the oil; this will help the fritters stay together in one piece. Cover the whole surface of the pan with fritters. Fry for 2 minutes on medium heat, or until the fritters are golden brown and crispy. Using a slotted spoon, transfer the cooked fritters to a dish.
5. When all of the fritters have been fried, turn up the heat to high to bring the oil back up to 400°F (200°C).
6. **For the dressing,** while the oil comes to temperature, place the glutinous rice in a small saucepan set on medium-low heat and toast for about 3 minutes, shaking frequently, until the rice turns light golden. Grind with a mortar and pestle or pulse in a spice grinder to yield a slightly coarse powder.
7. Tip this into a small bowl along with the onion, sugar, lime juice, vegetarian fish sauce, cilantro, mint, chili flakes, and ¼ cup (60 ml) water. Add more lime juice, vegetarian fish sauce, or sugar to taste.
8. Line a dish with paper towel. Carefully add all the fritters back to the hot oil and fry for 30 seconds, or until the fritters turn a deep golden brown and become extra-crispy. Using a slotted spoon, transfer them to the prepared dish.
9. Place the fritters on a serving dish and serve immediately with the dressing.

Fried Cauliflower with Gochujang Glaze

SERVES 4

FRIED CAULIFLOWER

Oil, for deep-frying

2 tablespoons salt

½ cup (120 ml) sour cream

2 cups (250 g) all-purpose flour

¼ cup plus 2 tablespoons (40 g) cornstarch

1 cauliflower (1 pound/450 g), cut into 1-inch (2.5 cm) florets

GOCHUJANG GLAZE

3 tablespoons Korean chili paste (gochujang/고추장; see page 20)

2 tablespoons honey

2 tablespoons ketchup

1 tablespoon apple cider vinegar

2 garlic cloves, finely grated

1 teaspoon sesame seeds, toasted

2 green onions, thinly sliced on the diagonal and soaked in water for 5 minutes to form curls

Cauliflower is a vegetable that unexpectedly shines when deep-fried. Its craggy surface is ideal for grabbing onto the dredge, and it turns tender within minutes of hitting the oil. Here, I coat the fried cauliflower florets in a sticky gochujang sauce and add a little sour cream to the dredge for a subtle cheese-like flavor that perfectly complements the glaze. Sliced into thick steaks instead of florets before being deep-fried and glazed, the cauliflower could transform a sandwich or burger.

1. **For the fried cauliflower,** fill a wok, deep skillet, or saucepan with 1½ inches (4 cm) of oil. Set the wok on high heat and heat the oil to 400°F (200°C).
2. While the oil heats up, whisk together 1 tablespoon of salt, the sour cream, and 1½ cups (360 ml) water in a large bowl.
3. In a large container, combine the remaining tablespoon of salt with the flour and cornstarch. Drizzle in 3 tablespoons of the sour cream mixture and whisk well to create small clumps.
4. Place the cauliflower first in the sour cream mixture and toss gently to coat well. Lift the florets out with your fingers and then place them in the container with the flour mixture. Cover and shake well to coat the cauliflower thoroughly.
5. Line a dish with paper towel. Working in batches to avoid overcrowding, carefully add the cauliflower to the hot oil. Deep-fry, stirring frequently, until the cauliflower is very light golden, crispy on the outside, and tender enough for a knife to slide through without any resistance, about 3 minutes. Using a slotted spoon, transfer the cauliflower to the prepared dish.
6. **For the gochujang glaze,** while frying the cauliflower, stir together the chili paste, honey, ketchup, apple cider vinegar, and garlic in a wide bowl to form a thick glaze.
7. When all of the cauliflower has been fried, transfer it to the glaze and toss well to coat the cauliflower evenly.
8. Sprinkle with the sesame seeds and green onion, and serve.

Hairil Sukaime

I grew up eating tempeh in Singapore, but as I'd never made it from scratch, it was eye-opening to chat with Hairil Sukaime, a descendant of one of Singapore's early tempeh artisans. During the Japanese occupation of Singapore, food was scarce, so the Javanese settlers started tapping into their expertise to produce tempeh with the minimal resources they had. The village they resided in—Kampung Tempeh—came to be named after their trade. During its heyday, the village was said to produce over five thousand pieces of tempeh daily, which were sold all over the island. In the 1980s, as Singapore rapidly urbanized, Kampung Tempeh, like hundreds of other traditional villages, was demolished and its inhabitants were forced to relocate into apartment buildings. The once flourishing tempeh-making cottage industry went into decline, though some artisans persisted in making their own tempeh at home.

What was it like growing up with tempeh being at the heart of your family?

The making, consumption, and appreciation of tempeh is in my family's blood, as we are Javanese. My paternal family had been making large quantities of tempeh from home since before I was born. It isn't an exaggeration when I say that a significant number of my family members were brought up on, and by, tempeh.

That tradition ceased in the early 2000s due to my family members' old age and health issues. In 2018, I picked up the craft. The process involves a lot of water, soybeans, patience, and elbow grease; however, seeing the tempeh develop its signature white mycelium and tasting the end product makes it rewarding.

What are the differences between traditional and industrialized tempeh production?

Tempeh-making was traditionally a manual operation with very little to no mechanical equipment used. Soybeans were hulled by being stepped on. The cooked and cooled beans were rubbed against waru (*Hibiscus tiliaceus*) and jati (teak) leaves before being packed. This acts as a process of inoculation known as usar, which loosely translates to "rub" or "rubbing." Scraps of older tempeh and leaves from previous batches were also used as starter culture as an alternative means of inoculation.

Leaves were used to wrap tempeh because they are naturally porous, and air circulation is one of the key factors that affects the fermentation process. The leaves of the simpoh air plant (*Dillenia suffruticosa*) have been used by tempeh makers in Singapore due to its abundance. The resulting tempeh has an imprint from the veins of the leaves.

Most tempeh manufacturers these days use commercially produced tempeh starters (*Rhizopus oligosporus*) and equipment, such as soybean hulling and automated tempeh-packing machines. Perforated plastic and biodegradable packaging are used in modern-day tempeh-making due to convenience.

How does homemade tempeh compare to commercial tempeh?

Homemade tempeh tastes so much better. I can't recall the exact flavor of the tempeh made by my late grandmother and aunts, but the fact that they did it for decades is a reflection of quality (similar to long-lasting hawkers and eateries).

Commercially made tempeh suffers from an issue known as patah pinggang, which literally means "broken hip." This phrase describes tempeh where the mycelium fails to properly form, because the tempeh was not allowed to ferment in the right conditions. Tempeh suffering from patah pinggang tends to spoil faster, feel slimy, and have an unpleasant, pungent odor.

Is plant-based eating part of traditional Malay food culture? How does tempeh fit into the diet?

I don't think the Malay culture looks at food as being plant-based or non-plant-based. Food is seen as sustenance and fuel, and we have always been taught to be thankful and appreciative to have food to eat.

Tempeh has been a traditional ingredient in most Malaysian, Malay Singaporean, and Indonesian households for many years. In the past, tempeh, along with other tubers, vegetables, herbs, and non-meat ingredients served as staples when times were tough. Meat dishes were served exclusively during celebratory and commemorative events. I hope that with the increase in people consuming tempeh, there will be more people who want to study and make it, too.

Fried Tempeh with Sambal Kicap

SERVES 4

INSPIRED BY HAIRIL SUKAIME

TEMPEH

1 tablespoon ground turmeric

1 teaspoon salt

14 ounces (400 g) best-quality tempeh (see page 22), cut into 3-by-¼-inch (7.5 cm by 6 mm) pieces

Oil, for deep-frying

SAMBAL KICAP

3 red or green chiles, seeded, if desired, and roughly chopped

5 garlic cloves

¼ cup (60 ml) kecap manis (see page 19)

2 tablespoons lime juice

¼ teaspoon salt

"Good-quality tempeh tastes so fantastic on its own without the need for complex preparation. Deep-fried tempeh, especially when homemade, has such a rich and creamy flavor."—*Hairil Sukaime*

1. **For the tempeh,** stir together the turmeric, salt, and ¼ cup plus 2 tablespoons (90 ml) water in a medium bowl. Dip the tempeh slices into the turmeric mixture and roll to coat them on all sides. Set aside to marinate while you prepare the sambal.
2. **For the sambal kicap,** coarsely grind the chiles and garlic in a spice grinder or a mortar and pestle. Transfer to a small bowl and add the kecap manis, lime juice, and salt. Set aside.
3. Line a dish with paper towel. Fill a wok, deep skillet, or saucepan with 1½ inches (4 cm) of oil. Set the wok on high heat and heat the oil to 400°F (200°C). Working in batches to avoid overcrowding, carefully add the tempeh to the hot oil. Deep-fry, stirring frequently, until the tempeh is golden brown all over like hash browns, 3 to 4 minutes. Using a slotted spoon or tongs, transfer the tempeh to the prepared dish.
4. Serve with the sambal kicap on the side.

Typhoon Shelter Mushrooms

SERVES 4

Oil, for deep-frying

12.25 ounces (350 g) king oyster or oyster mushrooms

1½ teaspoons soy sauce

⅓ cup (40 g) potato starch

12 garlic cloves (about 1 head), chopped

1 red chile, chopped

½ teaspoon five-spice powder (see page 16)

¼ teaspoon salt

¼ teaspoon sugar

1 cup (20 g) Thai basil leaves (see page 23)

Typhoon shelter dishes are an important part of Hong Kong's culinary traditions. Typhoon shelters were established in Hong Kong to provide a safe harbor for boats and the people whose livelihoods relied on fishing. As the nation became affluent in the late 1800s and high-rent residences and luxury stores opened close to the shelters, fishermen seized the opportunity and fried their catch with garlic to appeal to the nouveau riche. The dishes became so popular that typhoon shelters were promoted as tourist spots. Today, these signature plates of seafood are served under a mountain of crispy garlic in seafood restaurants across Hong Kong. For a vegetarian version, I've substituted mushrooms for the seafood. While fermented black beans (dòu chǐ/豆豉) are a common ingredient in traditional typhoon shelter dishes, I use five-spice powder and Thai basil leaves instead as their perfume works wonderfully with garlic.

1. Fill a wok, deep skillet, or saucepan with 1½ inches (4 cm) of oil. Set the wok on high heat and heat the oil to 400°F (200°C).
2. While the oil heats, cut the mushrooms lengthwise into ⅓-inch-thick (8 mm) pieces. Place them in a large bowl and toss with the soy sauce and 2 tablespoons water. Add the potato starch and toss the mushrooms again to coat them in an almost imperceptible layer of the slurry.
3. Line a dish with paper towel. Working in batches to avoid overcrowding, carefully add the mushrooms to the hot oil. They will stick together as they hit the oil—use chopsticks to separate them as much as possible. Deep-fry, stirring frequently, until golden brown, crispy, and shrunken, 3 to 4 minutes. Using a slotted spoon, transfer the mushrooms to the prepared dish.
4. Carefully pour off most of the hot oil from the wok, reserving 3 tablespoons. Add the garlic and red chile and fry on low heat for 1 minute, until fragrant.
5. Before the garlic browns, add the fried mushrooms and toss thoroughly to coat them in the fragrant oil and aromatics. Then add the five-spice powder, salt, and sugar. Taste a piece of mushroom and season with five-spice powder or salt or add more sugar to taste.
6. When you are happy with the way the dish tastes, turn the heat up to high and stir-fry until the garlic turns golden brown but is not burnt, about 1 more minute. Add the Thai basil leaves and fry for 1 more minute, or just until the basil wilts. Transfer to a dish and serve immediately.

1
2
3
4

Vegetable Rolls, Two Ways

SERVES 4

FILLING

1 tablespoon oil

⅓ green cabbage (about 9 ounces/250 g), thinly sliced

1½ carrots, cut into thin matchsticks

½ cup (20 g) small dried black fungus (see page 15), soaked in water for 15 minutes, then drained and thinly sliced

1 tablespoon kecap manis (see page 19)

1 tablespoon soy sauce

1 tablespoon vegetarian oyster sauce or mushroom stir-fry sauce

1 teaspoon toasted sesame oil

½ teaspoon salt

A pinch of five-spice powder (see page 16)

DIPPING SAUCE

¼ cup (60 ml) Japanese rice vinegar or apple cider vinegar

3 tablespoons vegetarian fish sauce or soy sauce

1 tablespoon plus 1 teaspoon sugar

3 garlic cloves, finely chopped

1 bird's-eye chile, minced

SPRING ROLLS

2 tablespoons all-purpose flour

7 spring roll wrappers, or fewer, depending on how many spring rolls you intend to make, measuring 8 inches (20 cm) square

Oil, for deep-frying

SUMMER ROLLS

7 dried rice paper sheets, or fewer, depending on how many summer rolls you intend to make, measuring 8½ inches (22 cm) in diameter

The phrase "vegetarian bee hoon" might not sound particularly appetizing, but when I was younger, it was all I wanted for breakfast. The thin vermicelli noodles were fried in soy sauce and served with braised cabbage and gluten-based mock meat fragranced with five-spice powder and sesame oil. That memory inspires this vegetable filling, which can be used to make spring or summer rolls. The rolls are delicious on their own, but serving them with herbs, a vinegary dip, and iceberg lettuce transforms them into a satisfying meal. A note on spring roll wrappers: You can use any size you like, but rolls made with larger wrappers tend to split less during cooking.

1. **For the filling,** set a large skillet on high heat and add the oil, cabbage, carrots, and soaked black fungus and fry until the cabbage and carrot wilt and become tender, about 4 minutes.
2. Add the kecap manis, soy sauce, vegetarian oyster sauce, sesame oil, salt, and five-spice powder. Stir-fry for 1 to 2 more minutes, then turn off the heat and allow the mixture to cool completely.
3. **For the dipping sauce,** stir together the Japanese rice vinegar, vegetarian fish sauce, sugar, garlic, and bird's-eye chile in a small bowl. Set aside.
4. **To make spring rolls,** combine the all-purpose flour with 3 tablespoons water in a small saucer to form a loose paste.
5. On a clean surface, lay one spring roll wrapper with one corner facing you, so that it looks like a diamond. Place roughly ¼ cup (60 g) of filling about 2 inches (5 cm) away from the bottom corner. Roughly shape the filling into a log. ① Fold the bottom corner over the filling and roll, as if you are making a burrito. ② Fold the left and right corners of the wrapper over the filling, smear the top corner with some flour slurry, ③ and continue rolling the spring roll up into a cigar shape. ④
6. Line a dish with paper towel. Fill a wok or large saucepan with 2 inches (5 cm) of oil and set it on high heat. Allow the oil to heat to 400°F (200°C). Working in batches to avoid overcrowding, carefully add the spring rolls to the hot oil. Deep-fry until golden brown and crispy, turning the rolls occasionally to encourage even browning, about 4 minutes. Using a spider skimmer or tongs, transfer the rolls to the prepared dish.

RECIPE CONTINUED →

ASSEMBLY

1 small head of lettuce, preferably iceberg, leaves separated

A handful of cilantro or mint leaves

7. **To make summer rolls,** briefly hydrate a sheet of the rice paper in a large bowl of room temperature water—just a few seconds will do. Lay it on a clean work surface and place ¼ cup (60 g) of filling about 2 inches (5 cm) from the bottom. Fold the bottom of the rice paper over the filling. If the rice paper still feels brittle and is not yet pliable, give it a few seconds to hydrate. Fold the left and right sides of the rice paper over the filling, then continue rolling the summer roll up into a cigar shape. ⑤

8. **For assembly,** slice the rolls into bite-size pieces, if desired, ⑥ and enjoy them with the dipping sauce, ⑦ lettuce, and cilantro leaves.

7

HAINANESE FRIED EGGPLANT, PAGE 219

Charred & Grilled

Charred Brussels Sprouts with Grapefruit and Yuba

SERVES 2 TO 3

BRUSSELS SPROUTS

12.25 ounces (350 g) brussels sprouts, trimmed and halved

2 tablespoons oil

½ teaspoon salt

TOFU STICKS

2 dried tofu sticks (fǔ zhú/腐竹; about 1.5 ounces/40 g; see page 16)

Oil, for deep-frying

DRESSING

3 tablespoons Japanese pickled ginger, chopped

3 tablespoons Kewpie mayonnaise

1 tablespoon plus 1½ teaspoons soy sauce

2 teaspoons Japanese rice vinegar

1½ teaspoons toasted sesame oil

¾ teaspoon sugar

ASSEMBLY

1 large grapefruit

A handful of nori strips (see page 21)

Brussels sprouts can be polarizing because of their inherent bitterness. However, I find that when you crank up the heat and roast them to the point where you fear they might burn, they become mellower and develop a delicious char from edge to edge. When I prepared this dish for my in-laws' Christmas party, it won over my brussels sprouts–hating cousin-in-law. The older family members praised how brilliantly the dried tofu sticks, or yuba, shapeshifted into crunchy "croutons" that added fragrance and texture to the salad. If you have the choice, the best tofu sticks to use for this salad are the flat and broad ones, rather than the narrow, bunched-up variety. In place of grapefruit, pomelo is also fabulous if it is available in your region.

1. **For the brussels sprouts,** preheat the oven to 445°F (230°C). Meanwhile, in an oven-safe skillet, preferably made of cast iron, toss together the brussels sprouts, oil, and salt.
2. Place the brussels sprouts cut side down in the pan and set on high heat for 3 to 4 minutes, or until the cut sides turn a light gold color. Transfer the pan to the oven and roast for 10 to 15 minutes, until the brussels sprouts are tender and charred.
3. **For the tofu sticks,** prepare a steaming setup by placing a trivet in a wok or large saucepan. Fill with enough water to come up just below the level of the trivet. Cover with a lid and set on high heat. When the water comes to a boil, place the dried tofu sticks on a heat-safe dish and set it on the trivet. Cover with the lid again and steam on high heat for 5 to 10 minutes. Once the tofu sticks have softened up nicely, remove them from the steamer and snip them into 2-inch (5 cm) lengths with a pair of scissors.
4. Line a dish with paper towel. Fill a wok or large saucepan with 2 inches (5 cm) of oil and set it on high heat. Allow the oil to heat to 300°F (150°C). Carefully add the tofu sticks and deep-fry for about 1 minute, turning occasionally with tongs, until they puff and blister. They should develop hardly any color. If the oil is too hot, the tofu sticks will brown too quickly and blisters will not form. Remove the fried tofu sticks from the pan using a spider skimmer or tongs and transfer them to the prepared dish.
5. **For the dressing,** mix together the Japanese pickled ginger, Kewpie mayonnaise, soy sauce, Japanese rice vinegar, sesame oil, and sugar in a small bowl. Add more soy sauce, rice vinegar, or sugar to taste.
6. **For assembly,** remove the skin and pith of the grapefruit with a knife. Peel and cut the grapefruit into segments, then cut each segment crosswise into thirds.
7. Place the grapefruit in a serving bowl or on a platter and toss with the brussels sprouts and tofu sticks. Drizzle with the dressing and sprinkle with the nori strips. Serve.

Grilled Corn with Coconut Cream and Green Onion

SERVES 4

COCONUT MIXTURE

3 tablespoons oil

6 green onions (about 6 ounces/ 170 g), thinly sliced

4 garlic cloves, finely chopped

1 cup (240 ml) coconut cream (see page 14)

1 tablespoon vegetarian fish sauce or soy sauce

1½ teaspoons sugar

CORN

4 ears corn, shucked

A handful of roasted peanuts, chopped

A sprinkle of cayenne pepper

A generous squeeze of lime or lemon juice

In Thailand and Cambodia, corn is grilled on the street over coals while being basted with salted coconut cream. The Thais have a penchant for infusing pandan into the coconut cream for khao phot ping (ข้าวโพดปิ้ง), while in Cambodia, green onion is used in poat ang (ពោតអាំង). This dish calls for a short list of ingredients, but the end result is so rich and savory that it evokes cotija-sprinkled street corn from Mexico. This is a great dish to cook on the grill during summer, but in inclement weather, you can also grill your corn directly on the stove or roast it in your oven on the highest temperature setting.

1. **For the coconut mixture,** add the oil and green onions to a saucepan set on high heat. Fry until the green onions wilt and begin to brown, 3 to 4 minutes, then add the garlic, and fry for a few seconds to release its fragrance.
2. Add the coconut cream, vegetarian fish sauce, sugar, and ½ cup (120 ml) water, and bring the mixture to a boil before turning off the heat. Add more fish sauce or sugar to taste.
3. **For the corn,** preheat a grill or set a cast-iron skillet on high heat, and add the corn. Grill, turning occasionally with tongs, until the corn begins to char, about 4 minutes. Then brush the corn all over with half of the coconut mixture and continue to grill until well charred, about 3 more minutes.
4. Transfer the corn to a platter and spoon over the remaining coconut mixture. Top with the roasted peanuts and cayenne pepper and drizzle with the lime juice. Serve.

Wayan Kresna Yasa

Wayan Kresna Yasa—chef and coauthor of *Paon: Real Balinese Cooking*—was born on the island of Nusa Penida in Bali. He trained and worked in the United States for six years, cooking at Acadia in Chicago and New York's Blue Hill at Stone Barns. As the global executive chef and culinary director for Potato Head, he opened Tanaman—a plant-based restaurant that was named one of the best new restaurants by *Condé Nast Traveler* in 2020. He is currently the executive chef and owner of HOME by Chef Wayan located in the village of Pererenan on the southwest coast of Bali.

What was your relationship with vegetables growing up?

In Bali, every household has a garden where families can grow vegetables for consumption or for offering to the gods in ceremonies. Vegetables are eaten on a daily basis with every meal. The most well-known vegetable dish from Bali is probably gado gado. Peanuts, garlic, and chiles are fried until crispy, then everything is ground into a creamy peanut sauce with a mortar and pestle. Some kecap manis is added for sweetness, then blanched green beans, bean sprouts, and cabbage are tossed with the sauce. There is also lawar, a traditional ceremonial dish of young jackfruit tossed with grilled coconut and bumbu Bali, a spice paste of fourteen ingredients. Everyday vegetable dishes include stir-fried fern tips and sambal eggplant.

It is a shame that families living in the cities have a very different diet these days. As busy working individuals who may not have time to cook, they tend to rely on fast food meals that often do not come with vegetables. Over time, people get used to the absence of vegetables in their diet. I was born and raised on the island of Nusa Penida, without the luxury of fast food options, so I always enjoyed vegetables as part of my meals.

What are your thoughts on the plant-based food scene in Bali?

The food that you see in most plant-based eateries in Bali tends to be Western-style (salad, raw bars, green juices) to drive tourism. It might be because tourists are not familiar with vegetable-based Balinese food and are not brave enough to try it.

The upside of Western culture arriving in Bali is that it has shown us that we can create dishes with raw vegetables. In traditional Balinese food culture, all vegetables have to be cooked and are never raw, except for cucumber. If I were to bring my mother a Western-style salad, she would probably say that I'm a rabbit.

What perspectives did you glean from your experience working in Western kitchens like Blue Hill at Stone Barns?

In my twenty months of working there, I learned that a flavorful vegetable dish does not start in the kitchen, but in the garden. I saw how important it was for farmers to be educated about flavor and texture—things that a chef would look out for.

In Indonesia, we do not have things like romaine, beets, or celery in our cuisine. Our farmers grow these Western vegetables, but tend not to eat them. This is problematic because they do not know what to look out for taste-wise, and often focus on growing the biggest vegetables they can. For example, they strive toward growing a four-pound cabbage without knowing that the cabbage has optimal flavor at three months old. On the other hand, they are experts at growing local produce that they eat, like fern tips and long beans.

The experience also gave me an appreciation for the natural cooking equipment that imparts so much flavor in traditional Balinese cooking. In Western kitchens, a combination oven is used for steam-braising, while Balinese cooks are able to achieve the same result by stuffing meat or vegetables in bamboo. Using a dangdang (traditional rice steamer) in place of an electric rice cooker adds a distinctive flavor and aroma to the finished rice. Also, when meat or vegetables are wrapped in leaves instead of parchment or foil, they benefit from a unique fragrance.

Urab Kacang

SERVES 3 TO 4

*BY WAYAN KRESNA YASA**

SAMBAL GORENG

½ cup (120 ml) coconut oil

3 shallots, thinly sliced into rings

10 garlic cloves, thinly sliced

1.75 ounces (50 g) bird's-eye chiles, thinly sliced

1½ teaspoons salt

URAB

7 ounces (200 g) long beans

5.25 ounces (150 g) bean sprouts

1.6 ounces (45 g) mature coconut flesh or grated coconut (see page 18)

1 tablespoon plus 1½ teaspoons lime juice

2 teaspoons coconut sugar

"Urab kacang is a green bean and charred coconut salad tossed with deep-fried sambal. Like most Balinese food, this recipe is fairly labor-intensive. However, it is easy to execute."—*Wayan Kresna Yasa*

1. **For the sambal goreng,** set a wok on medium heat and add the coconut oil and shallots. Line a dish with paper towel. Sauté the shallots until the edges turn golden, about 3 minutes. Remove them from the pan using a slotted spoon and transfer them to the prepared dish.
2. Add the garlic to the wok, and fry until the edges turn golden, 1 to 2 minutes, then remove them with the slotted spoon and set aside with the fried shallots.
3. Add the bird's-eye chiles to the wok, and stir-fry for 1 to 2 minutes until they wilt, then remove them with the slotted spoon and set aside with the fried shallots and garlic. Transfer the fried aromatics to a large bowl and toss everything by hand until well-combined. Season with the salt.
4. **For the urab,** fill a medium saucepan with salted water and set it on high heat. When the water boils, add the long beans and blanch for 2 to 3 minutes, or until they are tender. Remove them from the saucepan and place in ice water to cool completely. Cut the beans into 2-inch (5 cm) pieces and set aside.
5. Bring the water in the saucepan back to a boil and add the bean sprouts. Cook for 1 minute, or until the sprouts are crisp-tender, then drain the saucepan's contents through a colander set in the sink. Leave the bean sprouts in the colander as they cool down to allow excess water to drain.
6. Meanwhile, on an open fire or on the stovetop using a stainless-steel grill net, grill the mature coconut flesh. Once the coconut meat releases a sweet toasty aroma and the flesh is darkened but not burnt, 3 to 4 minutes, remove it from the fire. Allow it to cool completely before grating it using the smallest holes of a box grater. If using grated coconut, stir-fry in a dry saucepan on high heat for 5 minutes, or until golden.
7. Add the coconut, vegetables, and 2 tablespoons of sambal goreng to a large bowl, along with the lime juice and coconut sugar—any leftover sambal goreng can be enjoyed as a condiment alongside meals with rice. Massage thoroughly with your hands. Season with salt or add more lime juice or coconut sugar to taste before serving.

* Adapted from *Paon: Real Balinese Cooking* by Wayan Kresna Yasa and Tjok Maya Kerthyasa, copyright © 2022. Published by Hardie Grant Publishing.

Potato Salad with Nori and Charred Green Onion

SERVES 4 TO 6

PICKLED RED ONION

½ small red onion, finely diced

1 tablespoon plus 1½ teaspoons Japanese rice vinegar

2 teaspoons sugar

½ teaspoon salt

MAYONNAISE

1 tablespoon oil

4 green onions (about 4 ounces/ 115 g), trimmed and halved lengthwise

3 nori sheets (see page 21)

¼ cup plus 2 tablespoons (85 g) mayonnaise

1 tablespoon soy sauce

ASSEMBLY

2 pounds (900 g) baby potatoes or larger potatoes cut into 1½-inch (4 cm) chunks

5 eggs

2 tablespoons toasted sesame oil

1 teaspoon Japanese seven-spice seasoning (shichimi togarashi/ 七味唐辛子; see page 19)

1 green onion, thinly sliced

I fell in love with making potato salad when I moved to the Netherlands because the potatoes here are so creamy and rich-tasting. Success lies in taking care to cook the spuds just right—long enough for a fork to slide into them with little effort, but not so long that they fall apart and develop a coating of starch when they hit the colander. As a change from the typical dressing of dill, mustard, and mayonnaise, I often go with this nori and charred-green onion mayonnaise. A few spoonfuls of sharp pickled onion liven up the deep charred flavors.

1. **For the pickled red onion,** combine the red onion, rice vinegar, sugar, and salt in a small bowl. Set aside to pickle while you prepare the mayonnaise.
2. **For the mayonnaise,** add the oil to a large saucepan and set it on high heat. When the oil is hot, add the green onions cut side down. Cook the green onions without turning them, pressing them down with a spatula as they cook. They should make a sound like the air going out of a balloon. When they are visibly wilted and charred in spots, about 90 seconds later, flip them and cook for 1 minute on the other side. Once thoroughly charred, transfer them to a food processor or blender.
3. Rip up the nori sheets with your hands and add them to the food processor or blender along with the mayonnaise. Blend until completely smooth. Transfer this paste to a large bowl and stir in the soy sauce. Place a fine-mesh strainer on top of the bowl and stir in the red onion pickling liquid, setting the pickled red onion aside for garnish. Add more soy sauce to taste.
4. **For assembly,** place the potatoes in a medium pot and cover them with salted water by a couple of inches. Cover and bring to a vigorous simmer over high heat. This will take approximately 5 minutes. Add the eggs and turn the heat down to medium. Cook for 6½ minutes to cook the potatoes and perfectly hard-boil the eggs. The potatoes should be fork-tender but still hold their shape.
5. Transfer the eggs to a bowl of cold tap water to cool down. Drain the potatoes and add them to the mayonnaise in the bowl. Toss well to coat. Transfer the potatoes to a serving platter. Peel the eggs and halve them. Top the potato salad with the eggs, drizzle with the sesame oil, and sprinkle with the Japanese seven-spice seasoning, green onion, and the reserved pickled red onion. Serve.

1
2
3
4

Grilled Rice Paper with Tofu Sisig

SERVES 2

TOFU

Oil, for deep-frying

12.25 ounces (350 g) extra-firm tofu (see page 23), cut into ½-inch (1.25 cm) cubes

1 small red onion, finely diced

6 garlic cloves, chopped

2 tablespoons plus 1½ teaspoons soy sauce

½ teaspoon sugar

A few cracks of freshly ground black pepper

1½ green chiles, minced

GRILLED RICE PAPER

¼ cup (60 g) Kewpie mayonnaise

Two 8½-inch (22 cm) dried rice paper sheets

2 egg yolks

2 green onions, thinly sliced

½ bird's-eye chile, thinly sliced

Juice of 2 calamansi limes

In the Philippines, traditional sisig is made by chopping up the fleshy portions of a boiled pig's head. Soy, chiles, and chopped onions are added, and the dish is finished on a sizzling plate with raw egg and a squeeze of calamansi. Here, the same flavors feature in the format of bánh tráng nướng—a Vietnamese street food with grilled rice paper and toppings. You might be skeptical about eating dried rice paper, but when grilled, it forms a crispy base in mere minutes. Scaled up, this is a fabulous dish for barbecuing with family and friends in summer—part of the excitement is the urgency required to spread the yolk over the rice paper and sprinkle the tofu over it all in the time it takes for the rice paper to crisp. If you want to be traditional, look for Silver Swan soy sauce, which is available at Filipino grocery stores. Otherwise, regular soy sauce works well.

1. **For the tofu,** fill a wok or large saucepan with 2 inches (5 cm) of oil and set it on high heat. Allow the oil to heat to 400°F (200°C). Dab the tofu thoroughly with paper towel to get rid of excess moisture. Working in batches to avoid overcrowding, carefully add the tofu to the hot oil. Deep-fry, stirring frequently, until the tofu develops a light golden brown exterior, about 3 minutes. Carefully pass the contents of the pan through a fine-mesh strainer set over a bowl, and set the fried tofu aside.
2. Place the pan back on high heat without washing or wiping it, and add half of the red onion. Fry until the onion softens, around 2 minutes, then add the garlic, and fry briefly until it releases its fragrance, about 30 seconds.
3. Return the fried tofu to the pan, and add the soy sauce, sugar, and black pepper. Toss the tofu thoroughly. Season with pepper or add more soy sauce or sugar to taste. Turn off the heat and stir in the green chiles and remaining red onion.
4. **For the grilled rice paper,** either turn a charcoal grill on high or set a cast-iron skillet over high heat. As it heats, add the mayonnaise to a piping bag fitted with a small tip or a ziplock bag with a corner snipped for piping. Working with one rice paper sheet at a time, place the paper directly on the hot grill or skillet and immediately top it with one of the egg yolks. Break the yolk and spread it all the way to the edges. ① It is normal for the sides of the rice paper to curl up slightly.
5. Before the egg yolk sets, spoon over half of the tofu mixture, and spread it out to form an even layer. ② Allow the rice paper to continue cooking for 2 minutes or so, or until the base is golden and crispy. Transfer it to a serving plate. Grill the second rice paper with the rest of the ingredients.
6. Pipe the Kewpie mayonnaise over the tofu, then sprinkle with green onions, bird's eye chile, and calamansi lime juice, dividing the mayonnaise and toppings between the two grilled rice papers. ③ Use scissors to snip the rice paper into slices like a pizza, and serve. ④

Bryan Koh

Bryan Koh is the author of five cookbooks and has long been a champion of underrepresented Asian cuisines. *Milk Pigs & Violet Gold: Philippine Food Stories* and *0451: Mornings Are for Mont Hin Gar: Burmese Food Stories* were such important tomes that they won the Best Food Book Award at the Philippine National Book Awards and third in the Best Asian Cookbook category at the World Gourmand Cookbook Awards, respectively. What I especially appreciate about Koh's work is the way it highlights plants that are neglected in modern diets, such as banyan tree buds and frangipani flowers. In Brian's words, "We have lost appreciation for plants with challenging flavor profiles and textures. They can seem intimidating, but one can unlock their magic with a little know-how."

Growing up, what was your relationship with vegetables?

My mother never forced us to eat vegetables and played a large part in my enjoyment of them. Meat and seafood were mostly used as a seasoning agent. Bitter gourd or French beans would be stir-fried with a little minced pork to add umami, for instance.

A favorite childhood dish was pinakbet, a vegetable-forward stew that contained a small amount of pork and fermented anchovy paste or fermented shrimp (*Acetes*) for seasoning. Vegetables were viewed as a great source of pleasure.

How has your perspective on vegetables evolved with research and travel?

In Myanmar, I was bowled over by how the Burmese could turn anything into a salad. They are magicians. Burmese salads are called a thoke (အသုပ်), which means to not just toss, but also to caress and gently massage. This is why hands are the best tool for the job.

What I found exciting about these salads was how the use of chickpea powder or crushed, roasted peanuts could result in something so lusciously rich, nutritious, and delicious. While Thai salads often have distinctive layers of sweetness, acidity, and funk, I find Burmese salads more intriguing; you wonder what is in them, as no particular voice is prominent. It's a symphony.

To me, what sets Burmese salads apart from most of their regional counterparts is the use of more oil than acid (similar to Western salads). Most of the time, the oil used is hsi chet (ဆီချက်), which means "cooked oil" or "oil cooked with seasonings"—usually garlic, chile, onion, or ground turmeric. If something punchy like fermented tea leaves (lahpet/လက်ဖက်) or fermented ginger (gyin/ဂျင်း) is in the salad, a very good peanut oil would suffice.

The way the Burmese would use buds and leaves for texture rather than taste was also a revelation. Texture has always been a big part of Asian culture—ingredients like shark's fin or jellyfish are really quite flavorless on their own—but to encounter such texture in the context of a salad was very unusual to me.

What did you learn from your experience in Borneo?

The way Borneans would use fruit in savory foods is an approach echoed in Peninsular Malaysia. In Sarawak and Sabah, fresh, ripe durian would be turned into a sambal. The Iranun, many of whom live in the area around Kota Belud, would incorporate unripe bananas and papayas into soups and spicy stews. It revealed to me a more malleable way of looking at food. Outside of Asia, a vegetable being used in something sweet, or a fruit being used in something savory might be regarded as a novelty, but for many Asian food cultures, it is a way of life.

How do you approach cooking for vegetarians or vegans?

Despite the existence of vegan versions of products on the market, it can be difficult replicating the flavor of fish sauce or bagoong (fermented fish paste). It is much easier to cook a dish from a cuisine that is vegan in the first place, like a salad from Kachin or Shan State in Myanmar, where fermented soybeans and soy are used as seasonings.

Whether I am cooking traditional vegan dishes or not, I try to make them as interesting and vivid as possible by adding different textures and packing them with umami. I enjoy being lavish with herbs, as long as they enhance and do not take away from the vegetable itself.

1
2
3
4

Kulawong Talong

SERVES 3 TO 4

*BY BRYAN KOH**

BURNT COCONUT MILK

1 pound plus 1.5 ounces (500 g) grated coconut (see page 18)

EGGPLANT

3 Japanese or Lebanese eggplants

2 tablespoons oil

1½ small red onions, finely chopped

One ¾-inch (2 cm) piece of ginger (7.5 g), finely chopped

4 garlic cloves, finely chopped

3 tablespoons apple cider vinegar or cane vinegar

½ teaspoon salt

A pinch of sugar

1 green bird's-eye chile, thinly sliced

A handful of thinly sliced red onion

A few cracks of freshly ground black pepper

"Asia has so much to offer in terms of plant-based cooking, and burnt coconut milk is something that can really elevate vegetable dishes. Grated coconut is charred by applying chunks of charcoal to it, then it is moistened with water and the milk is wrung out. One of the most well-known dishes prepared with burnt coconut milk is kulawo, which comes from Quezon, in the Philippines. The following method is designed for those of us who lack coals or the nerve to handle them."—*Bryan Koh*

1. **For the burnt coconut milk,** place a wok or saucepan on high heat until it smokes, then add the grated coconut. Cook without stirring until the base begins to char, about 5 minutes. Redistribute the coconut and leave it again until its base chars. Repeat this several times until about a fifth of the coconut is scorched. ①
2. Tip the coconut into a bowl and sprinkle ¾ cup plus 2 tablespoons (200 ml) water over it. Leave for a minute before squeezing the liquid through a piece of muslin into a bowl. You should get approximately 1¼ cups (300 ml) of burnt coconut milk. ② Set aside.
3. **For the eggplant,** char the eggplants directly on a gas stove burner on high heat, turning occasionally with tongs, until tender and charred, 5 to 10 minutes. Alternatively, broil the eggplants on a foil-lined rimmed baking sheet until tender and charred on all sides, 10 to 20 minutes, turning occasionally. Transfer to a container and cover with a lid until cool enough to handle. Peel off and discard the charred skin and set aside the eggplant.
4. Add the oil to a saucepan or wok set on medium heat. Once hot, add the chopped red onions, ginger, and garlic and fry until soft and aromatic, 1 to 2 minutes.
5. Add the coconut vinegar and allow to bubble and boil for 1 to 2 minutes to remove the metallic edge. Add the burnt coconut milk, salt, and sugar. Simmer, uncovered, for 15 minutes, or until the sauce reduces to a light creamy consistency.
6. Add the eggplants, along with the green bird's-eye chiles. Turn off the heat and season with salt or add more sugar to taste.
7. Transfer to a serving dish and garnish with the red onion and black pepper. Serve.

* Adapted from *Milkier Pigs & Violet Gold: Philippine Food Stories* by Bryan Koh, copyright © 2020. Published by Xochipilli. Distributed by Marshall Cavendish.

Umeboshi Onigiri with Marinated Yolk and Shiso

MAKES 6 ONIGIRI

6 eggs

¼ cup (60 ml) soy sauce

2 tablespoons mirin

1 tablespoon black rice

1½ cups (300 g) Japanese or Korean short-grain rice

½ cup (100 g) unsalted butter

Pitted flesh of 3 Japanese salted plums (umeboshi/梅干し; see page 18), chopped

6 shiso leaves (see page 22), thinly sliced

I avoided making onigiri for a long time because I thought shaping them by hand would be difficult, but it's actually not! While onigiri are most commonly shaped into triangles, they can be round, too. Japanese salted plums (umeboshi/梅干し) and shiso make a classic flavor combination. A tablespoon of black rice is all it takes to stain the short-grain rice an attractive purple, which hints at the umeboshi. You could do without grilling the onigiri with soy, mirin, and butter, but I highly recommend this step as the toasty, caramelized crust is delightful. I typically enjoy these onigiri as part of a larger meal, or with simple toppings as ochazuke (お茶漬け). To turn them into an on-the-go snack, I bury the jammy marinated yolks in the center of the rice and wrap each onigiri in crispy seaweed.

1. Two or three days before you plan to serve, separate the egg yolks. The best tip I can give you is to use the freshest eggs you can find; less-than-fresh yolks are prone to breaking. With very fresh eggs, you can simply crack them into a bowl, then pick the yolks up with your fingers as if they are marbles. Place them in a small container, saving the whites for another use.
2. Add the soy sauce and mirin to the yolks. Cover the container and allow the yolks to cure in the refrigerator for 2 to 3 days. You are looking for the yolks to be thoroughly seasoned and take on a jammy texture.
3. In a bowl, rinse the black rice and short-grain rice thoroughly until the water runs clear. Drain and transfer to a rice cooker. Add 1⅔ cups (400 ml) water and cook according to your rice cooker's instructions. (See 3 for instructions on cooking rice without a rice cooker.)
4. In a saucepan, combine 2 tablespoons of the marinade from the yolks with the butter. Cook gently on low heat until the butter melts.
5. When all the water has been absorbed by the rice and the rice is tender, mix it gently with the Japanese salted plums. With moistened hands, divide the rice into 6 portions and form each into a patty.
6. Heat a charcoal grill or cast-iron skillet over high heat, and when hot, add the onigiri. Grill the onigiri, flipping occasionally and brushing with the butter mixture as you go to help with the caramelization.
7. When the onigiri are crispy and well-browned on both sides, about 3 minutes, top with the marinated egg yolks and shiso leaves and serve.

Sambal Goreng

SERVES 4

When people suggest that a vegetarian diet lacks protein, I point to sambal goreng. In this popular Indonesian, Singaporean, and Malaysian dish, protein comes in two main forms—tempeh and tofu—that are cut into small cubes, deep-fried, and stir-fried with lots of aromatics. While some cooks throw in prawns or beef to supplement the stew, the stars are resolutely these plant-based proteins. It was Nurdiana, a passionate home cook from Singapore, who first taught me to cook this dish. In her family's version, the aromatics are sliced finely rather than being ground into a paste so that each mouthful is a textured and varied experience. My own touch comes with the addition of lime leaves and a homemade spice paste.

TEMPEH, TOFU, AND BEANS

- Oil, for deep-frying
- 7 ounces (200 g) tempeh (see page 22), cut into ½-inch (1.25 cm) cubes
- 7 ounces (200 g) extra-firm tofu (see page 23), cut into ½-inch (1.25 cm) cubes
- 5.75 ounces (165 g) green beans, thinly sliced into 2-inch (5 cm) lengths on a diagonal

ASSEMBLY

- ¼ cup plus 1 tablespoon (75 g) sambal (see page 71)
- 5 shallots, thinly sliced
- 4 garlic cloves, thinly sliced
- 2 red chiles, thinly sliced
- 2 thick coins of galangal (see page 17), bruised
- 2 makrut lime leaves (see page 20), torn
- 1 stalk of lemongrass, bottom half only (see page 20), finely chopped
- ½ cup (120 ml) coconut cream (see page 14)
- 2 tablespoons plus 1½ teaspoons tamarind concentrate (see page 22)
- 1 tablespoon sugar
- 2 teaspoons salt
- Cooked rice, for serving

1. **For the tempeh, tofu, and beans,** fill a wok or large saucepan with 2 inches (5 cm) of oil and set it on high heat. Line a dish with paper towel. Allow the oil to heat to 400°F (200°C). Carefully add the tempeh to the hot oil and deep-fry, stirring frequently, for 3 to 4 minutes or until golden brown. Using a slotted spoon or spider skimmer, transfer the tempeh to the prepared dish.
2. Repeat the process with the extra-firm tofu. When the tofu is light golden brown, 3 to 4 minutes, transfer it to the dish with the tempeh. Set aside.
3. Bring a saucepan of salted water to a boil over high heat. Blanch the green beans for 2 minutes, or until crisp-tender, then drain and set aside.
4. **For assembly,** combine the sambal, shallots, garlic, red chiles, galangal, lime leaves, and lemongrass in a large saucepan or wok set on medium heat.
5. Sweat the aromatics for 3 minutes or until they turn soft and translucent, then add the fried tempeh, tofu, coconut cream, tamarind concentrate, sugar, salt, and ¾ cup (180 ml) water. Bring to a simmer. Add the blanched green beans and stir them through.
6. Season with salt or add more sugar or tamarind concentrate to taste. It should taste like a harmonious blend of salty, sweet, tangy, smoky, spicy, and rich flavors. Serve with hot rice.

Jenny Lau

Jenny Lau is a British Chinese Londoner with roots in Malaysia and Hong Kong, and the author of *An A–Z of Chinese Food (Recipes Not Included)*. Lau started *Celestial Peach*—her blog and Instagram account—as a way to investigate health and longevity through a vegan Chinese diet. Now, it is a platform that champions stories about Asian food, people, and culture. It is her inventive creations such as perilla furikake, fig leaf–wrapped tofu misozuke, and Yunnanese oil-preserved mushrooms that made Lau one of the first people I approached when I was writing this cookbook.

How did your interest in a vegan Chinese diet begin?

It was an oblique journey. Typical of my Cantonese and Malaysian-Chinese heritage, I used to love eating meat, especially all the spare parts (chicken feet, fish eyes; you name it, I ate it). As I approached my thirties, I became invested in health as both sides of my family have not been without their sicknesses. I started a dedicated yoga practice almost eight years ago and it made me consider vegetarianism. Part of embodying yoga is to study the philosophies—one of which is ahimsa (non-harming).

I have elderly aunts who are vegan Buddhists and they used to take me to restaurants that served Cantonese dishes prepared with imitation meat (as well as omitting alliums—the "five pungent spices"—for their ability to stimulate sexual passions, temptations, and rage). That was eye-opening for someone like me who had previously considered meat a nonnegotiable ingredient in Chinese cooking.

I realized that vegetarianism and wellness exist as a subset of Chinese cuisine. I have since been combining the principles of Chinese cooking with the philosophies of harmony and balance to explore how Chinese food can be healthy and plant-based.

Has it been challenging to eat a more plant-based diet while cooking from your heritage?

Not at all. If you were to adapt a pork-based dish, ask yourself, what is the role of the pork here? It's going to be either flavor, nutrients, texture, color, or even some kind of traditional symbolism. Once you deconstruct it, you can have so much fun with "substitutes." You can even omit it. Who's going to judge you?

Tofu is my playground. For every cut of chicken, there is just as much variety in tofu textures and flavors.

For people who want meat analogs, there is an impressive range of mock meat products available. OmniPork has been a game changer. I think it comes from making their products meat-like in order to convert Chinese meat-lovers, as opposed to veggie sausages and fake bacon which are designed to appease vegans.

What is the key to making vegetable dishes special?

Umami and texture. You find umami in mushrooms or fermented soy. What I love about a lot of Asian cuisines is the playful approach to texture. Your mouth needs to have fun while eating. Chewy, slurpy, crunchy, smooth—all of these textures challenge your teeth and your digestive system, and I'm sure the playful process signals to your brain that you're enjoying your food and maybe don't need to eat so much.

I am exploring dishes that combine different vegetable cooking methods to create a multi-layered texture dimension. Think: crunchy, steamed broccoli topped with slow-braised mushrooms in a thick, cornstarch-based gravy, on a crispy golden noodle nest. It might take more time and effort, but it makes a standout dish.

What's one interesting thing you've learned on this journey?

The way you slice cucumbers changes the way your salad tastes. Smashed cucumber is a very popular dish. For a show-stopping piece, try the accordion cut—it looks mind-bogglingly impressive (while being quite easy to execute) and creates lots of crevices for soaking up dressing and hiding crunchy salad accoutrements like fried shallots, crushed peanuts, or toasted seeds.

Tempeh Satay with Sambal Matah

SERVES 4 TO 6

INSPIRED BY JENNY LAU

SATAY

¾ small red onion, roughly chopped

6 garlic cloves

3½ red chiles, roughly cut

One 1½-inch (4 cm) piece of ginger (15 g), roughly cut

One ½-inch (1.25 cm) piece of galangal (10 g; see page 17), roughly cut

¼ cup (60 ml) melted coconut oil

2 teaspoons ground turmeric

1 teaspoon ground coriander

¼ teaspoon ground nutmeg

4 makrut lime leaves (see page 20), torn

2 stalks of lemongrass, bottom half only, (see page 20), bruised

4¼ cups (1 L) coconut water

8 ounces (225 g) tempeh (see page 22), cut into 1-inch (2.5 cm) squares, about ⅓ inch (8 mm) thick

2 teaspoons salt

SAMBAL MATAH

½ small red onion, finely diced

1½ red or green chiles, or a combination of both, seeded and thinly sliced

1 stalk of lemongrass, bottom half only, (see page 20), finely chopped

2 makrut lime leaves (see page 20), thinly sliced

Petals of ½ ginger flower (see page 18), minced

3 tablespoons coconut oil

3 tablespoons lime juice

¾ teaspoon salt

ASSEMBLY

¼ cup plus 1 tablespoon (75 ml) kecap manis (see page 19)

"My friend Kenn Lam, a talented Singaporean artist, shared a recipe for ayam betutu (Balinese spiced chicken). I made a vegan version using tempeh on one of my barbecue nights by wrapping it in banana leaves, partially steaming, then grilling it. The spices together with the pre-steaming gave it a delicate, aromatic vibe, but the sambal matah really made it."—*Jenny Lau*

1. **For the satay,** coarsely grind the red onion, garlic, red chiles, ginger, and galangal in a small food processor, blender, or mortar and pestle.
2. Add the coconut oil to a medium pot set on high heat. When the coconut oil melts, set half of it aside for later. Add the coarse aromatic paste to the pot and fry for 3 to 5 minutes, or until it is highly fragrant.
3. Add the turmeric, coriander, nutmeg, lime leaves, lemongrass, coconut water, tempeh, and salt to the pot. Bring the mixture to a boil on high heat, then turn the heat to low. Simmer, covered, for 30 minutes, then drain the tempeh and let it cool in the colander.
4. **For the sambal matah,** mix together the red onion, chiles, lemongrass, lime leaves, and ginger flower petals together in a heat-safe bowl.
5. Heat the coconut oil in a pan until just beginning to smoke, then pour the oil over the aromatics. Stir well and add the lime juice and salt.
6. When the tempeh is cool enough to handle, thread it onto wooden skewers and brush with the reserved coconut oil. Grill over charcoal or sear in a cast-iron skillet on high heat, flipping occasionally, until the tempeh is browned on both sides and charred in places, about 3 minutes.
7. **For assembly,** brush the tempeh all over with the kecap manis. Cook for another 1 to 2 minutes until the satay looks glazed. Remove the satay from the grill and brush on extra kecap manis for shine. Transfer to a serving plate and spoon over the sambal matah. Serve.

Smoky Eggplant Raita with Focaccia

SERVES 8

FOCACCIA

2¾ cups (345 g) all-purpose flour

1 teaspoon (5 g) salt

2 teaspoons (10 g) sugar

1 teaspoon (5 g) active dry yeast

1¼ cups (300 ml) warm water

3 tablespoons plus ¼ cup (60 ml) extra-virgin olive oil

2 teaspoons mustard seeds

2 teaspoons sesame seeds

2 teaspoons cumin seeds

A handful of curry leaves (see page 15)

1 green chile, chopped

6 garlic cloves, thinly sliced

RAITA

4 Japanese or Lebanese eggplants

1 cup (300 g) Greek yogurt

2 teaspoons salt

2 teaspoons garam masala (see page 17)

¼ cup (60 ml) chili oil (see page 14)

2 teaspoons black mustard seeds

2 teaspoons cumin seeds

A large handful of curry leaves (see page 15)

At Carlton Wine Room in Melbourne, where I once worked, the focaccia was always made in-house and, for a time, I was the one responsible for preparing it every morning. It was pure therapy to press the olive oil into the risen dough, and I began thinking about other oil possibilities. Here, the focaccia is topped with bloomed spices and curry leaves and served alongside a charred eggplant raita, as a hat-tip to the stracciatella topped with green onion oil that accompanied the bread at Carlton Wine Room. The strands of smoky eggplant really remind me of the stringy qualities of that cheese.

1. **For the focaccia,** in a large bowl, stir together the flour, salt, sugar, and yeast. Gradually add the warm water and stir until everything is thoroughly combined. You are looking for a very moist, loose dough. Allow it to proof, covered, for 1 to 2 hours depending on your climate, or until the dough has doubled in size and the top is dappled with pockmarks.
2. Pour 3 tablespoons of the olive oil into an 11-inch (28 cm) cast-iron pan or round cake pan, coating the bottom evenly. With a spatula or dough scraper, transfer the dough to the pan. With your oiled fingers, lift the edges of the dough and fold them toward the center. Flip the dough over so that it is fully coated in oil. With your fingers, dimple the dough thoroughly so that it stretches to the edges of the pan. Allow the dough to rest, uncovered, for another 1 to 2 hours, or until very puffy and doubled in size.
3. While the dough rests, place the remaining ¼ cup (60 ml) of olive oil in a small saucepan and set it on medium heat. Add the mustard seeds and toast them for 20 seconds, or until they splutter, then add the sesame seeds, cumin seeds, curry leaves, green chiles, and garlic. Fry for another 30 seconds, or until the sesame seeds are golden and the curry leaves shrivel. Turn off the heat and set the mixture aside.
4. Preheat the oven to 400°F (200°C). Drizzle the cooled oil mixture evenly across the rested dough. Dimple the dough sparingly with your fingers so as to not deflate it while gently pushing the garlic slices into the dough. Bake for 20 minutes, or until golden brown and well-risen, then allow the focaccia to cool in the pan.
5. **For the raita,** char the eggplants directly on a gas stove burner on high heat, turning occasionally with tongs, until tender and charred, 5 to 10 minutes. Alternatively, broil the eggplants on a foil-lined rimmed baking sheet for 10 to 20 minutes, or until tender and charred on all sides, turning occasionally. Transfer to a container and cover with a lid until cool enough to handle.
6. Peel off the charred skin and discard. Chop the flesh and mix with the Greek yogurt, salt, and garam masala. Spoon the raita into a small serving dish.
7. In a small saucepan, heat the chili oil, then add the black mustard seeds. When the mustard seeds pop, around 15 seconds, turn off the heat, step back, and carefully add the cumin seeds and curry leaves. The curry leaves will splutter aggressively, so be careful.
8. Drizzle the tempered spices over the raita. Slice the focaccia into 8 wedges with a bread knife and serve it with the raita.

Hainanese Fried Eggplant

SERVES 4

FRIED EGGPLANT

4 Japanese or Lebanese eggplants

Oil, for deep-frying

½ teaspoon salt

½ teaspoon freshly ground black pepper

All-purpose flour, for dredging

1 egg, beaten

Panko, for crumbing

SAUCE

1 tablespoon oil

1 small red onion, thinly sliced

3 garlic cloves, minced

½ cup (80 g) peas, fresh or frozen

¼ cup plus 3 tablespoons (100 ml) ketchup

2 tablespoons soy sauce

2 tablespoons vegetarian Worcestershire sauce

1 teaspoon toasted sesame oil

¼ teaspoon salt

1 tablespoon cornstarch

Singapore is home to a diverse Chinese population whose ancestors hail from different regions in China. One of these communities is the Hainanese. As latecomers to Singapore, when the Hainanese first arrived other industries had already been occupied by other communities, so they often found employment as cooks or servants for British families. Through these jobs, the Hainanese immigrants were exposed to British cuisine, which they adapted by adding ingredients and using techniques that they were familiar with. One of their famous inventions is the Hainanese pork chop, which is breaded with cream crackers, deep-fried, and served with a cornstarch-thickened sauce made with ketchup and soy sauce. This charred eggplant dish takes inspiration from that original East-meets-West dish, though I prefer to use panko for the extra crunch it provides, and it's just as delicious with rice as it is with boiled vegetables and roasted potato wedges. It is an especially great way to get children to eat vegetables.

1. **For the fried eggplant,** char the eggplants directly on a gas stove burner on high heat, turning occasionally with tongs, until tender and charred, 5 to 10 minutes. Alternatively, broil the eggplants on a foil-lined rimmed baking sheet for 10 to 20 minutes, or until tender and charred on all sides, turning occasionally. Transfer to a container and cover with a lid until cool enough to handle.
2. Fill a wok or large saucepan with 2 inches (5 cm) of oil and set it on high heat. Allow the oil to heat to 400°F (200°C). While the oil heats up, peel the charred skins off the eggplants with your fingers and discard. With a fork, flatten the flesh gently to encourage the eggplants to split open, being careful not to mash them.
3. Season the eggplants on both sides with the salt and black pepper, then line up three shallow bowls of the flour, beaten egg, and panko. First, dredge them in the flour. Dust off excess flour, then dip in the egg wash and toss in the panko. Press the panko onto the eggplant with your fingers to help it adhere.
4. Line a dish with paper towel. Working in batches to avoid overcrowding, carefully add the eggplants to the hot oil. Cook, turning occasionally with tongs, until they turn golden brown on both sides. This will take 3 to 4 minutes in total. Using a spider skimmer or slotted spoon, transfer the eggplants to the prepared dish to drain before moving them to a serving platter.
5. **For the sauce,** set a saucepan on medium heat and add the oil, red onion, and garlic. Sweat for 2 to 3 minutes until lightly softened, then add the peas, ketchup, soy sauce, Worcestershire sauce, sesame oil, salt, and ½ cup plus 2 tablespoons (150 ml) water. Turn the heat to low and cook, covered, until the onion is tender, 2 to 3 minutes.
6. Remove the lid and bring the mixture to a boil on high heat. Meanwhile, in a small bowl, stir together the cornstarch and ¼ cup (60 ml) water.
7. Add the slurry to the pan, stirring, until the liquid thickens to a gravy. Season with salt to taste before pouring the gravy over the eggplant. Serve.

HASSELBACK POTATOES WITH SALTED EGG SAUCE, PAGE 225

Roasted & Baked

Savory Corn and Bell Pepper Cake with Guacamole

SERVES 8

VEGETABLES

2 bell peppers

1 cup (180 g) fresh or frozen corn kernels

1½ green chiles, thinly sliced

¾ cup (15 g) cilantro leaves, roughly chopped

1 teaspoon salt

BATTER

1¼ cups (190 g) stone-ground whole grain corn flour (see headnote)

¾ cup (105 g) all-purpose flour

½ cup (100 g) sugar

1 teaspoon baking soda

1 teaspoon Kashmiri chili powder

1 teaspoon ground turmeric

½ teaspoon salt

1¼ cups (300 ml) buttermilk

½ cup (112 g) unsalted butter, melted, plus more for greasing

2 eggs

2 tablespoons plus 1½ teaspoons honey

GUACAMOLE

Flesh of 1½ ripe avocados (12.75 ounces/360 g)

Half a 14-ounce (400 g) can of black beans, rinsed and drained

1 tomato, diced

½ small red onion, chopped

½ cup (10 g) cilantro leaves and tender stems, roughly chopped

1 tablespoon plus 1½ teaspoons lime juice

2 teaspoons ground cumin

1½ teaspoons salt

This savory cornbread was a happy accident made by substituting finely milled corn flour for coarse cornmeal when making Friends & Family owner and baker Roxana Jullapat's cornbread from her cookbook *Mother Grains: Recipes for the Grain Revolution*. What emerged was more like cake than bread, with the most tender and airy crumb. I tinkered further by incorporating Indian-inspired flavors, such as cilantro, green chiles, and ground turmeric. It was my husband Wex's idea to pair the cornbread with guacamole. Together, it makes a divine brunch. If you don't have a cast-iron pan, use a cake pan or loaf pans—the recipe is very forgiving. I like to use Bob's Red Mill whole grain corn flour. Leftover cornbread stays moist for a day or two when wrapped tightly and kept at room temperature.

1. Preheat the oven to 350°F (180°C).
2. **For the vegetables,** char the bell peppers directly on a gas stove burner on high, turning them occasionally with tongs, until their skin has blackened all over, 5 to 10 minutes. Alternatively, broil the bell peppers on a foil-lined rimmed baking sheet for 10 to 20 minutes, or until tender and charred on all sides, turning occasionally. Transfer to a container and cover with a lid until cool enough to handle.
3. Set a large skillet on high heat, and when hot, add the corn. Spread the kernels in a single layer and cook, without stirring, for 3 minutes, or until charred on the underside. Give the corn a quick stir, then transfer to a medium bowl with the green chiles and cilantro leaves.
4. When the peppers have cooled, peel off the blackened skins and discard with the stems and seeds. Chop the flesh roughly and stir into the corn mixture with the salt.
5. **For the batter,** in a large bowl, whisk together the corn flour, all-purpose flour, sugar, baking soda, chili powder, turmeric, and salt.
6. In another bowl, whisk together the buttermilk, butter, eggs, and honey. Pour the wet ingredients and vegetable mixture into the flour mixture and stir to combine.
7. Preheat an 11-inch (28 cm) cast-iron skillet on high heat for a few minutes, then brush with more melted unsalted butter. Wipe off any excess grease with a paper towel, pour in the batter, and bake for 20 to 25 minutes until lightly golden brown and a cake tester emerges clean.
8. **For the guacamole,** mash the avocado roughly with a fork in a medium bowl, then stir in the black beans, tomato, red onion, cilantro, lime juice, cumin, and salt.
9. Slice the cornbread and serve it with the guacamole.

Hasselback Potatoes with Salted Egg Sauce

SERVES 4

POTATOES

2 pounds plus 3 ounces (1 kg) baby potatoes, preferably Desiree or Yukon Gold

¼ cup (60 ml) melted ghee (see page 18)

1 teaspoon salt

SAUCE

¼ cup (60 g) ghee (see page 18)

½ bird's-eye chile, cut into 2 or 3 pieces

2 sprigs of curry leaves, left on the stem (see page 15)

1 large garlic clove, chopped

4 cooked salted egg yolks (see headnote), mashed

2 tablespoons milk powder

½ cup plus 1 tablespoon (135 ml) evaporated milk

1 teaspoon sugar

½ teaspoon salt

ASSEMBLY

A small handful of chives, finely chopped

When raw duck eggs are buried in salted charcoal and left alone for weeks, something miraculous happens. The salt seeps into the porous shell and cures the egg within, enhancing the yolk's oiliness and giving it a Parmesan-like flavor over time. When the charcoal is washed off and the eggs are cracked, you'll find a yolk the color of urchin roe. Salted eggs are sold raw or cooked; the former is usually still covered in salted charcoal. Raw salted egg yolks are also sometimes sold in individual vacuum-sealed packets. Here, when cooked and mashed into curry leaf–scented butter, the yolk practically melts. A dousing of evaporated milk tames its funk and allows everything to cohere into a lush, voluptuous sauce, perfect for tossing with battered vegetables, such as lotus root or pumpkin—or for spooning over the Hasselback potatoes in this easy but impressive side. While cutting thin slices in each potato might seem fussy, once baked these cuts expand to form crevices for the sauce to flow into.

1. **For the potatoes,** preheat the oven to 445°F (230°C). Trim a small slice off one side of each baby potato so it sits flat and does not wobble when placed cut-side down on your cutting board. Place each potato horizontally between two chopsticks and make vertical slices, as thin as you can, all along the potato. The chopsticks will prevent you from cutting all the way through and keep the base intact.
2. Grease a large oven-safe pan, preferably cast-iron, with 2 tablespoons of the melted ghee. Transfer the potatoes to the pan and drizzle with the remaining melted ghee, then sprinkle with the salt.
3. Roast the potatoes for 30 to 35 minutes, or until tender and golden brown.
4. **For the sauce,** set a saucepan over medium heat and add the ghee, bird's-eye chile, and curry leaves. Heat until the ghee melts and the curry leaves pop, about 30 seconds. Remove the curry leaves and chile—you can save these for another dish or to use as a garnish.
5. Add the garlic to the pan, and fry until fragrant, around 20 seconds. Add the mashed salted egg yolks and milk powder and stir to combine. Cook until the yolks gently foam, about 2 minutes.
6. Add the evaporated milk, sugar, and salt and bring the mixture to a simmer. Continue to cook until the sauce becomes smooth and thick, about 2 minutes. Turn off the heat, then season with salt or add more sugar to taste. You might also want to loosen the sauce with more evaporated milk, bearing in mind that the sauce will continue to thicken as it cools.
7. **For assembly,** spoon the sauce over the potatoes liberally and garnish with the chives.

John Chantarasak

Since 2019, chef and cofounder of AngloThai John Chantarasak has embraced a primarily plant-based diet in the interest of health and sustainability. For inspiration, he visited villages populated by the Lahu and Akha tribes, whose diets are heavily plant-based and centered on foraged ingredients. While he still eats meat and seafood on occasion, Chantarasak regularly taps into his Thai and British heritage to create dynamic vegetable dishes, such as som tum (**ส้มตำ**) made with rainbow carrots, kohlrabi, and radish. His breadth of knowledge served as inspiration for his book *Kin Thai: Modern Thai Recipes to Cook at Home*.

How has your upbringing impacted your diet?

My family has always eaten in a balanced way and this stems from the way my mother grew vegetables to feed us as children.

There are vegans in our family on my wife's side, so we've been exposed to that lifestyle for a few years. For family gatherings, we tend to cook vegan meals rather than making separate dishes for different diets and it's really broken down the negative stigma associated with a meatless diet.

How did your time with the Lahu and Akha tribes impact you?

These tribes live and survive off the land, as they have access to very few modern conveniences such as supermarkets. The tribespeople also do not earn much money as they work for themselves to live. There is little disposable income to spend on luxury foods that cannot be gathered or farmed.

Their knowledge of the forests and jungles is incredible. It made me realize that nearly all plants have a use, be that for food, materials, or medicine. These experiences made me more aware of my own local environment and seasonality. Even though I live in central London, I manage to find areas to forage for seasonal ingredients like wild garlic, three-cornered leeks, mushrooms, elderflower, and so on.

Has it been easy for you to conceptualize Thai-inspired dishes without meat or seafood?

The concept of vegetarianism and veganism didn't exist in commercial Thailand until very recently and many traditional Thai dishes contain some form of animal protein. Cooking meatless versions of protein-based dishes is not always that straightforward and requires practice, but there is usually something that exists that can bring those same flavor profiles to these dishes. Soybeans are building blocks of flavor for vegan and vegetarian dishes, so I cook with different kinds of soybeans quite a lot.

What is a Thai cooking technique that could improve the way we cook vegetables at home?

Live-fire cooking has existed in Thailand for centuries and is still a very prevalent cooking method today. The best way to get the most out of cooking over an open fire is to think about the life stages of the fire and how it can be utilized at various times. The obvious way to cook with fire is to grill food over intense, direct heat. Vegetables like peppers and eggplants can be cooked directly on hot coals to burn and blacken the skins and to produce steamed, smoky flesh that is delicious in salads.

Coals can also be dispersed to give off less heat and slow down the rate of cooking for larger vegetables. At the end of a dinner service, I tend to bury celeriac, pumpkin, and potatoes in the dying embers and let them cook gradually overnight for use in dishes the next day.

1
2
3
4

Gaeng Tay Po

SERVES 4

*BY JOHN CHANTARASAK**

CELERIAC

1¼ cups (300 ml) coconut cream (see page 14)

3 pandan leaves (see page 21), knotted

1 tablespoon salt

1 pound plus 1.5 ounces (500 g) celeriac or turnips, cut into 2-inch (5 cm) pieces

RED CURRY

1¼ cups (300 ml) coconut cream (see page 14)

1 tablespoon coconut oil

¼ cup (60 g) vegan Thai red curry paste

Scant 1 cup (200 ml) coconut milk

1 tablespoon plus 1½ teaspoons granulated dark palm sugar (see page 15)

1 tablespoon vegetarian fish sauce or soy sauce

2 red or green chiles, thinly sliced on a diagonal

2 makrut lime leaves (see page 20), torn

1 makrut lime or Persian lime, halved

2 teaspoons tamarind concentrate (see page 22)

A handful of Thai basil leaves (see page 23)

Cooked rice, for serving

"This is a version of a Thai curry called gaeng tay po (แกงเทโพ) that I prepared as a vegan main course for a summer residency. I buried a whole celeriac in charcoal embers and left it to gently cook overnight. The next day, I peeled and quartered the celeriac, then cooked the quarters over very hot coals while basting them with salted coconut cream. The sides blackened and became highly seasoned while the inside remained creamy and soft. The celeriac felt meaty and rich and matched the red curry wonderfully. The method outlined below has been adapted for a domestic kitchen."—*John Chantarasak*

1. **For the celeriac,** preheat the oven to 375°F (190°C).
2. In a large saucepan, combine the coconut cream, pandan leaves, and salt. Bring the mixture to a boil and cook on high heat for 2 to 3 minutes until reduced by a quarter.
3. Dip the celeriac pieces into the thick coconut cream to coat thoroughly on all sides, then transfer them to a roasting tray. ① Roast for 30 minutes, or until deeply golden and completely cooked through. ②
4. **For the red curry,** combine the coconut cream and coconut oil in a large saucepan set on medium heat. Cook for about 3 minutes, or until the cream separates and the surface develops an oily sheen. ③
5. Add the Thai red curry paste and cook for 5 minutes to release its fragrance, then add the coconut milk, palm sugar, vegetarian fish sauce, and scant 1 cup (200 ml) water. Bring to a simmer and cook for another 5 minutes to reduce the mixture slightly.
6. Add the roasted celeriac to the curry, along with the chiles, lime leaves, and makrut lime. Cook for 1 to 2 minutes so that the lime imparts a pleasant tart brightness to the sauce. Be sure not to overboil or stew the makrut lime, as it will become unpleasantly bitter. The curry should become creamier as it simmers.
7. Turn off the heat and let the curry stand for a few minutes, then add the tamarind concentrate and Thai basil leaves. Stir to wilt the herbs, then remove the pandan leaves and transfer the curry to a serving dish. Serve with the cooked rice. ④

* Adapted from *Kin Thai: Modern Thai Recipes to Cook at Home* by John Chantarasak, copyright © 2022. Published by Hardie Grant Books.

Turmeric Carrots with Dill and Mung Bean Jelly

SERVES 3 TO 4

MUNG BEAN JELLY

⅓ cup (45 g) mung bean starch

½ teaspoon salt

A pinch of baking soda

CARROTS

1 tablespoon plus 1½ teaspoons vegetarian fish sauce or soy sauce

One 1-inch (2.5 cm) piece of galangal (20 g; see page 17), roughly cut

1 tablespoon potato starch

1 tablespoon ground turmeric

1 tablespoon yogurt or coconut cream (see page 14)

¼ cup (60 ml) oil

9 ounces (250 g) young carrots, trimmed and halved lengthwise

2 green onions, thinly sliced on a diagonal

¼ cup plus 2 tablespoons (7 g) dill fronds

DRESSING

3 tablespoons lime juice

3 tablespoons sugar

2 tablespoons apple cider vinegar

2 tablespoons vegetarian fish sauce or soy sauce

3 garlic cloves, finely grated

½ red chile, chopped

ASSEMBLY

¼ cup (30 g) roasted peanuts, chopped

In Asia, we do love our jellies. There are, of course, sweet jellies, but we also appreciate jellies in our savory dishes. Often, these are bland gels that are made by heating a slurry of water and starch—liáng fěn (凉粉) in China, cheongpo-muk (청포묵) in Korea, and laphing (ལ་ཕིང) in Tibet are just a few. These jellies are appreciated for their refreshing, slippery texture that cools one down in hot weather, and neutral flavor, which allows them to complement a multitude of dressings. In this dish, mung bean jelly tossed in nu'ó'c châ'm, a classic Vietnamese dressing, accompanies roasted carrots. Inspired by the Hanoi dish chả cá lã vọng, where fish is marinated in turmeric and fried with dill and green onion, these carrots are definitely not shy in flavor. It is worth seeking out galangal, as it lends the carrots a shrimpy, fried fish flavor.

1. **For the mung bean jelly,** the night before you plan to serve, add 1⅓ cups (320 ml) water to a saucepan set on medium-low heat. In a small bowl, stir together the mung bean starch, salt, and ⅓ cup plus 1 tablespoon (95 ml) water.
2. When the water in the saucepan is barely simmering but warm enough for small bubbles to appear on the sides and bottom, add the baking soda. Give the mung bean starch mixture a stir, then add it to the pot while whisking. Cook gently, stirring, until the mixture begins to thicken. Reduce the heat to low and cook until the gel turns from white to translucent and begins to bubble, about 4 minutes.
3. Transfer the mixture to a rectangular container or loaf pan. Allow to cool completely, then refrigerate overnight. The gel can be made up to three days in advance and kept refrigerated in an airtight container.
4. **For the carrots,** preheat the oven to 445°F (230°C). Line a baking sheet with parchment paper. In a small blender or spice grinder, blend the vegetarian fish sauce, galangal, potato starch, turmeric, yogurt, and 1 tablespoon of the oil until a fibrous paste forms.
5. Toss the baby carrots in the paste on the prepared baking sheet. Roast the carrots in the oven for 10 to 15 minutes or until they are tender, but not mushy. Set aside.
6. **For the dressing,** stir together the lime juice, sugar, apple cider vinegar, vegetarian fish sauce, garlic, and red chile in a bowl.
7. When the jelly has set, run a knife along its sides to loosen it from the container. Flip the pan upside down onto a cutting board to unmold it. Cut the jelly in half lengthwise, then cut it crosswise into ½-inch (1.25 cm) slices. Toss the jelly with the dressing and place the slices on a serving platter, reserving any dressing left in the bowl.
8. Heat the remaining 3 tablespoons oil in a skillet set on high heat. When the oil begins to shimmer, add the carrots and sear them on both sides until well caramelized, about 2 to 3 minutes. Add the green onions and dill fronds and toss gently; the herbs will wilt slightly as they make contact with the hot pan.
9. **For assembly,** place the carrots and wilted herbs on top of the mung bean jelly. Drizzle any remaining dressing over everything and sprinkle with the roasted peanuts.

1
2
3
4

Podi-Rubbed Roasted Cauliflower

SERVES 4

CAULIFLOWER

¼ cup (75 g) salt

8 garlic cloves, crushed

1 green chile, roughly cut

1 tablespoon plus 1½ teaspoons sugar

1 tablespoon plus 1½ teaspoons garam masala (see page 17)

One 2-inch (5 cm) piece of ginger (20 g), cut into thick coins

1 large cauliflower, trimmed

¼ cup (60 ml) ghee (see page 18), melted

PODI

3 tablespoons split chickpeas (chana dal/चना दाल)

1 teaspoon ghee (see page 18)

½ cup (80 g) raw peanuts, with or without skin

A handful of curry leaves (see page 15)

¼ teaspoon asafoetida (hing/हींग; see page 14)

1 tablespoon Kashmiri chili powder

1 teaspoon dark brown sugar or coconut sugar

1 teaspoon ground coriander

1 teaspoon ground cumin

¼ teaspoon salt

ASSEMBLY

¼ cup plus 1 tablespoon (75 ml) yogurt

½ teaspoon salt

¼ teaspoon garam masala (see page 17)

A handful of crispy gram flour noodles (sev/सेव; see page 14)

A handful of pomegranate seeds

A small handful of dried rose petals, optional

A handful of mint leaves, thinly sliced

I never understood the hype when it came to whole roasted cauliflower until I learned to brine the cauliflower before roasting—a tip I picked up from *Matty Matheson: A Cookbook*. Just like brining a chicken, this seasons and flavors the vegetable to its core. I also make a paste out of ghee and podi (பொடி), a south Indian spice blend, and rub it all over the nooks and crannies, so that the cauliflower develops a deeply flavorful crust, which is what makes this version so compelling. Don't be afraid to deeply char the cauliflower—rather than tasting acrid, it will have a far more complex flavor and even develop a delicate crunch.

1. **For the cauliflower,** the night before you plan to serve, combine the salt, garlic, green chile, sugar, garam masala, ginger, and 3 quarts (3 L) water in a pot. Bring to a simmer on high heat to dissolve the salt and sugar, then turn off the heat and let cool completely.
2. Add the cauliflower, and top it with a weight, such as a small plate, so that it is completely submerged in the brine. Cover the pot and refrigerate the cauliflower overnight, or up to 24 hours.
3. The next day, drain the cauliflower and allow it to sit in a colander for 2 to 3 hours. This allows any brine trapped in its crevices to drain.
4. **For the podi,** toast the split chickpeas in a skillet set on medium heat for 3 minutes, or until the dal is highly aromatic and has turned a shade darker. Tip them into a blender.
5. Place the skillet back on the stove and add the ghee and peanuts. Fry on medium heat until the peanut skins begin to peel or the skinless peanuts turn golden, 3 to 4 minutes. Add the curry leaves and asafoetida. Continue to stir-fry the mixture for a further 1 to 2 minutes, or until the curry leaves shrivel up, before adding it to the blender.
6. Let the mixture cool completely, then add the chili powder, brown sugar, coriander, cumin, and salt. Pulse everything to a coarse rubble, then season with salt or add more sugar to taste.
7. Preheat the oven to 445°F (230°C). Line a baking sheet with parchment paper. In a small bowl, stir together a generous ½ cup (75 g) of the podi and melted ghee to form a paste.
8. Place the cauliflower on the prepared baking sheet. With your hands, rub the paste all over the florets, giving equal attention to the underside of the cauliflower. ①
9. Roast for 40 minutes, or until well-charred and a knife slides into the cauliflower's core easily. ② If the charring happens too quickly, tent the cauliflower with foil for the remaining roasting time. Transfer the roasted cauliflower to a serving plate.
10. **For assembly,** stir together the yogurt, salt, garam masala, and 2 tablespoons water in a small bowl. Drizzle the mixture liberally over the cauliflower. Top with the crispy gram flour noodles, pomegranate seeds, dried rose petals (if using), and mint. Serve.

O Tama Carey

O Tama Carey has an inverse relationship with vegetables compared to other people I know. When the chef-owner of Lankan Filling Station was growing up, she always tended toward vegetables even though she was never vegetarian. It was only through a cooking job in London that she began to appreciate meat and offal. Still, her meals at home remain vegetable-centric. Her cookbook *Lanka Food: Serendipity & Spice* reflects her relationship with greens as it's filled with an array of vegetarian and vegan recipes. When not pounding spices at her restaurant, you'll find Carey writing for *The Saturday Paper*.

How do vegetables feature on a Sri Lankan table?

There's sambol (සම්බෝල), which encompasses a whole range of chili condiments and more salady things as well. Pol sambol (පොල් සම්බෝල) is the most common one; this is coconut-based, and is quite tangy with lime juice. Seeni sambol (සීනි සම්බෝල) is a caramelized onion number. There are also many super fresh-tasting sambols made with cucumber. Regardless of the type of sambol, it is always a condiment for you to add at whim to your meal.

Mallung (මැල්ලුම්) is a vegetable dish served at room temperature like a salad. It often features a leafy green, but you could make it with anything from leek to green papaya. It is briefly cooked, usually without any fat, because the coconut in the dish is what lends it fattiness. The cabbage mallung that we serve at the restaurant is super simple, just four or five ingredients, but people always comment on how delicious it is.

We also have achcharu (අච්චාරු), an umbrella term that refers to pickles that are served as condiments. In Sri Lanka, where you would have an abundance of tropical fruits, preserving is a big part of the food culture. You could get whole limes, split them into quarters, and pack them in salt. Traditionally, you would leave them out to dry in the sun until they get quite dark before storing them in vinegar. What you end up getting is this really tangy lime pickle (lunu dehi/ලුණු දෙහි) that I love. Like preserved lemons, the rind of the lime pickles is what you use. We finely dice it with some onions, season it with fresh lime juice, and eat it as a condiment with rice. The pickled pulp can be quite overpowering but can be used to season dishes. At Lankan Filling Station, we often make a lime pickle mayonnaise.

How has your experience with Asian food informed the way you use and consume vegetables?

Meals tend to be a collection of dishes in Asian cuisines, and for that reason, the notion of balancing flavors and textures is inherent in a lot of Asian cooking. Balance comes from having vegetable and meat dishes, gentle and rich dishes, texturally soft and crunchy dishes. There are so many ways you can create harmony in a dish and all those components are equally important. Animal protein is viewed more as part of a larger meal, rather than being the star. In a Sri Lankan banquet, there is often just one meat or seafood dish alongside a whole range of vegetable dishes.

Why do you think vegetables get such a bad reputation?

With a piece of meat, you cook it and it's done. But with vegetables, sometimes you need a bit more thought and imagination. At home, on a good night, a typical meal would have three dishes, each focusing on one vegetable and having a few different textures. One vegetable could be roasted, another could be a raw salad, and the final dish could be stir-fried cabbage or warm grains. I find two hot dishes and one cold dish to be a good guide to give you sufficient textural and flavor variety. This way, you don't feel like you are lacking in anything.

Deviled Cashews

SERVES 6 TO 8

*BY O TAMA CAREY**

2½ cups (400 g) raw cashews

2 tablespoons plus 1½ teaspoons ghee (see page 18)

1 tablespoon black mustard seeds

A large handful of curry leaves (see page 15)

1 tablespoon flaky sea salt

2½ teaspoons Korean chili flakes (gochugaru/고춧가루)

1 tablespoon Kashmiri chili powder

"This enticing snack is simple to make and a perfect nibble with drinks. The nuts should have an almost sweet flavor and be on the verge of too salty and too hot. Make a larger batch if you like; the cashews keep well for weeks in an airtight container."—*O Tama Carey*

1. Preheat the oven to 300°F (150°C). Spread the cashews on a baking sheet, and roast for 12 to 15 minutes, giving them a toss 2 to 3 times throughout the process, until they are pale golden all over. Set aside to cool.
2. Add the ghee to a large saucepan set on high heat. When the ghee has melted, add the black mustard seeds and fry, shaking the pan regularly, until the seeds just start to pop, around 20 seconds. Add the curry leaves and fry the leaves for 30 seconds, or until they take on a glassy appearance, stirring continuously.
3. Add the cooled cashews and 1½ teaspoons of the flaky sea salt to the saucepan. Stir well to coat the nuts. Continue to fry for 2 to 3 minutes, stirring occasionally, until they turn a deep golden color—a bit of charring is absolutely fine.
4. Stir in the chili flakes, and swiftly remove the pan from the heat. Add the chili powder and the remaining 1½ teaspoons of flaky sea salt and toss well to coat. Season with salt or add more chili powder to taste. Set aside until just cool enough that you can easily eat the nuts with your fingers. Serve.

* Adapted from *Lanka Food: Serendipity & Spice* by O Tama Carey, copyright © 2022. Published by Hardie Grant Books.

Pumpkin and Pearl Couscous Salad

SERVES 6

PUMPKIN

1 pound (450 g) pumpkin, seeds discarded, cut into ¾-inch (2 cm) cubes

2 tablespoons olive oil

½ teaspoon salt

SALAD

2 cups (300 g) pearl couscous

¼ cup (60 ml) plus 2 tablespoons olive oil

Heaped ½ cup (90 g) raw cashews

½ cup (80 g) raisins

1 teaspoon cumin seeds

1 green chile, minced

1 tablespoon chopped ginger

½ teaspoon Kashmiri chili powder

1½ cups (40 g) loosely packed baby spinach

1 tablespoon plus 1½ teaspoons lemon juice

1 cup (20 g) chopped cilantro

1 teaspoon dark brown sugar or coconut sugar

½ teaspoon salt

My mother is a creature of habit. Whenever she tastes something she likes on a trip, she wants to frequent the same eatery to have it again on each subsequent visit. The first time she was in Melbourne, she loved the roasted pumpkin and chickpea salad at a café we took her to. The business has since changed hands, but she still mentions it whenever she visits. This is a very loose adaptation of that salad with influences from sabudana khichdi (साबूदाना खिचड़ी), a tapioca pearl dish enjoyed by Indian Hindus during religious fasts. To make it more substantial, you can cube and pan-fry some paneer to toss with the salad.

1. **For the pumpkin,** preheat the oven to 425°F (220°C), line a baking sheet with parchment paper, add the pumpkin, and toss with the olive oil and salt. Roast for 20 to 25 minutes, or until tender.
2. **For the salad,** bring a saucepan of salted water to a boil on high heat, then add the pearl couscous and cook for 8 minutes, or according to package instructions. When the couscous is tender, drain it in a colander set in the sink. Rinse thoroughly with water to get rid of excess starch, then set aside.
3. In a large saucepan, combine ¼ cup (60 ml) of the olive oil with the cashews. Stir-fry on high heat for 2 to 3 minutes, or until they begin to brown.
4. Add the raisins and continue stir-frying for 1 minute, or until the cashews are well-browned and the raisins puff up. Transfer to a bowl and set aside.
5. To the same saucepan, add the remaining 2 tablespoons of olive oil and the cumin seeds. When the cumin seeds begin to crackle, about 30 seconds, add the green chile, ginger, and chili powder, then add the couscous and mix well.
6. Turn off the heat and tip the spiced oil into the bowl with the raisins and cashews. Add the baby spinach, lemon juice, cilantro, brown sugar, and salt. Gently fold in the roasted pumpkin, and serve.

Spanakopita with Spiced Ghee and Fried Onions

SERVES 8

- 1 cup (240 g) ghee (see page 18)
- 1 red onion, thinly sliced
- One 1-inch (2.5 cm) piece of ginger (10 g), finely chopped
- 3 garlic cloves, chopped
- 2½ green chiles, minced
- 2 teaspoons ground coriander
- 2 teaspoons ground cumin
- 2 teaspoons Kashmiri chili powder
- 1 teaspoon freshly ground black pepper
- ½ teaspoon sugar
- A pinch of asafoetida (hing/हींग; see page 14)
- 9 ounces (250 g) feta, crumbled
- 7 ounces (200 g) ricotta
- 2 eggs, beaten
- ¼ teaspoon salt
- 8 ounces (225 g) frozen baby spinach, thawed in a colander and squeezed thoroughly to remove excess moisture
- ½ cup (10 g) cilantro leaves
- 10 sheets of phyllo pastry (see headnote), each approximately 17 by 11 inches (43 by 28 cm), thoroughly defrosted if frozen

It might not look like it, but this pie—inspired by saag paneer (साग पनीर), a rich, north Indian spinach dish with fried paneer—is one of the simpler pies that you can make. The only challenging step is frying the onions in ghee, but heating them up at the same time as the fat mitigates any mishaps. Once the onions are fried and the spices are bloomed, the pie comes together in a jiffy. Phyllo pastry is available at many supermarkets these days; if you have multiple brands to pick from, I recommend selecting one with the thinnest sheets of pastry for a spanakopita with the most satisfying crunch.

1. Add the ghee and red onion to a saucepan set on high heat. Cook the onion for 4 minutes, or until light golden brown, stirring from time to time.
2. Meanwhile, in a large bowl, combine the ginger, garlic, green chiles, coriander, cumin, chili powder, black pepper, sugar, and asafoetida.
3. When the onion has browned, pour it through a fine-mesh strainer set over a bowl. Press down on the onions with a spoon to expel all of the ghee. Transfer the fried onions and ¼ cup plus 3 tablespoons of the fragrant ghee to the spice mixture. Reserve the remaining ghee for later.
4. Thoroughly mix the onion mixture with the feta, ricotta, and eggs. Season with salt to taste. Add the baby spinach and cilantro, and mix everything thoroughly with your hands.
5. Preheat the oven to 350°F (180°C). Brush a 9-inch (23 cm) springform cake pan with some of the leftover ghee. Drizzle more of the ghee over 5 sheets of the phyllo pastry. ①② Rub the pastry with your hands to grease them evenly on both sides. ③ Line the cake pan with the pastry, allowing the sheets to overlap, so that you get some overhang. ④ The pastry should cling snugly to the sides and base of the pan; rub it with a little more ghee if it does not.
6. Transfer the spinach mixture to the pan, spreading it evenly with a spoon or your hands. ⑤ Lift the pastry overhang over the filling. ⑥
7. Drizzle the remaining 5 sheets of phyllo pastry generously with the leftover ghee. Rub the ghee evenly over the pastry and scrunch the sheets up lightly in your hands ⑦ before draping each loosely over the top. ⑧ With a sharp knife, cut the spanakopita into 8 wedges, like a cake. These cuts will prevent a mess of shards upon serving, once the pie has baked.
8. Bake for 45 to 60 minutes until the pastry is crispy and golden brown. The pie is delicate when hot, so rest it in the pan for at least 20 minutes before unmolding. Serve.

1
2
5
6

3
4
7
8

Petty Pandean-Elliott

Petty Pandean-Elliott is a champion of Indonesian food in the UK, having pioneered a modern approach to Indonesian culinary traditions through her cookbooks, newspaper columns, and magazine articles. It is clear that Elliott has a deep respect for nature, as she makes no secret how blessed the Indonesian archipelago is when it comes to biodiversity. She has been observing the rise of the plant-based movement in the UK and hopes to see the resurgence of plant-based culture in Indonesia. Her latest work is *The Indonesian Table*.

How are plants celebrated in Indonesian cuisine?

Indonesia is home to some of the largest tropical forests in the world and we are blessed with incredible biodiversity. For this reason, vegetables are a huge feature of our meals and are present in a dizzying array—from tubers (sweet potatoes, tapioca, taro) and pulses (sago, rice), to hundreds of different leaves.

While root-to-stalk eating has only just gained popularity in the West, all parts of the plant were utilized in my grandmother's era. People would eat papaya in its unripe and ripe forms, and also enjoy the flower and leaves. Beyond eating, plants would be fashioned into cooking equipment. Bamboo can be stuffed and used as a cooking vessel to perfume food as it cooks, and banana leaves are used as edible wrappers or fragrant serving plates.

Let's not forget tempeh—originating in Java, this fermented soybean product has become a crucial protein source in plant-based diets worldwide.

We have such a reliance on plants that I feel that if anyone would like to learn about living sustainably, Indonesia has that knowledge to tap.

How does sustainability factor into the Indonesian way of life?

Indonesian philosophy is all about living in harmony with nature, fellow humans, and the creator. This could be best explained through an Indonesian dish that is steeped in meaning—nasi tumpeng. In the center of the plate, you have a pointed cone of rice that symbolizes devotion to the creator of the planet who reigns over the universe. It also alludes to the mountainous landscape of many parts of Indonesia. Together, the rice and the dishes that accompany it on the same platter represent the collective responsibility that humans have to look after the environment and the respect that one should have for nature and other human beings.

How has modernization changed Indonesia's food culture?

I was lucky enough to have grown up experiencing the traditional food culture of Manado. I witnessed the importance of locality and traditional cooking techniques, such as cooking over a wood fire and wrapping food in leaves.

It worries me that the younger urban generation might not grasp the roots of our culture, and I am concerned about the rising consumption of convenience foods and the heavy use of plastic packaging.

Indonesians these days tend to cook and consume vast amounts of meat and seafood. While meat plays a key role in our traditional rituals, I find that people in the modern era have a tendency to flaunt their wealth through food. For me, it's important to find a balance so we can live in harmony with the planet.

Is it easy for you to cook plant-based Indonesian food?

Even though dishes like beef rendang are synonymous with Indonesian food, there are traditional plant-based versions of what we commonly consider to be meat-based dishes. When I was traveling in Padang in West Sumatra, which is well-known for rendang, I tasted a rendang made from twenty varieties of leaves in one village! It had such an amazing flavor. (Rendang actually refers to a cooking technique, where the coconut gravy is so reduced and concentrated that the mixture begins to exude coconut oil and fries in the coconut fat.)

The heart of Indonesian cooking does not lie in meat, but in freshly ground aromatics (bumbu), dried spices (rempah), and herbs. As long as you have a combination of all of these, whatever you cook—tofu, tempeh, vegetables—will taste delicious.

Petty Elliott

Pasties with Vegetables and Rice Noodles

MAKES 16 PASTIES

*BY PETTY PANDEAN-ELLIOTT**

PASTRY

3⅔ cups (450 g) all-purpose flour

1 tablespoon sugar

1 teaspoon salt

1¼ cups (250 g) unsalted butter, softened

¼ cup (60 ml) boiling water

1 egg, lightly beaten

FILLING

2 tablespoons oil

4 garlic cloves, finely chopped

1 small red onion, finely chopped

2 potatoes, cut into ⅓-inch (8 mm) cubes

3 carrots, grated

½ cup (75 g) thinly sliced green beans

1 small bundle (50 g) dried glass or rice noodles, soaked for 15 minutes, drained, then snipped into 1-inch (2.5 cm) lengths

1½ teaspoons salt

¼ teaspoon ground white pepper

2 green onions, thinly sliced

½ cup (10 g) chopped cilantro

ASSEMBLY

Flour, for dusting

1 egg, beaten

"This distant cousin of the empanada, pastel sayuran dan bi hun has an entirely different pastry texture and filling. Pasties were introduced to Indonesia by the Portuguese and were eventually made with local ingredients. You will find pasties in big cities across the archipelago. Traditionally, they are deep-fried, but this version is baked and delivers beautiful results. The pasties are best served with the peanut sambal included in this recipe, which I find integral to their enjoyment."—*Petty Pandean-Elliott*

1. **For the pastry,** mix together the flour, sugar, and salt in a large bowl. Add the unsalted butter and egg and combine the mixture, rubbing any large pieces of butter into the flour with your fingers, until you get a coarse rubble.
2. Gradually add the boiling water, kneading gently to form a soft, pliable dough. Divide the dough into 16 portions, each weighing roughly 1.75 ounces (50 g). Roll them into balls and refrigerate, covered, for 1 hour.
3. **For the filling,** place a large skillet or wok on medium heat and add the oil, garlic, and red onion. Sauté for 3 minutes, or until the onion turns soft and translucent.
4. Add the potatoes, and sauté for 2 to 3 minutes to soften slightly, then add ¾ cup (180 ml) water. Cook until most of the water has evaporated, about 5 minutes. If the potatoes are not tender by then, continue cooking with an additional splash of water.
5. Add the carrots, green beans, soaked glass noodles, salt, and white pepper. Cook for 3 minutes, or until the vegetables lose their raw crunch and the noodles become tender.
6. Turn off the heat and stir in the green onions and cilantro. Set the filling aside to cool. When the dough has fully rested, preheat the oven to 375°F (190°C). Line 2 baking sheets with parchment paper.

RECIPE CONTINUED →

PEANUT SAMBAL

3 tablespoons oil

1¼ cups (150 g) raw peanuts, with or without skin

3 shallots, finely chopped

2 garlic cloves, thinly sliced

3 red chiles, thinly sliced

2 bird's-eye chiles, coarsely chopped

2 makrut lime leaves (see page 20), torn

3 tablespoons coconut sugar

1 tablespoon kecap manis (see page 19)

Juice of 1 lime

1 teaspoon salt

7. **For assembly,** dust a clean work surface and rolling pin with flour. Flatten the dough balls and roll them out into 5-inch (13 cm) rounds. Place roughly 2 tablespoons of filling in the middle of each one. Fold the pastry over the filling to form a half-moon shape. ① Trim the excess dough with a pair of scissors ② and crimp the edges with your fingers to form a seam along the curved edge of the pasty. ③ You can also do this with a plastic crimper.
8. Place the pasties onto the prepared baking sheets, leaving 2 inches (5 cm) between each. Brush with the egg wash, ④ and bake for 20 minutes, or until the pasties are golden. Brush the pasties with any leftover egg wash, then bake for a final 5 minutes until bronzed and lacquered. Set aside to cool.
9. **For the peanut sambal,** add 2 tablespoons of the oil and the peanuts to a saucepan set on medium heat. Sauté for 3 to 4 minutes, or until the skins begin to peel or the skinless peanuts turn golden. Transfer them to a blender with a slotted spoon, leaving excess oil behind in the pan.

10. To the same saucepan, add the remaining 1 tablespoon oil, shallots, and garlic. Sauté until the shallots soften, 2 to 3 minutes, then add the red chiles, bird's-eye chiles, and lime leaves. Sauté for 1 to 2 minutes to release the fragrance of the lime leaves.
11. Transfer the aromatics to the blender with the peanuts, along with the coconut sugar, kecap manis, lime juice, salt, and ¾ cup plus 2 tablespoons (200 ml) water. Blend until smooth.
12. Season with salt or add more coconut sugar, kecap manis, or lime juice to taste, or adjust the consistency with more water. Serve the warm pasties with the peanut sambal as an afternoon snack.

Butternut Squash Dengaku

SERVES 4

DENGAKU MISO

⅔ cup (200 g) miso (see page 20)

¼ cup plus 2 tablespoons (90 ml) mirin

¼ cup plus 2 tablespoons (90 ml) sake

¼ cup plus 2 tablespoons (75 g) sugar

SQUASH

2 tablespoons olive oil

1 pound plus 1.5 ounces (500 g) skinless butternut squash, cut into 1½-inch (4 cm) cubes

ASSEMBLY

⅔ cup (60 g) walnuts

1 green onion, thinly sliced

A few shakes of Japanese seven-spice seasoning (shichimi togarashi/七味唐辛子; see page 19)

Dengaku (田楽) refers to grilling food with a savory miso paste (dengaku miso/田楽味噌), a method dating back to fourteenth-century Japan. The technique became a culinary sensation when chef Nobu Matsuhisa popularized it in his legendary black cod dish. Modern recipes for dengaku miso are quick, involving just a thorough mix of the ingredients. However, this was not quite the case at the Japanese café where I used to work. We would place a huge bowl of four ingredients—mirin, miso, sake, and sugar—over a double boiler, allowing the mixture to caramelize gently into a thick paste over the course of lunch service. This produced a dark, glossy potion that was so complex in flavor that anything we brushed with it and broiled tasted a perfect combination of sweet and savory. Having some on hand is a lifesaver for days when you're too tired to think of what to cook for dinner; jarred, it also makes a fabulous gift.

1. **For the dengaku miso,** set a medium saucepan of water on high heat. While you wait for the water to come to a simmer, whisk together the miso, mirin, sake, and sugar in a large heat-safe bowl. Set the bowl on top of the simmering water and cook for 30 minutes on medium-high heat, stirring from time to time. You are looking for the mixture to darken in color and take on the consistency of mayonnaise.
2. When the dengaku miso is ready, keep ⅓ cup (100 g) in the large bowl. The rest of the mixture can be kept in a jar for up to 2 weeks in the refrigerator.
3. **For the squash,** preheat the oven to 400°F (200°C) and line a baking sheet with parchment paper. Mix the olive oil into the miso in the bowl, then add the butternut squash. Toss thoroughly to coat the squash evenly, then transfer the cubes to the prepared baking sheet. Roast for 30 to 40 minutes until tender.
4. **For assembly,** while the squash is roasting, toast the walnuts in a pan set on medium-high heat. Shake the pan every once in a while so that the walnuts toast evenly. When they are fragrant, 3 to 4 minutes, turn off the heat and set the pan aside.
5. When the squash is cooked, remove the baking sheet from the oven. With your fingers, break the walnuts into rough pieces and sprinkle them over the squash, then toss everything together gently. Transfer the squash and walnuts to a serving dish and top with the green onion and Japanese seven-spice seasoning. Serve.

Kare-Kare-Style Roasted Sweet Potatoes

SERVES 2 TO 3

SWEET POTATOES

3 small sweet potatoes, unpeeled

INFUSED OIL

½ cup oil

1 small red onion, thinly sliced

1 stalk of lemongrass (see page 20), halved lengthwise and again crosswise

3 garlic cloves, bruised

1 teaspoon annatto powder (see headnote) or Kashmiri chili powder

SAUCE

1 tablespoon glutinous rice

2 tablespoons coconut cream (see page 14)

2 tablespoons natural peanut butter

1 tablespoon dark soy sauce

1 tablespoon sugar

1½ teaspoons vegetarian fish sauce or soy sauce

1 teaspoon finely grated ginger

½ teaspoon salt

2 tablespoons lime juice

ASSEMBLY

2 green onions, quartered lengthwise and cut into 4-inch (10 cm) lengths

People always ask me what's the one ingredient I recommend having on hand to cook more satisfying dishes. My answer is peanut butter. While I'm sure that the thought of peanut butter in savory dishes may be a leap for some, we embrace it in Asian cooking to add creaminess, richness, and a nutty flavor. Case in point: kare-kare, a Filipino beef braise with a velvety gravy that derives its depth from peanuts and toasted rice. Sweet potatoes' affinity for these flavors inspired me to conceive this interpretation of the classic dish. Annatto, or atsuete as it is known in the Philippines, gives kare-kare its characteristic reddish-orange hue, but you can substitute chili powder if you can't find it. If you have a peanut allergy, this dish is just as good made with other nut butters.

1. **For the sweet potatoes,** preheat the oven to 400°F (200°C). Scrub the sweet potatoes with a brush under running water, then wrap them in foil and place on a baking sheet. Bake for 50 minutes to 1 hour until fork-tender. Allow to cool completely.
2. **For the infused oil,** while the sweet potatoes cool, combine the oil, red onion, lemongrass, garlic, and annatto powder in a small saucepan. Set this on low heat and cook for 10 minutes, or until the garlic and onion crisp up and turn a rich golden color. Turn off the heat and let cool.
3. **For the sauce,** toast the glutinous rice in a small saucepan set on medium-low heat, shaking occasionally. When the rice turns golden and smells like popcorn, about 3 minutes, transfer it to a spice grinder or blender. Pulse until you get a slightly coarse powder; you want to retain some texture.
4. Tip the powder back into the saucepan. Add the coconut cream, peanut butter, dark soy sauce, sugar, vegetarian fish sauce, ginger, salt, and ¾ cup (180 ml) water. Stir and simmer on low heat for 2 minutes, or until the consistency resembles a thin gravy. Stir in the lime juice; the sauce will continue to thicken as it cools.
5. Discard the lemongrass from the saucepan with the infused oil. Pour the contents of the saucepan through a fine-mesh strainer set over a large skillet. Reserve the fried onion and garlic for garnish. Set the skillet on high heat.
6. Cut the sweet potatoes in half lengthwise and when the oil shimmers, add to the skillet, cut side down. Fry for 2 to 3 minutes on high heat, or until the sweet potatoes achieve a nice sear. Arrange the sweet potatoes attractively on a serving dish.
7. **For assembly,** add the green onions to the oil in the skillet, cut side down, and allow to sear on high heat for 30 seconds on each side, or until caramelized and slightly charred. Turn off the heat. Remove the green onions from the skillet and set aside.
8. Drizzle the sauce and the infused oil remaining in the skillet over the sweet potatoes. Top with the green onions and fried garlic and onion. Serve.

PANDAN NIÁN GĀO, PAGE 265

Sweetened

Bomboloni with Charred Banana Cream

MAKES 10 BOMBOLONI

BOMBOLONI

¼ cup (60 g) unsalted butter, melted and cooled

2 tablespoons plus 1½ teaspoons sugar

2 eggs

1 teaspoon salt

1 teaspoon active dry yeast

2 cups (250 g) bread flour

Oil, for deep-frying

BANANA CREAM

½ banana leaf

1 cup (240 ml) milk

2 large bananas

3 egg yolks

⅓ cup (40 g) all-purpose flour

2 tablespoons plus 1½ teaspoons coconut sugar

½ cup plus 2 tablespoons (150 ml) heavy cream

ASSEMBLY

Sugar, for tossing

Like rice, bananas are a key part of my Asian identity. Now that I live in the Netherlands, I miss strolling through Singapore's markets and eyeing all the banana varieties available. Banana leaves, too, are so integral to our lives that there is a lady at Tekka Market in Singapore who has sold only banana leaves since 1985. It is a shame that the use of banana leaves in desserts is not commonplace outside of Asia, despite the ubiquity of the banana as an ingredient. Filled with a cream made from both the leaf and the charred fruit, these bomboloni are wonderfully evocative of the tropics.

1. **For the bomboloni,** whisk together the butter, sugar, eggs, salt, yeast, and ¼ cup plus 1 tablespoon (75 ml) water. Sift in the bread flour and mix until a homogenous, wet dough forms. Cover the bowl and allow the dough to rest for 1 hour at room temperature, or until the dough has doubled in size.
2. With the help of a bench scraper, transfer the rested dough from the bowl to a floured work surface. Pick up the left side of the dough and stretch it to the left as far as it will go, then fold it onto itself. Repeat this process a few more times, alternately stretching the dough toward the right, top, and bottom, until the dough begins to resist.
3. Return the dough to the bowl, cover with plastic wrap, and refrigerate it for 24 hours.
4. **For the banana cream,** on the same day the dough is made, rinse and wipe the banana leaf, then combine it with the milk in a saucepan. Bring to a simmer on high heat, then turn off the heat and allow the milk to infuse while you grill the bananas.
5. Char the bananas with their peels on directly on a gas stove burner on high heat, turning occasionally with tongs, until the peels are completely charred, the bananas have split open, and the flesh within is tender, 5 to 10 minutes. Alternatively, broil the bananas on a foil-lined rimmed baking sheet for 5 to 10 minutes, or until tender and charred on all sides, turning occasionally. Set aside until cool enough to handle.
6. Peel off and discard the charred skin and mash the fruit thoroughly with a fork. Set aside.
7. In a bowl, stir together the egg yolks, flour, coconut sugar, and a pinch of salt with a spatula.
8. Return the saucepan of milk and banana leaf to a boil on high heat. Remove the banana leaf with a pair of tongs and drizzle the hot milk into the yolk mixture, whisking constantly to prevent the eggs from curdling. Place a fine-mesh strainer on top of the saucepan and pour the milk mixture through. Discard any residue.

RECIPE CONTINUED →

9. Cook the mixture on medium heat, stirring with a heat-safe spatula, for about 3 minutes, or until very thick. The cream should fall off a spoon in thick dollops. Mix in the mashed bananas. Press plastic wrap directly onto the surface of the cream to avoid the formation of a skin, and refrigerate.
10. After the dough has had its 24 hours of rest, whip the heavy cream to stiff peaks in a large bowl. Fold the cream into the fully chilled banana mixture, then transfer the mixture to a piping bag fitted with a large plain nozzle. Store in the fridge while you work on the bomboloni.
11. Divide the rested dough into 10 pieces, weighing roughly 1.75 ounces (50 g) each. With floured hands, shape the pieces by pulling the dough edges to the bottom to form a ball, and pinch well to seal.
12. Generously flour and line a baking sheet with parchment paper. Place the balls on top, spacing them 3 inches (7.5 cm) apart. Cover with a clean kitchen towel and proof in an enclosed space, like a cool oven, until the balls are doubled in size and look very puffy. This can take anywhere from 2 to 4 hours, depending on your climate.
13. When you are ready to fry the bomboloni, fill a wok or large saucepan with 2 inches (5 cm) of oil and set it on high heat. Line a dish with paper towel. Allow the oil to heat to 400°F (200°C). Working in batches to avoid overcrowding, carefully add the bomboloni seam side down to the hot oil. Deep-fry for about 2 minutes on each side, or until golden brown. Transfer the bomboloni to the prepared dish.
14. **For assembly,** toss the hot bomboloni in the sugar. Fill them with the banana cream by poking the nozzle of the piping bag into the light band around the doughnut's circumference. Squeeze the bag until you feel the doughnut bulge with cream. Alternatively, for more indulgence, I also like to split the bomboloni, pipe an obscene amount of cream onto one half, then sandwich it with the other half, like maritozzi (Italian cream buns). Serve immediately, preferably while the cream is cold and the doughnuts are still warm.

Matcha Ice Cream with Red Bean and Dango

SERVES 4

ICE CREAM

2 tablespoons plus 1½ teaspoons matcha powder

¾ cup (145 g) sugar

5 egg yolks

1 cup plus 1 tablespoon (250 ml) milk

2 cups plus 2 tablespoons (500 ml) heavy cream

RED BEAN PASTE

1½ cups (300 g) dried red beans, soaked overnight

¾ cup (145 g) sugar

DANGO

4.75 ounces (135 g) silken tofu (see page 23)

⅔ cup (100 g) glutinous rice flour (see headnote)

ASSEMBLY

¼ cup (35 g) roasted soybean powder (kinako/きなこ)

My weakness is a Japanese matcha dessert franchise called Tsujiri. Every time I walk past a store, I am tempted to buy one of their parfaits, which is a perfect harmony of matcha ice cream, red bean, Japanese rice balls (dango/団子), and roasted soybean powder (kinako/きなこ). It became such an expensive habit that I had to learn to make my own. Traditionally, shiratamako (白玉粉), flour made from Japanese short-grain glutinous rice, is used to make dango, but regular glutinous rice flour produces a satisfactory result. Plus, it is easier to source and kinder on the wallet.

1. **For the ice cream,** at least 2 days in advance, place the matcha powder in a small bowl. In a large bowl, whisk together the sugar, egg yolks, and a pinch of salt.
2. Add the milk to a saucepan set on medium heat. When the milk comes to a simmer, pour a small amount into the matcha powder and stir well to form a thick, well-dissolved paste. Pour the rest of the hot milk gradually into the egg mixture, whisking constantly to prevent the eggs from curdling. Combine the egg mixture and matcha paste in the saucepan.
3. Cook the mixture on low heat, stirring constantly, until it thickens enough to coat the spatula and reaches a temperature of 165°F (75°C). Turn off the heat and immediately whisk in the heavy cream. Pass the custard through a fine-mesh-strainer set over a container, discard any residue, and let cool completely. Store the custard, covered, in the fridge overnight.
4. The next day, churn the chilled custard in an ice cream maker. Alternatively, place the custard in the freezer, stirring every 30 minutes with a fork to break up any ice crystals, until the mixture is completely frozen.
5. **For the red bean paste,** drain the soaked red beans and place them in a medium pot. Cover generously with water and bring to a boil on high heat. Turn the heat to low and cook, covered, until the beans are tender, about 20 minutes.
6. When cooked, drain the beans and return them to the pot with the sugar and a pinch of salt. Cook on medium-high heat until the sugar completely melts and coats the beans, and the beans disintegrate into a chunky paste. Allow to cool and set aside.
7. **For the dango,** bring a pot of water to a boil on high heat. In a bowl, combine the silken tofu and glutinous rice flour. Knead for 2 minutes, or until a smooth dough forms. Pinch off small pieces roughly the size of a hazelnut. Roll into balls between the palms of your hands.
8. Add the balls to the boiling water and cook for 1 to 2 minutes, or until they float to the surface. Lift the dango out of the pot with a spider skimmer and transfer them into a bowl of cold water to cool completely. If not used right away, the dango can be stored like this for a few hours at room temperature or refrigerated with the water in a covered container for up to 2 days. The water helps to keep the dango separate and maintains their roundness.
9. **For assembly,** scoop the ice cream into small serving dishes. Spoon some red bean paste over the ice cream, top with the dango, and sprinkle generously with the roasted soybean powder.

C-Y Chia and Shane Stanbridge

C-Y Chia and Shane Stanbridge are business and life partners who ran the acclaimed food business S+M Vegan for almost a decade, and subsequently the Michelin and James Beard Foundation–recognized restaurant turned pop-up Lion Dance Cafe (LDC) in Oakland, California. Chia's Singaporean childhood and Teochew family recipes informed LDC's vegan perspective on hawker classics. Paired with Stanbridge's Italian roots and commitment to hospitality, the duo's small operation is an award-winning hotspot.

How do you tackle the misconception that vegan food is boring?

SS: We tell skeptics to just try our food! Cooking vegan is not just leaving the meat out and expecting the same outcome. The outdated idea that vegan food is not "real food" is a fundamental misunderstanding of what veganism is. Thankfully, the perception of vegan food in the San Francisco Bay Area has evolved.

CC: Most restaurants with the best vegan food are owned by chefs of color and represent a vast array of cuisines. On nights off, we get to choose between handmade tamales and tortillas dressed in expertly crafted salsas, richly spiced Eritrean and Ethiopian dishes piled high atop tangy injera (የእንጀራ), or fresh tofu with copious amounts of banchan (반찬).

Our focus is making bold, colorful, flavor-packed food that unapologetically tells our story as cooks who have our own specific journeys, are queer, and love to eat. It just happens that our food is vegan because it makes sense to us ethically. Many people don't even realize that our food is meatless.

What are some of your favorite ingredients and techniques that add layers to your food?

CC: When it comes to flavor, we use a lot of preserved ingredients to boost the savoriness and depth of our animal-free cooking.

Preserved radish (cài fǔ/菜脯) is extremely versatile. My aunties always have it around and it can be used in everything from Teochew chwee kueh (水粿), to omelets, to soups. Shane spends a lot of time learning different preservation and fermentation techniques and has been making preserved radish from scratch.

SS: Treating a vegetable as if it is a piece of meat is key. If you sear cauliflower like steak and finish it in the oven, it can be a very exciting vegetable. You can also add aroma to vegetables by wrapping them in fig, banana, or pandan leaves. We once grilled seitan in lotus leaf, and as the leaf burned, it infused the seitan with a pleasant fragrance.

Where does your playful and creative approach to vegan food come from?

CC: It's a matter of perspective. There are hundreds of vegetables, fruits, spices, nuts, seeds, grains, and legumes out there that can be combined and prepared in hundreds of ways. So, if anything, we feel overwhelmed by the abundance of possibilities. We have both learned a lot from well-regarded chefs in Paris, New York, and San Francisco, but the value of a thoughtfully prepared vegetable was first instilled in us by our families.

SS: My family has roots in Italy (Rome and Sicily), where for a long time, diets were significantly produce-based. There's a lot of pastas, breads, local produce, and olive oil. When animal-based ingredients are used, they function more as a flavor enhancer rather than a centerpiece. We've had some of the most striking and satisfying beans of our lives in Rome. They weren't labeled as vegan; they happened to be, as a result of cucina povera ("the food of the poor"). This way of cooking is similar to how C-Y's aunts cook—where the vegetables are stir-fried with a little bit of Chinese cured sausage or dried shrimp.

CC: Ultimately, we are inspired by the essential, less-celebrated cooks who came before us who shaped the cultures and traditions we reference—not just as professional cooks, but also as their descendants.

Pandan Nián Gāo

MAKES 14 PIECES

INSPIRED BY C-Y CHIA AND SHANE STANBRIDGE

- 1⅔ cups (250 g) glutinous rice flour
- ⅔ cup plus 2 tablespoons (160 g) sugar
- 1 teaspoon baking powder
- ¼ teaspoon salt
- 5 pandan leaves (see page 21) or fig leaves, snipped into small pieces
- 1¾ cups (420 ml) coconut milk
- 3 tablespoons melted coconut oil or grapeseed oil, plus more for greasing

"Nián gāo (年糕) is the chewy, gently sweet, glutinous rice cake that marks Lunar New Year. We wanted to scent ours with pandan and rich coconut milk to reference Nyonya kueh (bite-size snacks made with rice flour and coconut milk), and as a nod to the pandan that C-Y's aunt grows in her herb garden. We bake it in a rectangular pan (rather than steam it in a round pan) for crispy, browned edges on every slice. Nián gāo is often fried before serving so this felt obvious. It's a labor of love, but the intoxicating aroma of caramelized coconut that takes over the kitchen, alone, is well worth it."—*C-Y Chia and Shane Stanbridge*

1. Preheat the oven to 400°F (200°C). Line a 9 by 5-inch (23 by 13 cm) loaf pan with parchment paper and grease the bottom and sides well. In a large bowl, whisk together the glutinous rice flour, sugar, baking powder, and salt.
2. In a blender, blend the pandan leaves and coconut milk till homogeneous. Pour the coconut milk mixture through a fine-mesh strainer set over a medium bowl. With a spoon, push down on the pulp in the strainer to fully extract the liquid. Whisk in the melted coconut oil.
3. Make a well in the dry ingredients and pour in the wet ingredients. Whisk until thoroughly combined and smooth.
4. Pour in the batter and bake for 45 minutes, or until the cake is dramatically puffed and has a lovely golden brown top. A skewer inserted into the cake should emerge clean.
5. Allow the cake to cool in the pan for 10 minutes (it will deflate but that is to be expected). Run a knife along the sides of the loaf pan, then unmold the cake onto a wire rack to cool completely.
6. Cut the cake in half lengthwise with a serrated knife, then slice each half into 7 pieces to serve.

Green Pea Cookies

MAKES APPROXIMATELY 40 COOKIES

- ½ cup (100 g) dried green peas (see headnote)
- ½ cup (70 g) all-purpose flour
- 2 tablespoons (30 g) sugar
- ¼ teaspoon salt
- ⅓ cup (80 ml) to ½ cup (120 ml) melted coconut oil

For many Singaporeans and Malaysians, the act of baking and gifting cookies heralds the arrival of the Lunar New Year. Families will make a whole assortment of cookies, ranging from pineapple tarts (buttery cookies topped with firm orbs of pineapple jam) to love letters (delicate tuiles cooked in an iron mold set over charcoal). These green pea cookies are a more recent addition to the repertoire, plausibly created as a nut-free alternative to the traditional Chinese peanut cookies. Dehydrated green peas speckle the dough pistachio-green. While green pea flour can be found easily at baking specialty shops in Singapore, it is less common outside of Asia. To make it from scratch, some recipes recommend dehydrating frozen green peas in an oven, but a hack that I've discovered is to blitz dried green pea snacks (not green split peas!), available at Asian grocers. Just select peas with minimal additional flavorings—unless you want a savory note in your cookies (wasabi pea cookies, anyone?). Like many Chinese cookies, these are vegan and have a unique sandy yet melt-in-the-mouth texture.

1. Preheat the oven to 320°F (160°C). Line a baking sheet with parchment paper. Coarsely chop 2 tablespoons (25 g) of the dried green peas and set aside.
2. Pour the rest of the peas into a small blender or food processor, along with the flour, sugar, and salt and grind to a fine powder. Tip into a large bowl and stir in the chopped green peas.
3. Gradually add the coconut oil until the mixture resembles clumps of wet sand. Bring it together with your hands to form a crumbly but cohesive ball of dough. You might need slightly more or less coconut oil.
4. Roll generous teaspoonfuls of the dough into balls and place on the prepared baking sheet.
5. Bake for 15 to 20 minutes until the cookies are sandy to the touch and firm enough to pick up without disintegrating. The cookies will further firm up as they cool, but retain their crumbly texture when bitten into. Cool completely and store for up to 2 weeks in an airtight container.

Carrot Semolina Cake

MAKES ONE 9-BY-4-INCH (23 BY 10 CM) CAKE

BUTTER MIXTURE

⅓ cup (55 g) fine semolina

1¼ cups (250 g) light brown sugar

¾ cup plus 2 tablespoons (200 g) unsalted butter, softened, plus more for greasing

6 egg yolks

¾ teaspoon salt

4 carrots (10 ounces/280 g), coarsely grated

WET INGREDIENTS

¼ cup plus 1 tablespoon (75 g) crème fraîche

3 egg whites

1 tablespoon finely grated ginger

1 teaspoon vanilla extract

DRY INGREDIENTS

Scant 1 cup (85 g) walnuts

3 green cardamom pods

1¼ cups (160 g) all-purpose flour

⅓ cup (40 g) ground almonds

1 tablespoon (15 g) baking powder

2½ teaspoons ground cinnamon

½ teaspoon ground nutmeg

FROSTING

7 ounces (200 g) cream cheese, softened

7 tablespoons (100 g) unsalted butter, softened

3 tablespoons plus 1½ teaspoons (50 g) crème fraîche

3 tablespoons (40 g) sugar

1 tablespoon plus 1½ teaspoons rosewater

The carrot's affinity with sweet treats is no secret to Indian cooks, who have been making cardamom-scented carrot halwa for centuries. The unexpected ingredient in this carrot cake is semolina, which has long been a part of Indian stovetop desserts, but only made its way into cake with the arrival of the Portuguese in India. Everyone who has eaten my take on carrot cake has reported how good it is. I chalk it up to the teeny bit of crushed cardamom that lends the cake its haunting fragrance and the toasting of the semolina, which produces a toasty, popcorn-like background flavor.

1. Preheat the oven to 350°F (180°C). Grease a 9-by-4-inch (23 by 10 cm) loaf pan and line it with parchment paper.
2. **For the butter mixture,** place the semolina in a dry saucepan set on low heat. Toast, constantly stirring, for 5 minutes, or until it smells nutty and fragrant and darkens to the color of sand. Turn off the heat and allow the semolina to cool.
3. In a large bowl, cream the brown sugar and butter until the mixture turns pale and slightly airier, but is not whipped. Stir in the egg yolks and salt. Add the toasted semolina and stir until the mixture is thoroughly combined. Finally, stir in the carrot.
4. **For the wet ingredients,** whisk together the crème fraîche, egg whites, ginger, and vanilla in a medium bowl.
5. **For the dry ingredients,** toast the walnuts in a dry saucepan set on medium heat, shaking from time to time, for 5 minutes or until they smell fragrant. Crush the walnuts in a small food processor or with a mortar and pestle until fine and rubbly, then tip them into a medium bowl. The largest piece should be no larger than a pea.
6. Crack the cardamom pods in the mortar. Shake out the seeds and discard the empty pods. Grind the seeds into a powder and add them to the bowl with the walnuts. Whisk in the flour, ground almonds, baking powder, cinnamon, and nutmeg.
7. Stir in about one-third of the wet ingredients to the butter mixture, then add about one-third of the dry ingredients and stir to combine. Repeat, scraping down the bowl as necessary, until all of the ingredients are fully incorporated.
8. Scrape the batter into the prepared loaf pan. Bake the cake for 50 to 60 minutes until the surface is deeply brown and a cake tester inserted into the center of the cake emerges clean. If the top starts to brown too quickly, you can loosely cover the top with aluminum foil halfway through baking.
9. Allow the cake to cool in the pan for 15 minutes before running a knife along the sides and lifting it out of the pan. Cool the cake completely on a wire rack before slicing.
10. **For the frosting,** while the cake cools, combine the cream cheese, butter, crème fraîche, sugar, and rosewater in a large bowl. Stir until there are no streaks of butter or cream cheese. Place the frosting in the refrigerator until ready to use. If making the cake in advance, store the cake at room temperature and the frosting in the refrigerator. Bring the frosting to room temperature before frosting the cake.
11. When the cake has completely cooled, slice it in half horizontally. Slather the bottom half of the cake with half of the frosting. Place the top half of the cake on top of the frosting and spread the remaining frosting over the top. Serve at room temperature.

Kimberly Mendoza Camara

New York–based bakery Kora was founded in 2020 by chef Kimberly Mendoza Camara. It is named after Camara's late-grandmother, Corazon, and its celebration of Filipino food culture helps it stand apart from other bakeries. In the hands of this proud Filipina, fruit and vegetables such as corn, avocado, and sweet potato take the spotlight.

Where did the idea of using vegetables in your desserts come from?

My fondest food memories in the Philippines revolve around the fresh fruits and vegetables growing in the countryside. I could spend hours looking at the produce on display at the palengkes (markets). Most were probably just picked that morning from a few miles away.

I also love how everyone in the provincial countryside has fruit trees growing on their property. Whenever I wanted fresh buko, our neighbor would climb up a tree and throw a coconut down to me. Due to these experiences, I believe that we Filipinos feel a strong sense of connection to the land and the abundance of natural gifts it provides.

When I was coming up with my pastries, I wanted them to be a way for people to learn more about our food and for me to explore my culture a little more. As a pastry chef, highlighting produce through my desserts feels natural as this is a direct representation of my Filipino heritage.

Why do you think ube is so central to Filipino food culture?

Ube is uniquely Filipino, as the tuber is native to the country. Purple is historically associated with royalty and is a symbol of wealth, prosperity, and luxury in Biblical scriptures. As the Philippines is predominantly Catholic, ube is beloved in the country. Also, the vibrant and rich color speaks for itself—it is such a naturally spectacular crop!

These days, however, most people seem to be enamored only by the color rather than the flavor and texture ube has to offer. Ube in its natural state has a fruity earthiness that is reminiscent of vanilla. Just adding extract doesn't cut it for me. This is not to say that ube extract is bad—we certainly use it to enhance our ube-based desserts—but we always use it in combination with the ube flesh in some form for that extra dense starchiness and earthiness.

How does Kora champion vegetables?

Kamotecue is caramelized sweet potato served by the skewer on the streets of the Philippines. To emulate that experience at Kora, we roast sweet potato discs and sprinkle them with sugar which we then caramelize with a blowtorch. The caramelized sweet potato is rolled in toasted sesame before being inserted into our doughnuts as a crowning finish.

We also make a doughnut inspired by maja blanca, a Filipino coconut and corn pudding garnished with latik (deeply roasted coconut milk solids). This is made by cooking down coconut milk until the curds begin to separate from the coconut oil, roasting the coconut solids in their own fat. It provides a slightly bitter balance to many desserts and confections. To reimagine this dessert in doughnut form, we prepare a coconut and corn cream filling and top the doughnut with latik and a corn tuile.

What do you find the most rewarding about incorporating plants into your desserts?

It's extremely rewarding to educate people on how versatile an ingredient can be—to challenge the skeptic and maybe even convert them. In the West, the majority of people would think of avocados only in a savory application, whereas in the East, avocados are in desserts and beverages everywhere. It's about creating an offering that looks and sounds enticing enough for people to give it a chance, and then enamoring them with the flavors.

Ginataang Bilo-Bilo

SERVES 4

INSPIRED BY KIMBERLY MENDOZA CAMARA

GLUTINOUS RICE BALLS

⅔ cup (100 g) glutinous rice flour

1 tablespoon ube powder, optional

GINATAANG BILO-BILO

One 20-ounce (565 g) can of ripe jackfruit in syrup

3 tablespoons (40 g) sugar

¼ teaspoon salt

¼ cup (45 g) sago, the smallest you can find

10.5 ounces (300 g) root vegetables such as sweet potato, taro, ube, or tapioca, cut into ¾-inch (2 cm) dice

½ cup plus 2 tablespoons (150 ml) coconut cream (see page 14)

CARAMELIZED BANANA

1 tablespoon plus 1½ teaspoons unsalted butter or coconut oil

¼ cup (50 g) coconut sugar

¼ teaspoon salt

7 ounces (200 g) bananas, preferably a firm variety like saba bananas, cut diagonally into-½ inch (1.25 cm) slices

"The first recipe I ever learned from my grandmother, Corazon, is called ginataang bilo-bilo. It's a carb-heavy coconut dessert soup that is cooked with root vegetables, fruits, sago, and glutinous rice balls. The assortment of vegetables and fruits vary depending on the region and what you have on hand. I love that this is a creamy, luxurious dessert that has absolutely no dairy in it, but provides the same comfort and satisfaction (and probably calories!). It is particularly soothing on a cold day."—*Kimberly Mendoza Camara*

1. **For the glutinous rice balls,** mix together the glutinous rice flour, ube powder (if using), and ¼ cup plus 3 tablespoons (100 ml) water. Knead, adding a little more flour or water if necessary, until you have a pliable dough.
2. Divide the dough into heaping teaspoon pieces, and roll each into a ball. You will get roughly 25 to 30 balls. Set aside.
3. **For the ginataang bilo-bilo,** drain the jackfruit, reserving the syrup, then finely slice and set aside. Pour the syrup into a medium pot and add the sugar, salt, and 1.7 quarts (1.7 L) water.
4. Bring the liquid to a rolling boil on high heat, then add the sago. Stir immediately to prevent the sago from clumping. Cover and cook for 5 minutes before adding the root vegetables. Cook until the vegetables are tender, 10 to 15 minutes, before adding the glutinous rice balls.
5. When the rice balls float to the surface, about 3 minutes, turn the heat to low and stir in the coconut cream. Allow the mixture to come to a simmer, then turn off the heat. The soup will look rather thin but will thicken as it cools.
6. **For the caramelized banana,** add the butter to a saucepan set on high heat. Once the butter melts, add the coconut sugar and salt. Stir until the sugar melts and begins to bubble, then add the bananas. Toss the bananas in the caramel and cook for a further minute to glaze them.
7. Add the bananas and jackfruit to the ginataang bilo-bilo and season to taste with more sugar, if desired. Serve warm.

Chili-Flecked Jalebis with Mango Yogurt

SERVES 6 TO 8

MANGO YOGURT

Flesh from 2 ripe mangoes (about 9 ounces/250 g)

½ cup (120 ml) yogurt

2 tablespoons lime juice

1½ teaspoons sugar

JALEBIS

1 cup plus 3 tablespoons (150 g) all-purpose flour

3 tablespoons cornstarch

¼ teaspoon baking soda

¼ cup (60 ml) yogurt

A big pinch of saffron threads, steeped in ¾ cup (180 ml) hot water for at least 30 minutes

Oil, for deep-frying

SYRUP

1¾ cups (360 g) sugar

1 teaspoon lemon juice

3 green cardamom pods, crushed lightly

A pinch of saffron threads

2 tablespoons Korean chili flakes (gochugaru/고춧가루)

2 teaspoons Kashmiri chili powder

ASSEMBLY

A handful of pistachios, finely chopped

A handful of dried rose petals

Syrup-soaked fritters are popular throughout the Indian subcontinent, in countries such as Sri Lanka, India, Bangladesh, and Nepal. For jalebis (जलेबी), squeezing the batter into hot oil takes a little practice—optimally, you should work quickly so that each swirl consists of several concentric circles—but the more you make, the easier it gets. Once fried, the jalebi is soaked in a saffron syrup, which gives it a bright amber, glass-like appearance. The tricky part is getting the syrup consistency right; too thick and the jalebis won't absorb it well, too thin and the jalebis become soggy. It is, thus, best to use a thermometer to gauge when the syrup is ready. While it might seem odd to have chili in a dessert, it pays to keep an open mind, for the spicy kick of the jalebis is pleasurable, especially when chased with cold, tangy yogurt.

1. **For the mango yogurt,** in a blender, blitz the mango flesh and yogurt until smooth. Stir in the lime juice and sugar. The purée should taste acidic and only mildly sweet. Transfer the mixture to a container, cover, and chill in the refrigerator.
2. **For the jalebis,** whisk together the flour, cornstarch, and baking soda in a medium bowl and stir in the yogurt. Gradually whisk in the saffron and its soaking liquid. You want a batter that is thick but flows easily off a lifted whisk. You might require more or less water to achieve the right consistency.
3. Transfer the batter to a squeeze bottle equipped with a nozzle approximately 5 mm in diameter. Alternatively, you can use a piping bag with a nozzle of a similar size or a ziplock bag with about 5 mm cut from the corner for piping. Set the batter aside.
4. **For the syrup,** combine the sugar, lemon juice, green cardamom pods, saffron, and ¾ cup (180 ml) water in a saucepan.
5. On high heat, bring the mixture to 225°F (107°C). To test the consistency, drop a small spoonful of syrup into a bowl of cold water; it should form a single thread when pulled out gently.
6. Turn off the heat and stir in the chili flakes and chili powder. Set the syrup aside.
7. Meanwhile, fill a wok or large saucepan with 2 inches (5 cm) of oil and set it on high heat. When the oil reaches 350°F (175°C), working in batches, form swirls of the batter in the hot oil by quickly squeezing 3 to 4 concentric circles and piping a line through the circles to hold them together. You should be able to fry four or five at once. The batter should puff up within seconds.
8. Fry, flipping the jalebis occasionally, until they turn lightly golden, 2 to 3 minutes. With a pair of tongs, pick up a jalebi, shake off excess oil, and lower it into the warm syrup. Allow it to soak for a few seconds before placing it onto a wire rack to drain. If the syrup is too thin, the jalebis will absorb it excessively and become soggy. If the syrup is too thick, it will crystallize on the jalebis rather than being absorbed. Repeat until the batter is used up.
9. **For assembly,** divide the jalebis and cold mango yogurt between goblets or serving bowls, or arrange on individual dishes. Thin the yogurt with water if necessary, and spoon it over the jalebis. Scatter with the pistachios and dried rose petals, and enjoy.

Winter Melon Jelly with Passion Fruit and Peach

SERVES 4

- 10.5 ounces (300 g) winter melon, hairy melon, zucchini, or cucumber, cut into ½-inch (1.25 cm) cubes
- ¼ cup plus 2 tablespoons (75 g) coconut sugar
- 2½ teaspoons agar powder
- Pulp from 2 passion fruit
- 2 peaches, pitted and thickly sliced

Understanding food as medicine is something that was natural to me from an early age. My maternal grandmother regularly made desserts like tofu skin and gingko soup not simply because they tasted good, but because they were a cost-effective way to care for the health of the entire family. Our fridge at home used to be filled with a rotating line-up of my mom's "cooling teas," which worked as soothing remedies for Singapore's relentless tropical heat. Winter melon tea is one such "tea" that helps cool down the body in summer, and is so easy to love that there are cans of it sold from vending machines across the island. If you cannot source winter melon in your area, you can use other gourds such as hairy melon, zucchini, or cucumber.

1. In a saucepan, toss together the winter melon and coconut sugar. Set aside for 1 hour, stirring occasionally, to draw out the melon's liquid.
2. Cover the saucepan with a lid and place over the lowest heat setting of the smallest burner. Simmer for 1 hour, until the melon is tender and translucent.
3. Pour the contents of the saucepan through a colander set in a large bowl, pressing down on the melon to completely extract all of the "tea." Measure the extracted liquid and add water as needed to yield 3⅔ cups (870 ml).
4. We will be using only the extracted melon tea for this recipe; the melon flesh can be eaten or discarded. Pour the tea back into the saucepan and whisk in the agar powder.
5. Bring the liquid to a simmer on high heat. When the mixture comes to a boil, add more coconut sugar to taste.
6. Turn off the heat and pass the mixture through a fine-mesh strainer set over a large container or individual serving dishes. (A helpful tip here is to wash your strainer immediately with hot water; once the agar sets, the strainer will be a nightmare to clean.) Leave the mixture to cool at room temperature until set—about an hour or two. At this point, the jelly can be enjoyed at room temperature or stored in the fridge until thoroughly chilled.
7. To serve, if the jelly is set in one large container, rake a fork through the jelly to break it into small pieces, then spoon it into serving bowls. Top the jelly with the passion fruit pulp and peach slices and serve.

Zoey Xinyi Gong

Zoey Xinyi Gong's food is both beautiful to look at and good for you. Born in Shanghai, Gong is a Traditional Chinese Medicine (TCM) practitioner, chef, food therapist, registered dietitian, and educator based in Brooklyn, New York. She is also the cofounder of The Red Pavilion, a TCM teahouse by day and Asian neo-noir nightclub after dark. The food that she serves at her pop-up dinners, workshops, and events showcase a range of plants, including fruit, grains, Chinese herbs, and root vegetables that are anchored in Chinese tradition. In 2023, she published *The Five Elements Cookbook: A Guide to Traditional Chinese Medicine with Reci pes for Everyday Healing*.

What were your meals like in Shanghai compared to America?

In Shanghai, I hated eating vegetables and ate plenty of meat. My diet was very different from what my grandparents ate in their youth. They lived through famines and meat was consumed only once a year. With growing affluence and the impact of globalization, meat consumption has risen significantly in China in recent decades. Still, there was a lot of variety at the dinner table, and we ate according to the seasons. Dairy was almost non-existent in our meals and soy was a central part of our diet.

When I moved to the United States at sixteen, my diet changed from a Chinese diet to a very American one. I ate sweets like cakes and brownies, and way more meat and dairy than ever before. I started experiencing health issues like joint pain, rashes, and breast tumors. I soon figured out that my new diet was the culprit, and this led me to reclaim the eating habits that I had in China. In months, my health problems went away; the switch in my diet was an enlightening moment for me.

How is food used as medicine in Chinese culture?

Chinese medicine teaches that most of the qi, or life force, in our body is derived from our diet and emphasizes eating in relation to nature. Asians tend to eat more seasonally than Westerners because our food systems are way less industrialized; we cannot get everything all the time. There is a strong understanding that food is very much part of nature, so the way we eat should be dynamic and align with the seasons.

In spring, there's a lot of yang energy (yáng qì/阳气) in nature because it is the beginning of everything and things are growing. If you eat things that can facilitate this energy in your body, like ginger and sprouts, you will feel more energetic and less agitated.

Also, while fresh, seasonal ingredients have good qi, food that is produced from a factory or is old and stale does not—it can't supply you with the healthy energy that you need. It is, thus, important for us to find out what grows in our region and at what time of the year, and to try to eat these foods as much as possible.

Why do you think plants feature so heavily in Asian desserts?

Plants have many inherent health benefits; it's why our ancestors added them to desserts. My go-to is white fungus or tremella (bái mù ěr/白木耳), which is one of the trendiest superfoods in the West, known for its anti-inflammatory and anti-tumor benefits. I cook it with peach gum (táo jiāo/桃胶)—the gummy-textured resin of the peach tree—naturally sweet goji berries, and jujube dates. After a couple of hours, it becomes this hydrating little dessert that is vegan and gluten-free.

I grew up in Shanghai, where rice fields are abundant, and the rice gets turned into so many varieties of mochi. These include glutinous rice balls (tāng yuán/汤圆) that we add to sweet broth, and steamed glutinous rice cakes filled with adzuki beans or nuts. Sometimes, mugwort is added to the mochi to impart a fresh grassy taste and medicinal benefits. A lot of females have cramps because their uterus is "cold"; mugwort can warm it up and facilitate the movement of qi and blood in the body.

Steamed Mochi-Stuffed Dates

MAKES 20 STUFFED DATES

BY ZOEY XINYI GONG

- ¼ cup plus 1½ teaspoons (30 g) glutinous rice flour
- 3 tablespoons (20 g) rice flour
- 3 tablespoons (45 g) warm water
- 20 dried red dates or Medjool dates measuring 1¼ inches (3 cm) long, halved lengthwise and pitted
- 1 tablespoon (12.5 g) sugar
- 2 teaspoons dried osmanthus flowers, optional

"This is a traditional Shanghainese dessert that I grew up eating. It has a beautiful name in Chinese, "a heart too soft" (xīn tài ruǎn/心太软), due to the soft mochi center and naturally sweet flavor from the dates. If you don't have dried red dates, you can substitute Medjool dates in this blood-nourishing, naturally sweet dessert."—*Zoey Xinyi Gong*

1. Combine the glutinous rice flour and rice flour in a small mixing bowl. Gradually add the warm water until a smooth dough is formed.
2. Prepare a steaming setup by placing a trivet in a wok or large saucepan. Fill with enough water to come up just below the level of the trivet. Cover with a lid and set on high heat. While waiting for the water in your steamer to come to a boil, divide the dough into 20 pieces, each about the size of a grape. Roll the pieces into small oval strips and stuff them between the two halves of each of the dates.
3. When the water starts to boil, place the stuffed dates in a heat-safe dish and put it in the steamer. Cover and steam for about 8 minutes on high heat or until the mochi turns translucent.
4. In a saucepan, combine the sugar, dried osmanthus flowers, and ¾ cup plus 2 tablespoons (200 ml) water and bring to a boil on high heat. Add the steamed dates and cook for 1 minute, stirring to allow the dates to soak up the syrup evenly.
5. With a slotted spoon, transfer the dates to a serving dish. Serve warm.

Black Sticky Rice Pudding with Coconut Milk and Mango

SERVES 4

- 1 cup (200 g) black glutinous rice, soaked overnight
- 5 pandan leaves (see page 21), knotted
- 2 blocks (100 g) dark palm sugar (see page 15)
- ½ cup (120 ml) coconut milk
- ¼ teaspoon salt
- 1 ripe mango, peeled and thinly sliced
- 1 teaspoon sesame seeds, toasted

In Southeast Asia, rice is our staple food, so it isn't surprising that we would have our own version of rice pudding. Ours is made with black glutinous rice, which has been cultivated and savored across Asia for millennia. While white glutinous rice consists only of the rice grain's starchy endosperm, black glutinous rice retains the oil- and flavor-rich germ and black outer bran that provides fiber. This dessert is, as a result, the rare moment when the flavor of rice in its whole, nutritious form takes center stage, rather than functioning as a soothing backdrop for other flavors. It is rewarding to watch the dark purple grains transform—as they cook, they plump up and release their starch, turning from a loose, watery mixture to a velvety, cohesive mass. While this rice pudding is traditionally adorned only with a cascade of coconut milk, it is stunning as a backdrop for mangoes at their peak.

1. Drain the rice and place it in a medium pot along with the pandan leaves, palm sugar, and 1.4 quarts (1.4 L) water.
2. Bring to a boil, then simmer on low heat for 1 hour, covered. Stir from time to time to prevent the pudding from scorching on the bottom.
3. When the rice is tender and the mixture resembles a thick porridge, turn off the heat and remove the pandan leaves. Allow the porridge to cool slightly.
4. Meanwhile, stir together the coconut milk and salt in a small bowl.
5. Divide the pudding among serving bowls, drizzle with the coconut milk, top with the mango, and sprinkle with the sesame seeds. Serve.

Blackberry and Peach Gum Shortcake

SERVES 6

CREAM

9 ounces (250 g) cream cheese, at room temperature, diced

2 eggs

½ cup (120 ml) heavy cream

½ cup (100 g) sugar

2¼ teaspoons all-purpose flour

COMPOTE

¼ cup (50 g) sugar

1 ounce (30 g) dried peach gum (táo jiāo/桃胶; see headnote), soaked overnight, drained

10.5 ounces (300 g) blackberries, fresh or frozen

2¼ teaspoons cornstarch

1 tablespoon lemon juice

SHORTCAKE

1 cup (125 g) all-purpose flour

1 tablespoon sugar

1 teaspoon baking powder

¼ cup (55 g) unsalted butter, chilled and cubed

½ cup (120 ml) plus 1 tablespoon heavy cream

The surprise element of this deconstructed shortcake is peach gum (táo jiāo/桃胶), the amber, gem-like crystals that form on a peach tree when its bark is wounded. Soaked in water, these swell to many times their original size and develop a delicate, silky texture when cooked. While traditionally added to Chinese dessert soups, I've found that they are wonderful when cooked with fruit and sugar, resulting in something that sits between compote and gelatin-set jelly. Peach gum is available in the dried section of Asian grocers, or you can choose to omit it—the result will be a standard blackberry compote, which lacks the unique soft chew of the peach gum, but it will still work in the shortcake. In place of whipped cream, I complete the shortcake with a cheesecake cream that mimics the gooey center of Basque cheesecake.

1. **For the cream,** a few hours or up to a day before you plan to serve, blend the cream cheese, eggs, heavy cream, sugar, flour, and a pinch of salt until completely smooth.
2. Transfer the mixture to a large heat-safe bowl and set over a pot of simmering water. Cook on medium-high heat, stirring frequently to prevent the eggs from curdling. The mixture will liquefy and then thicken up, about 5 minutes. When it reaches 165°F (75°C), turn off the heat and allow it to cool completely. Transfer to the refrigerator to chill thoroughly.
3. **For the compote,** the next day, combine 1 tablespoon of the sugar, the soaked peach gum, and 2 cups plus 2 tablespoons (500 ml) water in a saucepan. Bring to a boil, then turn the heat down to low and simmer, covered, for 30 minutes. The peach gum should lose its brittle texture and turn tender and chewy. Drain, discarding the liquid.
4. In the empty saucepan, combine the blackberries, remaining 3 tablespoons of sugar, and 2 tablespoons water. Set on medium-low heat and cook until the blackberries release their juices, 3 to 5 minutes.
5. In a small bowl, mix together the cornstarch and 2 tablespoons water. Turn the heat to low and add the cornstarch slurry to the saucepan, stirring constantly. The juices should thicken up almost immediately. Turn off the heat and stir in the peach gum and lemon juice.
6. **For the shortcake,** preheat the oven to 425°F (220°C) and line a baking sheet with parchment paper. In a large bowl, whisk together the flour, sugar, and baking powder, and a pinch of salt. Use your fingers to rub in the butter until a coarse rubble is formed. Stir in ½ cup (120 ml) of the heavy cream until just combined.
7. Divide the dough into 6 pieces, weighing about 1.25 ounces (35 g) each. Form each piece into a ball, then flatten them into ½-inch-thick (1.25 cm) discs. Place on the prepared baking sheet and brush with the remaining heavy cream.
8. Bake for 10 to 12 minutes until the shortcakes are golden brown. Place a generous dollop of the compote and chilled cream in each serving bowl. Top with a shortcake and serve immediately.

BLACKBERRY AND
PEACH GUM SHORTCAKE,
PAGE 285

Further Reading

If your appetite has been whetted by these flavor combinations and techniques from Asia, here is a list of other titles that will inspire you:

- *Asian Green: Everyday Plant-Based Recipes Inspired by the East* by Ching He Huang (Kyle Books, 2021)
- *East: 120 Easy and Delicious Asian-Inspired Vegetarian and Vegan Recipes* by Meera Sodha (Flatiron Books, 2020)
- *East Meets Vegan: The Best of Asian Home Cooking, Plant-Based and Delicious* by Sasha Gill (The Experiment, 2019)
- *Ever-Green Vietnamese: Super-Fresh Recipes, Starring Plants from Land and Sea* by Andrea Nguyen (Ten Speed Press, 2023)
- *Every Grain of Rice: Simple Chinese Home Cooking* by Fuchsia Dunlop (Bloomsbury Publishing, 2019)
- *From Gujarat with Love: 100 Authentic Indian Vegetarian Recipes* by Vina Patel (Pavilion Books, 2021)
- *Jackfruit and Blue Ginger: Asian Favourites, Made Vegan* by Sasha Gill (Murdoch Books, 2019)
- *Kansha: Celebrating Japan's Vegan and Vegetarian Traditions* by Elizabeth Andoh (Ten Speed Press, 2010)
- *Mission Vegan: Wildly Delicious Food for Everyone* by Danny Bowien (Ecco, 2022)
- *Mumbai Modern: Vegetarian Recipes Inspired by Indian Roots and California Cuisine* by Amisha Dodhia Gurbani (Countryman Press, 2021)
- *Plant-Based India: Nourishing Recipes Rooted in Tradition* by Dr. Sheil Shukla (The Experiment, 2022)
- *Prashad: Indian Vegetarian Cooking* by Kaushy Patel (Hodder & Stoughton, 2012)
- *Prashad at Home: Indian Cooking from Our Vegetarian Kitchen* by Kaushy Patel (Headline Home, 2015)
- *Tenderheart: A Cookbook About Vegetables and Unbreakable Family Bonds* by Hetty Lui McKinnon (Knopf, 2023)
- *The Korean Vegan Cookbook: Reflections and Recipes from Omma's Kitchen* by Joanne Lee Molinaro (Avery, 2021)
- *The Modern Tiffin: On-the-Go Vegan Dishes with a Global Flair* by Priyanka Naik (S&S/Simon Element, 2021)
- *The Vegan Chinese Kitchen: Recipes and Modern Stories from a Thousand-Year-Old Tradition* by Hannah Che (Clarkson Potter, 2022)
- *To Asia, With Love: Everyday Asian Recipes and Stories from the Heart* by Hetty Lui McKinnon (Prestel, 2021)
- *Vegan JapanEasy: Classic & Modern Vegan Japanese Recipes to Cook at Home* by Tim Anderson (Hardie Grant London, 2020)
- *Vegetarian Chinese Soul Food: Deliciously Doable Ways to Cook Greens, Tofu, and Other Plant-Based Ingredients* by Hsiao-Ching Chou (Sasquatch Books, 2021)
- *Vegetarian Viêt Nam* by Cameron Stauch (W. W. Norton & Company, 2018)

Acknowledgments

For two years, the idea for this book sat in my computer gathering virtual dust—until the support of countless others helped shape it into something even greater than my solitary vision. Now, as *PlantAsia* finds a larger, global audience with this new edition, I'm overwhelmed by this turn of events and humbled by the collective effort that made it possible.

To Gan Chin Lin, whose interview opened the door to this new chapter in *PlantAsia*'s history: Thank you for your generosity and unwavering support.

To The Experiment—my editor Sara Zatopek, whose respect for the book's cultural integrity has been a huge blessing; copy editor Ally Mitchell, whose meticulous edits helped make the book more user-friendly; designer Beth Bugler, who wove my feedback into the design of the book with such grace; and the rest of the team for ushering this book into its next chapter.

To my original collaborators: Jess Ho, your editorial vision laid the foundation. Shreya Parasrampuria, your art still breathes life into these pages. Yong Wen Yeu, Joey Song, and Christopher Toh, your steadfast friendship buoys me.

To the voices who entrusted me with their stories—Cameron Stauch, Sunny Lee, Ivy Chen, Vasunthara, Maori Murota, Sonoko Sakai, Gayan Pieris, Minal Patel, Jihee Shin, Cathy Erway, Cathie Carpio, Julie Kleeman and Yeshi Jampa, Andrea Quynhgiao Nguyen, R. G. Enriquez-Diez, Hairil Sukaime, Wayan Kresna Yasa, Bryan Koh, Jenny Lau, John Chantarasak, O Tama Carey, Petty Pandean-Elliott, C-Y Chia and Shane Stanbridge, Kimberly Mendoza Camara, and Zoey Xinyi Gong—your wisdom now travels farther. This book is a testament to your legacies and generosity.

To the readers of my newsletter, my first cookbook *Wet Market to Table*, and *PlantAsia*'s earliest supporters: Your enthusiasm fuels this journey. You are for whom the work is all worth it.

To the students in my cooking classes: You taught me the value of empathy as a cookbook author, and that food is a conduit for pleasure, connection, and community.

Finally, to my family and closest friends: Wex Woo, Nancy Cheong, Cathy Cheong, Chia Swee Hoon, Grandma, Amy Cheong, Amelia Chia, Samuel Chia, Ernest Chia, Eileen Ng, Woo Keng Ghee, Woo Sian Boon, Joey Song, Dawn Chan, Francine Sim, Rachel Leng, Christopher Toh, Joel Quek, Ian Ong, Kevin Wong, Baey Yue-Guang, and Prongs—your love and support is the bedrock of my life and makes everything possible.

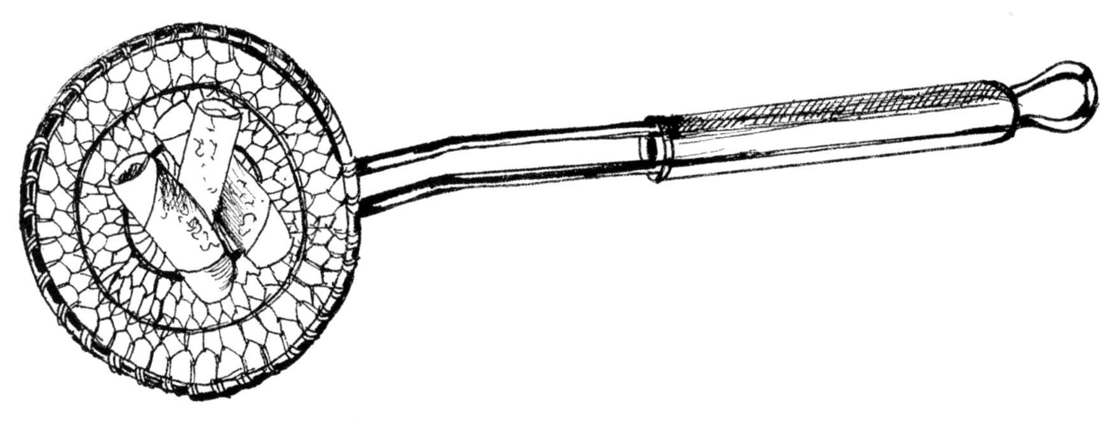

VEGETABLE ROLLS,
TWO WAYS, PAGE 187

Index

D

F

J

K

L

M

T

U

W

Z

LIST OF RECIPES

AF ALLIUM-FREE RECIPES
VG VEGAN RECIPES
VGO VEGAN-OPTION RECIPES
V VEGETARIAN RECIPES

INTERVIEWS

About the Author

PAMELIA CHIA is a Singaporean culinary teacher and food writer based in the Netherlands. With a background in food science and experience cooking in professional kitchens, Pamelia is passionate about Asian culinary traditions and providing a platform for cooks from the region to share their knowledge. She's the author of the cookbook *Wet Market to Table: A Modern Approach to Fruit and Vegetables* and the weekly Asian food newsletter *Singapore Noodles*. If you try any of the recipes in this book, she would love to see what you create! Tag her on Instagram at @pameliachia or use the hashtag #PlantAsiaCookbook.